lonely planet

INDIA

Christabel Lobo, Margot Bigg, Joe Bindloss, Puneetinder Kaur Sidhu, Joanna Lobo, Charukesi Ramadurai, Paul Stafford, Jenny Walker

Meet our writers

Christabel Lobo

@whereschristabel

Christabel is a writer and illustrator based between South India, the UAE and Washington, DC.

Margot Bigg

@margotbigg

Margot lived and worked in Delhi for six years and continues to visit regularly.

Joe Bindloss

@joe_on_travel

Joe has been writing about Asia since the 1990s, and he was formerly Lonely Planet's Destination Editor for the Indian Subcontinent.

Puneetinder Kaur Sidhu

@cuttinglooseinsta

Puneetinder is a travel and food writer and lives by one motto: Travel. Eat. Write. Repeat.

Previous spread Pattabhirama Temple complex, Hampi (p232)

IMAGESOFINDIA/SHUTTERSTOCK

Mumbai
Nashik 3h
or 5h
Pune
Western India 190
Bhubaneswar
Hyderabad
Visakhapatnam
Ratnagiri
Bay of Bengal
Southern India 212
Chennai
ANDAMAN & NICOBAR ISLANDS (INDIA)
Lakshadweep (India)
Ooty (Udhagamandalam)
Ooty 3h
Salem
Coimbatore
Madurai
Lakshadweep Sea
SRI LANKA
Colombo
0 500 km
0 250 miles

Start the day at a chai stall or temple gate. Wander forts, palaces and ancient temples still used for worship and daily life. Eat with your hands from banana leaves, steel plates and street carts. Ride slow trains into hill stations, tea gardens and desert towns. Glide by boat through mangroves, rivers and backwaters. Sit in on cooking, craft and music traditions passed down from one generation to the next. Time your visit to festivals that remake cities overnight.

This is India.

TURN THE PAGE AND START PLANNING YOUR NEXT BEST TRIP →

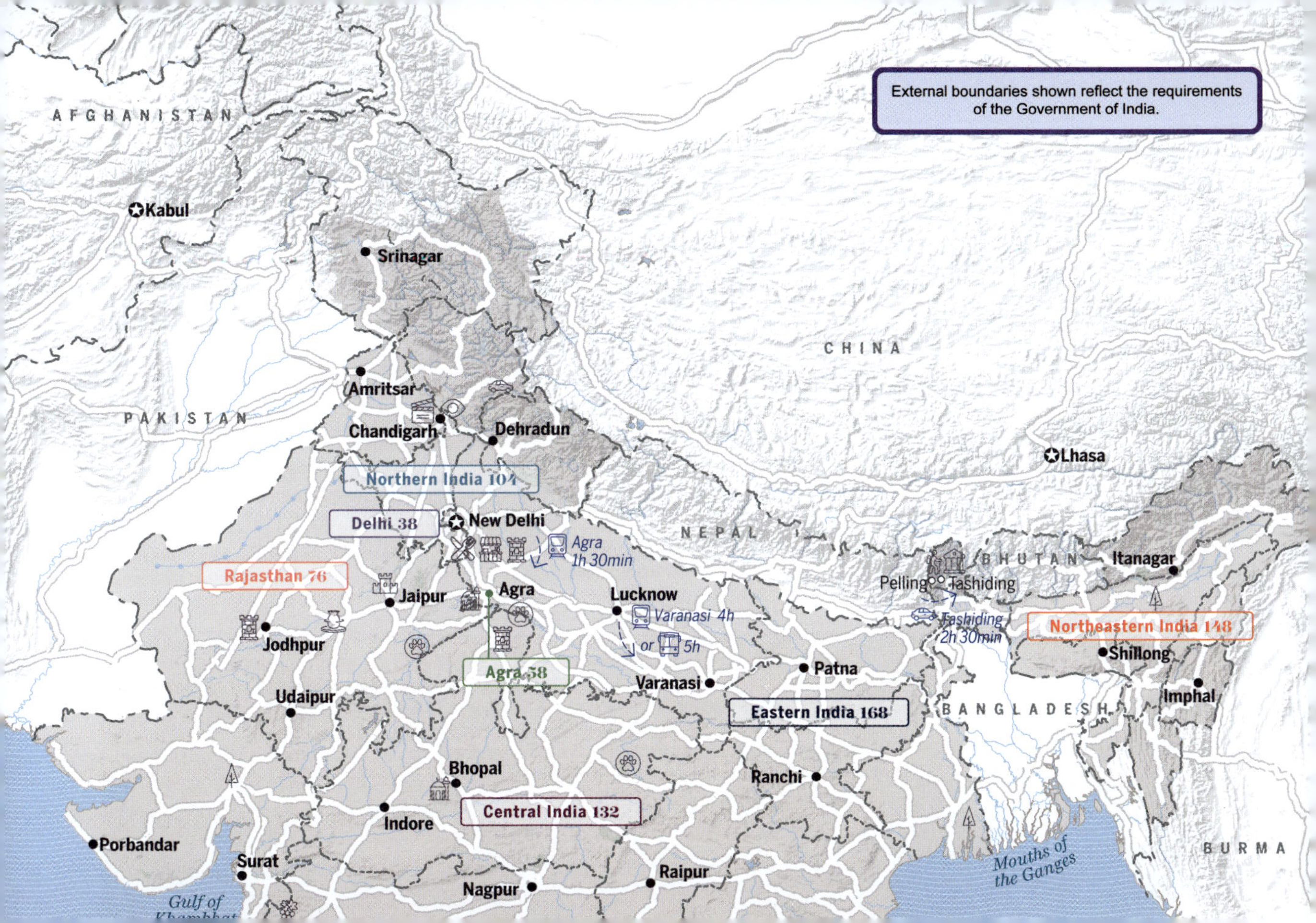
External boundaries shown reflect the requirements of the Government of India.
AFGHANISTAN
Kabul
Srinagar
PAKISTAN
Amritsar
Chandigarh
Dehradun
CHINA
Lhasa
Northern India 104
Delhi 38
New Delhi
Agra
1h 30min
NEPAL
BHUTAN
Itanagar
Pelling
Tashiding
Tashiding
2h 30min
Rajasthan 76
Jaipur
Agra
Lucknow
Varanasi 4h
or 5h
Northeastern India 148
Shillong
Jodhpur
Agra 58
Varanasi
Patna
Imphal
Udaipur
Eastern India 168
BANGLADESH
Bhopal
Ranchi
Central India 132
Indore
Porbandar
Surat
Raipur
Nagpur
BURMA
Mouths of the Ganges
Gulf of Khambhat

Joanna Lobo

@thatdoggonelady

Joanna Lobo is a freelance journalist, editor, and author based in Goa who enjoys writing about food, travel and everything that makes her heart happy. .

Charukesi Ramadurai

@charukesi

Charukesi writes about travel, culture, wildlife and conservation (among other things) for various publications around the world.

Paul Stafford

@paulrstafford

Paul is based in Birmingham, UK, but when not entangled in a web of words and pictures he is travelling for Lonely Planet.

Jenny Walker

@jennywalkertravel

Dr Jenny Walker is a higher education consultant, an author of an academic book on desert travel literature, and co-author of a guide to Oman.

Contents

SCOTTYELLOX/SHUTTERSTOCK

Amber Fort (p87), Jaipur

ESSAY

VISUAL GUIDES

AFGHANISTAN
Kabul
OMAN
Arabian Sea
Jodhpur
Udaipur
Porbandar
Surat
Gulf of Khambhat
Mumbai
Pune
Ratnagiri

Ranthambhore National Park

Ruins and tigers

Ranthambhore's dry forests are threaded with ruined facades, step-wells and a hilltop fort, remnants of its princely past. Tigers move through this open terrain alongside lakes and scrub, making sightings feel sudden and exposed instead of hidden deep in the jungle.

3hr from Jaipur

▶ p85

Bandhavgarh & Kanha National Parks

Waiting for Wildlife

These neighbouring reserves offer classic Central Indian landscapes, a sal forest, grassland clearings and winding tracks. Safaris are repetitive by design, with long stretches of waiting punctuated by brief, charged moments – a mark in the dust, a movement in tall grass.

4hr from Jabalpur

▶ p138

WILDLIFE WONDERS

India offers some of the world's most compelling wildlife encounters. Tigers emerge from dry forests at dawn, rhinos graze on floodplains reshaped each monsoon and mangroves breathe with the shifting tides. From national parks and dense mangroves to rainforest hills and island reefs, wildlife experiences here demand patience, timing and respect, making sightings feel intimate rather than guaranteed.

Nilgiri Biosphere

Mist and movement

The Western Ghats hold some of the country's oldest rainforests. In **Eravikulam National Park**, part of the Nilgiri Biosphere Reserve, rolling grasslands and shola forests are home to the endangered Nilgiri tahr and the rare purple Kurinji flower.

4hr from Kochi

▶ p236

Kaziranga National Park

Grasslands and giants

These **vast grasslands** are reshaped each year by the Brahmaputra's floods. One-horned rhinos graze in the open alongside buffalo and deer, while birdlife gathers in the wetlands.

3hr from Guwahati

▶ p160

Sundarbans National Park

Life by the tide

Exploring the **Sundarbans** (pictured left) means travelling by boat through a shifting network of creeks and mangrove islands. There are no roads and few clear sightlines. Wildlife encounters are shaped by the tides as much as luck.

3hr from Kolkata

▶ p172

Andaman Islands

Remote blue waters

The **Andamans** reward travellers who like their wildlife half above, half below the surface. Snorkel coral reefs, kayak through mangroves or travel farther to quieter islands where diving, surfing and empty beaches await.

2hr from Chennai

▶ p228

India has over 7500km of coastline, with pockets suitable for surfing and diving.

India's Himalayan trekking routes pass through forest, alpine meadows and high passes, often taking seven to ten days.

Many experiences are seasonal or weather dependent

KO BACKPACKO/SHUTTERSTOCK

ADRENALINE **ADVENTURES**

India's massive scale and varied terrain create the perfect conditions for adventure seekers. Long coastlines support surfing and diving, mountain ranges offer trekking and high-altitude trails, while rivers and deserts allow for slow-burn, physical challenges rather than extreme sports. Experiences run the gamut, with many activities locally run.

Best Adventure Experiences

- **Trek from Yuksom beneath Khangchendzonga, the world's third-highest mountain (pictured; p154)**
- **Surf world-class breaks at Butler Bay in the Andamans (p228)**
- **Dive coral reefs off Havelock Island with certified guides (p228)**
- **Kayak Kerala's backwaters and lagoons beyond houseboat routes (p225)**
- **Ride camels on an overnight safari from Jaisalmer's still-inhabited fort (p96)**

MADE BY HAND

India is renowned for its craft traditions, which remain an integral part of daily life. Temple towns feature carved stone and painted ceilings, while market streets are lined with textiles, leather goods and clay idols. In cities, printers, weavers and metalworkers work by hand in open workshops. In rural areas, pottery, embroidery and weaving continue at home, using locally sourced materials.

CLOCKWIES FROM LEFT: TUUL & BRUNO MORANDI/GETTY IMAGES, HARI MAHIDHAR/SHUTTERSTOCK

HAAT BAZAARS

In Bastar, weekly markets rotate between villages, showcasing Adivasi crafts, including Ghadwa bell-metal castings. They're best visited through locally arranged community-led tours.

Best Craft Experiences

- Watch clay idols being shaped in Kumartuli, Kolkata (p182)
- See banana fiber artisans at work in Anegundi (p233)
- Explore puppet makers and miniature painting schools in Udaipur (p100)
- Learn the art of *ajrakh* block printing with natural dyes in Ajrakhpur (p196)
- Browse craft markets in Northeastern India (p162)

KACHCH CRAFT VILLAGES

In Kachch, craft traditions are organised by community. Villages specialise in embroidery, weaving, *ajrakh* printing or rogan painting, often practised within families.

Above left Ajrakh block printing (p197)
Left Bell-metal castings (p145)

Delhi
Street food and snacks

Delhi's food culture thrives on its street-food snacks. You'll find crisp *chaat* (fried dough snacks) drenched in sweetened yogurt and chutneys, alongside dumplings, kebabs and slow-cooked nihari (stews).

✈ *2½hr from Goa*

▸ p44

Goa
Fiery feasts

Goan cuisine is a mix of coastal delicacies and Portuguese colonial influence. Vinegar, coconut and chilli define dishes like fish curry and seafood with tamarind.

✈ *1hr from Mumbai*

▸ p204

FLAVOURS OF **THE LAND**

Eating in India is rarely detached from place. What ends up on your plate reflects altitude, rain, soil and work. Travel across the country and you'll taste it – fresh cheese made in Himalayan villages, milk sweets shaped daily in Kolkata, coffee grown under forest shade in the south and spice-laden dishes emerging from kitchens across Mumbai and Delhi.

Kumaon

Mountains of cheese

High in the western Himalayas, short summers shape local dairy practices. Milk is processed into fresh cheese, yoghurt and ghee. Try them in simple meals in homestays and eateries across the region.

1hr from Delhi

▸ p117

Kolkata

City of sweets

Confectioners in Kolkata turn milk into spongy, syrup-soaked desserts. Try popular items like *mishti doi* (sweet curd), *rasgulla* (dessert dumplings; pictured) and *sandesh* (sweet desserts).

2½hr from Delhi

▸ p177

Puducherry

Butter and batter

Puducherry's food reflects its French colonial past alongside Tamil cooking. Bakeries sell croissants and baguettes, while nearby restaurants serve *idli* (fermented rice cake) and dosa.

3hr from Chennai

▸ p226

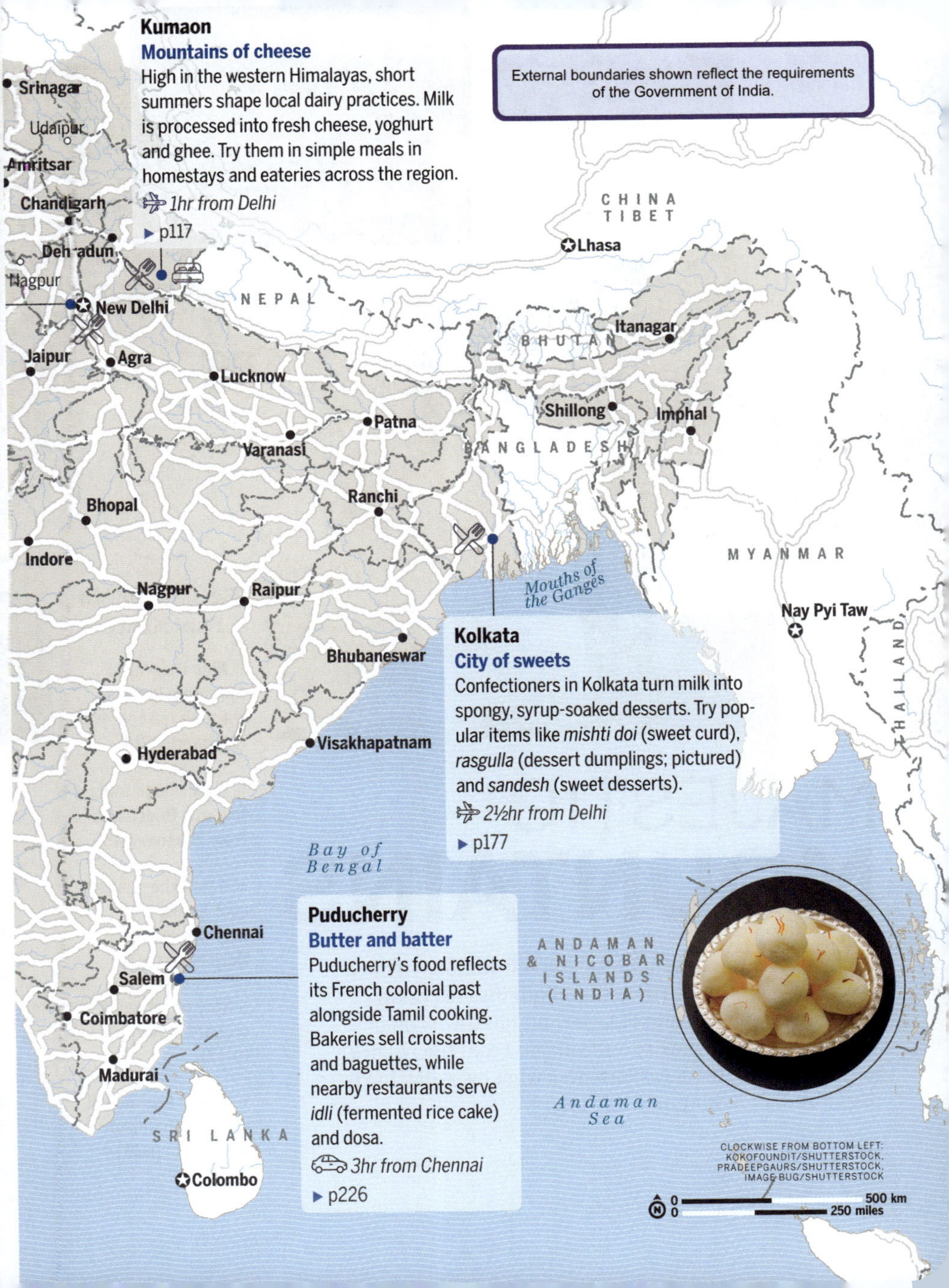

CLOCKWISE FROM BOTTOM LEFT: KOKOFOUNDIT/SHUTTERSTOCK, PRADEEPGAURS/SHUTTERSTOCK, IMAGE BUG/SHUTTERSTOCK

- The mountain regions range from low-elevation hill stations to high Himalayan passes.
- Travel times are slow, with winding roads, especially at altitude.
- Weather and altitude shape access year round.

MAJESTIC MOUNTAINS

India's mountain towns and hill stations invite a slower pace of travel. Toy trains climb into tea estates, footpaths link mountain villages and hill towns offer stunning views at sunrise and sunset. From the Nilgiris to the eastern Himalayas, discover what everyday life is like in India's mountains.

Best Mountain Experiences

- ▶ **Ride the Nilgiri Mountain Railway through tea country (pictured; p218)**
- ▶ **Walk village trails towards Goecha La from Yuksom (p155)**
- ▶ **Watch the sunrise over Khangchendzonga from Darjeeling (p174)**
- ▶ **Stay on an apple orchard in Kotkhai (p113)**
- ▶ **Take in Aravalli hill views from Rajasthan's forts (p89)**

DETHAN PUNALUR/GETTY IMAGES

ALONG THE COAST

India's coastline stretches from palm-lined beaches and fishing villages to coral reefs, mangroves and island forests. Swim, surf or dive in the Andamans, kayak through Kerala's backwaters or spend slow days eating seafood along Goa's sandy shores.

Best Coastal Experiences

- Surf Karnataka's reef and beach breaks in Udupi and Kodi Bengre (p231)
- Paddle Kerala's backwaters by kayak (p225)
- Eat your way through Goa's beachside tavernas and markets (p204)
- Travel between Andaman Islands by ferry (p228)

CLOCKWISE FROM LEFT: KIRTI BHOLE/SHUTTERSTOCK, VKILIKOV/SHUTTERSTOCK

↖ MUST TRY

Goan cuisine highlights seafood. Flavours are spicy and sour, influenced by local produce and colonial Portuguese rule, alongside local spirits like feni.

★ MARINE LIFE

The Andaman Sea boasts a vibrant marine life, from dugongs and dolphins to reef sharks and manta rays.

Above left Seafood platter, Goa (p204)
Left Dugong (p228)

Delhi

Capitals collide

Delhi has served as a capital multiple times. Walk Old Delhi near the Mughal-era Jama Masjid and Chandni Chowk (pictured left), then cross into New Delhi's wide avenues for a stark contrast that shows how power reshaped the city without erasing what came before.

3hr from Bengaluru

▸ p38

Jaipur

Planned city

Unlike older cities that grew organically, Jaipur was planned from the start. Walking through the centre makes orientation easy, with sightlines to gates, palaces and bazaars (pictured left) that were designed to manage trade, processions and daily traffic.

5hr from Delhi

▸ p82

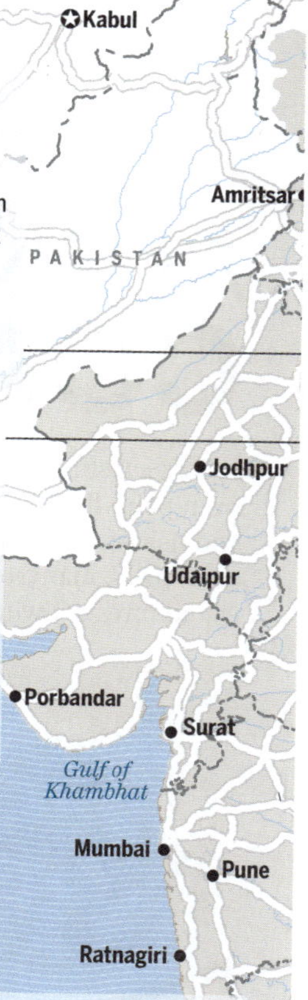

LAYERS OF TIME

India's past isn't something you step into briefly and leave behind. In many cities, temples still draw crowds at dawn, forts shape neighbourhoods and old streets continue to organise daily movement. Travelling through these places rewards walking, repetition and time. It's not just about ticking off monuments, but noticing how facets of history are still being used today.

Hampi

Walk the ruins

Once the capital of the Vijayanagara Empire, Hampi today is a stunning mix of temples, bazaars and royal buildings scattered across a rocky landscape. It's best experienced on foot or by bicycle, to get a sense of the sheer scale of the ruined city.

6hr from Bengaluru

▸ p232

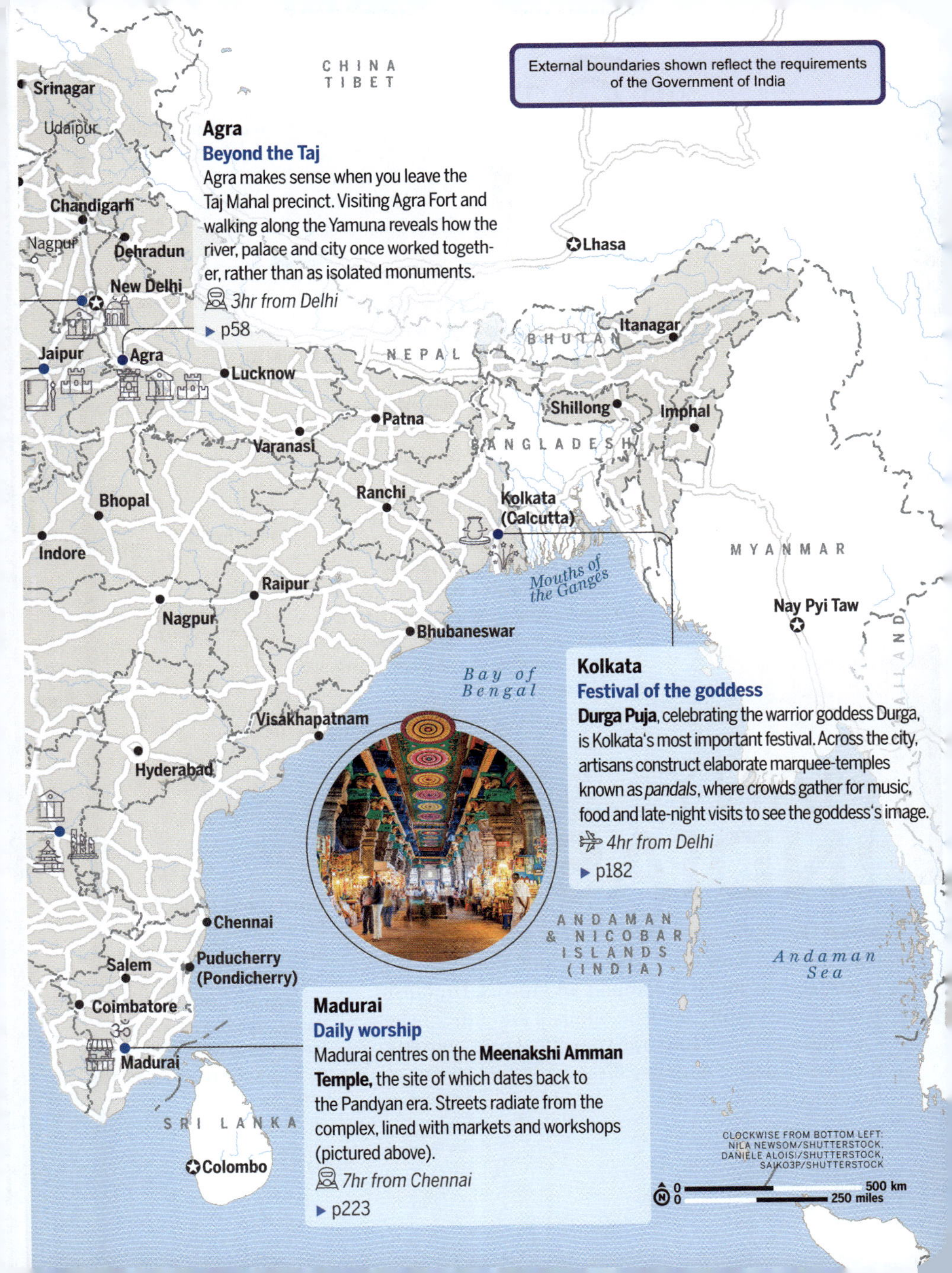

Agra

Beyond the Taj

Agra makes sense when you leave the Taj Mahal precinct. Visiting Agra Fort and walking along the Yamuna reveals how the river, palace and city once worked together, rather than as isolated monuments.

3hr from Delhi

▶ p58

Kolkata

Festival of the goddess

Durga Puja, celebrating the warrior goddess Durga, is Kolkata's most important festival. Across the city, artisans construct elaborate marquee-temples known as *pandals*, where crowds gather for music, food and late-night visits to see the goddess's image.

4hr from Delhi

▶ p182

Madurai

Daily worship

Madurai centres on the **Meenakshi Amman Temple,** the site of which dates back to the Pandyan era. Streets radiate from the complex, lined with markets and workshops (pictured above).

7hr from Chennai

▶ p223

CLOCKWISE FROM BOTTOM LEFT: NILA NEWSOM/SHUTTERSTOCK, DANIELE ALOISI/SHUTTERSTOCK, SAIKO3P/SHUTTERSTOCK

Ajmer Sharif Dargah

Sufi pilgrimage

The dargah of **Khwaja Muin-ud-Din Chishti** is one of South Asia's most important Sufi shrines. The complex fills daily with prayer, ritual offerings and commemorations.

3hr from Japiur

▶ p91

Ranakpur Jain Temple

Symmetry in marble

The 15th-century **Chaumukha Mandir** is a forest of carved white marble. Its hundreds of columns, motifs and figures reflect Jain ideas of restraint.

2hr from Udaipur

▶ p91

Kwan Kuang Temple

Mumbai's only Chinese temple

In Mazagaon, Kwan Kuang Temple has murals of Chinese deities, calligraphy, paintings and a brass bell. Visit during Chinese New Year, when the space fills with offerings, incense and worshippers.

16min from Colaba

▶ p198

MANY **INDIAS**

Over millennia, faiths, languages and communities have taken root in India, shaping landscapes as much as temples and towns. Hinduism, Islam, Christianity, Jainism, Sikhism and other belief systems are woven into everyday life. From marble temples to desert dargahs, discover India's stories of tolerance and diversity.

Great Living Chola Temples

Stone and scale

Begin at Thanjavur's Brihadishwara Temple, where an 80-ton granite dome crowns a 66m tower. Nearby Gangaikonda Cholapuram and Darasuram reveal intricate carvings, frescoes and courtyard spaces set amid paddy fields.

7hr from Chennai

▶ p220

Jama Masjid

Urban devotion

One of India's largest mosques (pictured below right) anchors Delhi's streetscape. Nearby, Sikh, Catholic and Bahai sites showcase the city's religious diversity.

22min from Hauz Khas

▶ p48

Notre Dame des Anges

Christian worship

Notre Dame des Anges (pictured left) reflects Puducherry's history as a French colonial settlement. The 19th century church is an active place of worship for local Tamil and Franco-Indian congregations.

3hr from Chennai

▶ p226

CLOCKWISE FROM BOTTOM LEFT: PHILIPPE MARION/GETTY IMAGES,RUDIERNST/SHUTTERSTOCK, SURENDRA/SHUTTERSTOCK,GABRIELA BHASKAR FOR LONELY PLANET

Winter in India is peak travel season. The dry weather and comfortable temperatures appeal to both domestic and international travellers.

Higher Himalayan regions see snowfall, while lower elevations remain cold but accessible for travel and trekking.

↑ Wildlife watching

National parks reopen after the monsoon, with winter offering popular – though sometimes leafy – conditions for wildlife viewing.

↖ Harvest time

Coffee cherries are picked across the Western Ghats with estates in Karnataka, Kerala and Tamil Nadu at their busiest.

Western Ghats

NOVEMBER

Average daytime max: 14°C (57°F)
Days of rainfall: 5
(Gangtok)

DECEMBER

Average daytime max: 21°C (70°F)
Days of rainfall: 1
(Agra)

India in WINTER

FROM LEFT: SOURABH BHARTI/SHUTTERSTOCK, JOHN NOBLE, PRADEEPGAURS/SHUTTERSTOCK, DINODIA PHOTOS/ALAMY BACKGROUND: RUDRA NARAYAN MITRA/SHUTTERSTOCK

Festival season

Winter coincides with Christmas, New Year and a dense calendar of regional religious and cultural festivals across India.

↑ Expect delays

In northern India, foggy mornings in December and January can delay trains and flights, especially around Delhi.

↖ Pongal

Tamil Nadu's four-day harvest festival in January celebrates the winter crop, with temple rituals, decorated homes and communal meals.

Tamil Nadu

JANUARY-EARLY FEBRUARY

Average daytime max: 25°C (77°F)
Days of rainfall: 2
(Shillong)

Average daytime max: 26°C (79°F)
Days of rainfall: 3
(Kolkata)

Demand for accommodation peaks during winter, particularly from December to February. View tours and overnight adventures in advance at lonelyplanet.com/destinations/india.

Packing Notes
Light layers for cool mornings; winter gear when travelling in the north. Don't forget sunscreen.

Spring's mild days make long visits to exposed sites more comfortable than in peak summer heat.

Across northern and central India, spring brings fresh growth, clearer skies and ideal conditions for walking and sightseeing.

With dry weather and new vegetation, spring offers good conditions for wildlife travel before the summer heat intensifies.

↖ Holi

Spring's most exciting festival sees streets erupt in colour and crowds as winter gives way to warmer days across India.

↖ Losar

Tibetan Buddhist communities in the Himalayas mark the Lunar New Year with monastery rituals, masked dances and family gatherings.

LATE FEBRUARY

Average daytime max: 31°C (88°F)
Days of rainfall: 1
(Chattisgargh)

India in SPRING

FROM LEFT: PAPRI/SHUTTERSTOCK, STANZINN/SHUTTERSTOCK, SIDDHARTH_TIWARI 36/SHUTTERSTOCK, PRADEEPGAURS/SHUTTERSTOCK
BACKGROUND: AYUSH TRIPATHI 740/SHUTTERSTOCK

↘ Gangaur

Celebrated in early spring, this Hindu festival honours marital devotion with processions, music and decorated idols.

↖ Shivratri

This major Hindu festival draws pilgrims to temples and river towns, particularly in northern and central India.

MARCH

Average daytime max: 28°C (83°F)
Days of rainfall: 9
(Kodagu)

Average daytime max: -4°C (21°F)
Days of rainfall: 2
(Ladakh)

After peak winter travel across India, spring offers lively festivals with slightly fewer crowds.

Packing Notes
Light layers for warm days but cool evenings. Comfortable shoes for festivals and long sightseeing days.

Demand for accommodation peaks from April to June, especially during school holidays. Book tours and overnight adventures in advance.

Hit the trails

Summer is peak time for hiking at altitude in Himachal Pradesh and Uttarakhand. The lower valleys remain hot and humid.

↗ Mango Season

From Alphonso in Maharashtra to Langra in Uttar Pradesh, summer is mango season. It's celebrated in homes and on menus nationwide.

↖ Buddha Purnima

Observed in April or May, this major Buddhist festival draws pilgrims to Bodhgaya, marking the Buddha's birth, enlightenment and death.

Bodhgaya

APRIL

Average daytime max: 32°C (89°F)
Days of rainfall: 1
(Delhi)

MAY

India in SUMMER

FROM LEFT: IMAGE BUG/SHUTTERSTOCK, CASPER1774 STUDIO/SHUTTERSTOCK, SANTHOSH VARGHESE/SHUTTERSTOCK
BACKGROUND: ARUN SAMBHU MISHRA/SHUTTERSTOCK

Wildlife spotting

Pre-monsoon heat in Central and Eastern India improves wildlife sightings, as animals gather near water before seasonal park closures.

↗ Thrissur Pooram

One of India's most spectacular temple festivals, marked by elephants, percussion ensembles and fireworks in Kerala between April and May.

Kerala

Humidity hits

Summer brings uncomfortably high heat and humidity across southern India, with sightseeing best planned early or late in the day.

JUNE

Average daytime max: 39°C (102°F)
Days of rainfall: 2
(Jaipur)

Average daytime max: 35°C (95°F)
Days of rainfall: 10
(Shimla)

April and May are the hottest months, ideal for beach days in Goa and Karnataka before the monsoons set in.

Packing Notes
Loose linens and plenty of sunscreen for sightseeing days. A light jacket helps in the hills.

Monsoons lower temperatures transform the countryside. But days are shaped by sudden downpours and humidity.

Heavy rain closes many national parks between July and September, especially in central India. Plan wildlife trips for other seasons.

↗ Rath Yatra

Held during the monsoon, this chariot festival draws crowds to coastal temple towns, rain or shine.

↘ Goa's Monsoon Festivals

Seasonal celebrations mark the rains, from São João to mud and fishing festivals rooted in local agrarian rhythms.

Goa

JULY

Average daytime max: 29°C (84°F)
Days of rainfall: 27
(Goa)

AUGUST

Average daytime max: 35°C (95°F)
Days of rainfall: 10
(Chennai)

India in MONSOON

FROM LEFT: RICHARD I'ANSON/GETTY IMAGES, MATHEWJOSEK/ALAMY, HARDIK DEDHIA/SHUTTERSTOCK
BACKGROUND: K_CHAUHAN/SHUTTERSTOCK

Travel troubles

In the Western Ghats, Himalayas and the Northeast, landslides and washouts can stretch short distances into long travel days.

Outside major festivals, the monsoon brings fewer visitors, easier hotel bookings and a slower pace of life in many regions.

In Tamil Nadu and across the Deccan Plateau, it rains mostly in bursts, with clearer spells between showers.

SEPTEMBER

Average daytime max: 29°C (84°F)
Days of rainfall: 15
(Kochi)

OCTOBER

Average daytime max: 20°C (68°F)
Days of rainfall: 7
(Darjeeling)

Monsoons slow road and rail travel in many regions, with delays common during heavy downpours.

Packing Notes
A rain jacket, quick-dry clothing and a waterproof daypack are essential. As is insect repellent.

GOLDEN TRIANGLE
Trip Builder

TAKE YOUR PICK OF MUST-SEES AND HIDDEN GEMS

Linking Delhi, Agra and Jaipur, the Golden Triangle is India's most travelled route. Sights here showcase Mughal power, Rajput ambition and fantastic street culture, with fast trains and worthwhile detours. Plenty of surprises await if you slow the pace and step slightly off the beaten path.

Trip Notes

Hub towns Delhi, Jaipur

How long Allow 7-10 days for core stops; up to two weeks if adding wildlife reserves or rural Rajasthan.

Getting around Trains are fast and efficient between major cities. Hire a car with a driver for day trips to smaller towns.

Tips Start early to beat crowds at major sights. October to March offers the best weather. Winter fog can delay trains in northern India.

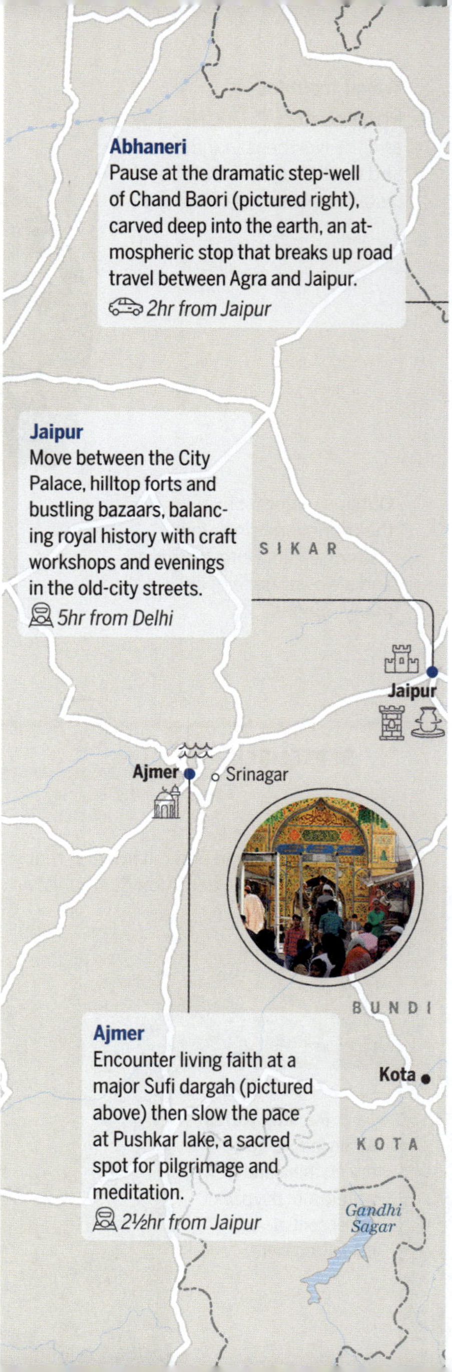

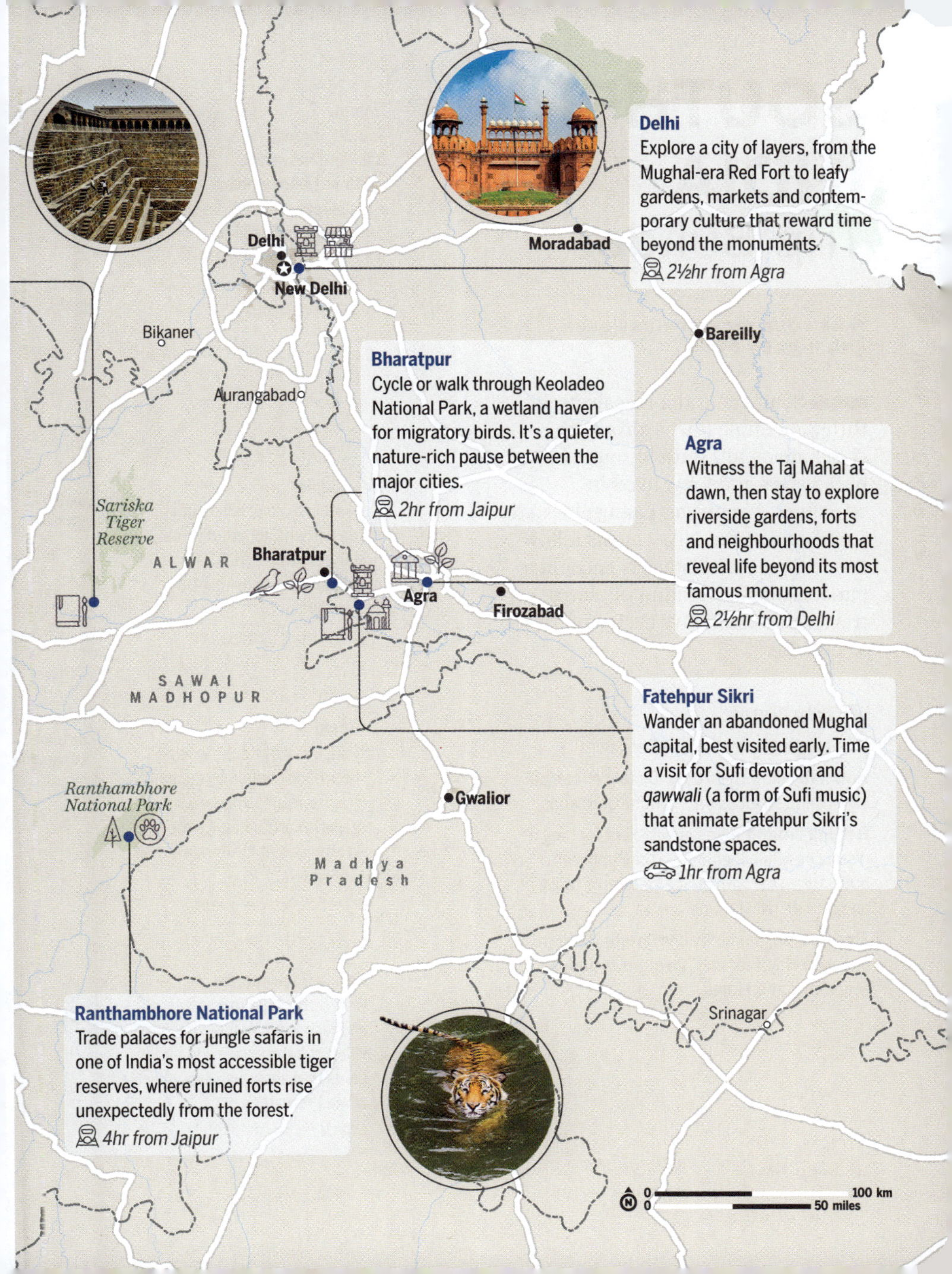

Delhi
Explore a city of layers, from the Mughal-era Red Fort to leafy gardens, markets and contemporary culture that reward time beyond the monuments.
2½hr from Agra

Bharatpur
Cycle or walk through Keoladeo National Park, a wetland haven for migratory birds. It's a quieter, nature-rich pause between the major cities.
2hr from Jaipur

Agra
Witness the Taj Mahal at dawn, then stay to explore riverside gardens, forts and neighbourhoods that reveal life beyond its most famous monument.
2½hr from Delhi

Fatehpur Sikri
Wander an abandoned Mughal capital, best visited early. Time a visit for Sufi devotion and *qawwali* (a form of Sufi music) that animate Fatehpur Sikri's sandstone spaces.
1hr from Agra

Ranthambhore National Park
Trade palaces for jungle safaris in one of India's most accessible tiger reserves, where ruined forts rise unexpectedly from the forest.
4hr from Jaipur

SOUTHERN INDIA
Trip Builder

TAKE YOUR PICK OF MUST-SEES AND HIDDEN GEMS

Southern India reveals itself through temple towns alive with ritual, misty hill stations, quiet backwaters and long, lived-in coastlines. Languages change by state – and sometimes city – meals follow the seasons and distances encourage patience. Pick a handful of places, travel lightly and give each stop time to breathe.

Trip Notes

Hub towns Chennai, Kochi, Bengaluru

How long Allow 10-14 days. Distances can be significant, so focus on a handful of regions.

Getting around Trains are efficient for long distances, while flights save time between hubs. Hire a car with driver for temple trails and remote hill stations.

Tips Heat and humidity can be intense from March to May. Festivals affect travel and accommodation rates.

CLOCKWISE FROM TOP LEFT: FABIO LAMANNA/SHUTTERSTOCK, VM2002/SHUTTERSTOCK

Hampi
Wander through boulder-strewn hills scattered with temples and palaces of a vast, ruined imperial capital. It's best explored slowly on foot or by bicycle.
9hr from Bengaluru

The Nilgiris
Cool off in a misty hill country of tea gardens, forested slopes and the historic UNESCO mountain railway linking Ooty to the highlands.
3hr from Coimbatore

Kochi
Pause in Fort Kochi, a neighbourhood shaped by ancient trading routes, modern art galleries and cafes. Also a starting point for Kerala's vast waterways.
1hr from Bengaluru

Kerala Backwaters
Drift through palm-lined canals and lagoons in Alappuzha, passing villages, lighthouses and paddy fields that showcase everyday life along the water's edge.
1½hr from Kochi

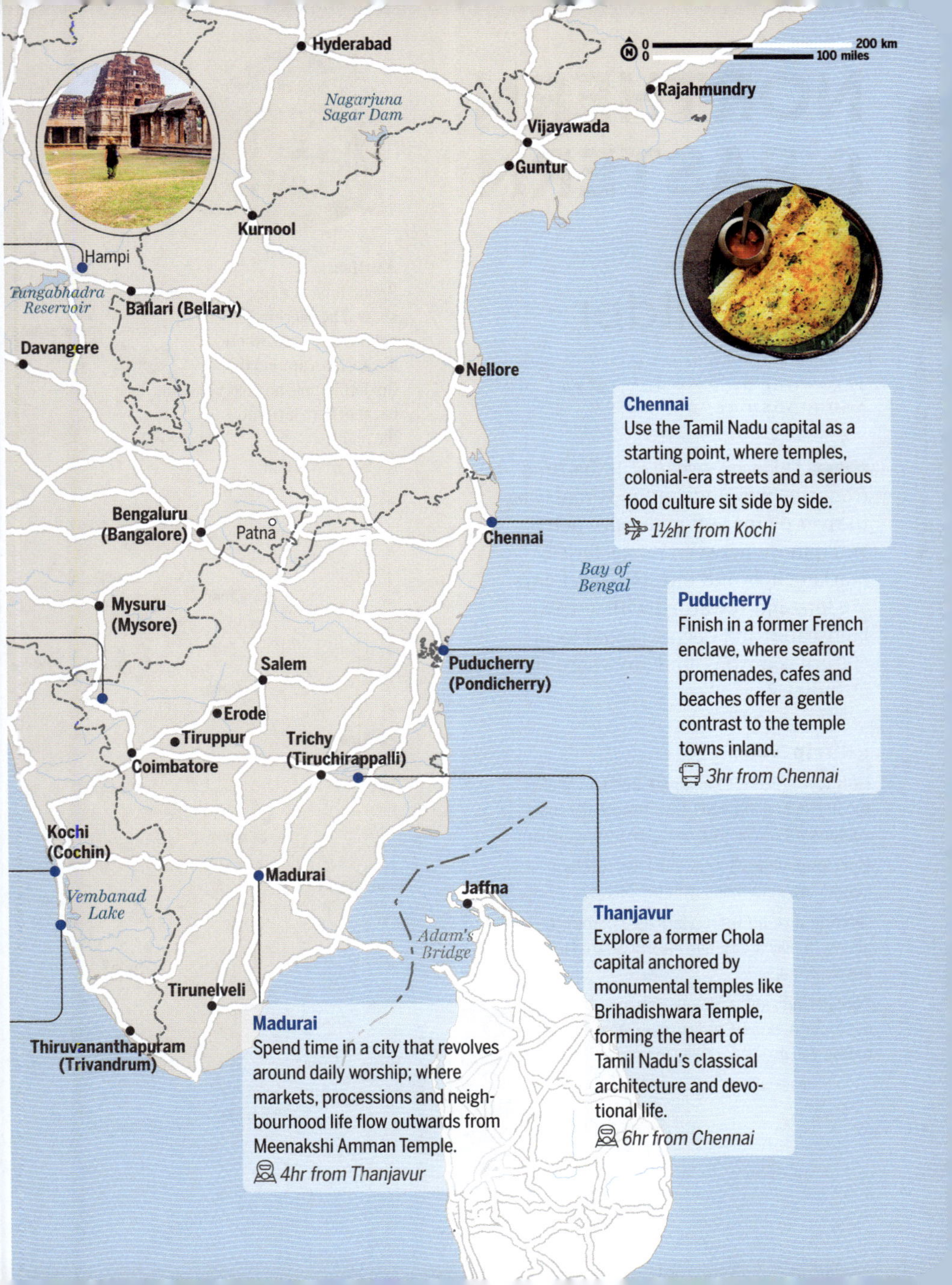
Hyderabad
0 200 km
0 100 miles
Rajahmundry
Nagarjuna Sagar Dam
Vijayawada
Guntur
Kurnool
Hampi
Tungabhadra Reservoir
Ballari (Bellary)
Davangere
Nellore
Chennai
Use the Tamil Nadu capital as a starting point, where temples, colonial-era streets and a serious food culture sit side by side.
1½hr from Kochi
Bengaluru (Bangalore)
Patna
Chennai
Bay of Bengal
Mysuru (Mysore)
Puducherry
Finish in a former French enclave, where seafront promenades, cafes and beaches offer a gentle contrast to the temple towns inland.
3hr from Chennai
Salem
Puducherry (Pondicherry)
Erode
Tiruppur
Trichy (Tiruchirappalli)
Coimbatore
Kochi (Cochin)
Madurai
Jaffna
Vembanad Lake
Adam's Bridge
Thanjavur
Explore a former Chola capital anchored by monumental temples like Brihadishwara Temple, forming the heart of Tamil Nadu's classical architecture and devotional life.
6hr from Chennai
Tirunelveli
Madurai
Spend time in a city that revolves around daily worship; where markets, processions and neighbourhood life flow outwards from Meenakshi Amman Temple.
4hr from Thanjavur
Thiruvananthapuram (Trivandrum)

NORTHERN & EASTERN INDIA
Trip Builder

TAKE YOUR PICK OF MUST-SEES AND HIDDEN GEMS

This vast sweep of India runs from the highlands in the Himalayas to river plains and mangrove deltas. You'll move between monasteries, market cities and forests. Travel days are long but rewarded with surreal landscapes and deeply rooted local culture you won't find anywhere else in India.

Trip Notes

Hub towns Delhi, Chandigarh and Leh anchor the north. Kolkata and Guwahati are the main eastern gateways, with Gangtok linking Sikkim.

How long Allow 10 days. Take two weeks if combining mountains with the plains.

Getting around Trains work best across the plains. In hilly areas, hire cars or shared jeeps are essential.

Tips Permits and advisories change frequently in border regions. Confirm with local operators before you go – especially in the Northeast.

CLOCKWISE FROM TOP LEFT: SAIKO3P/SHUTTERSTOCK, PAPRI/SHUTTERSTOCK, PAUL STAFFORD, PAPRI/SHUTTERSTOCK

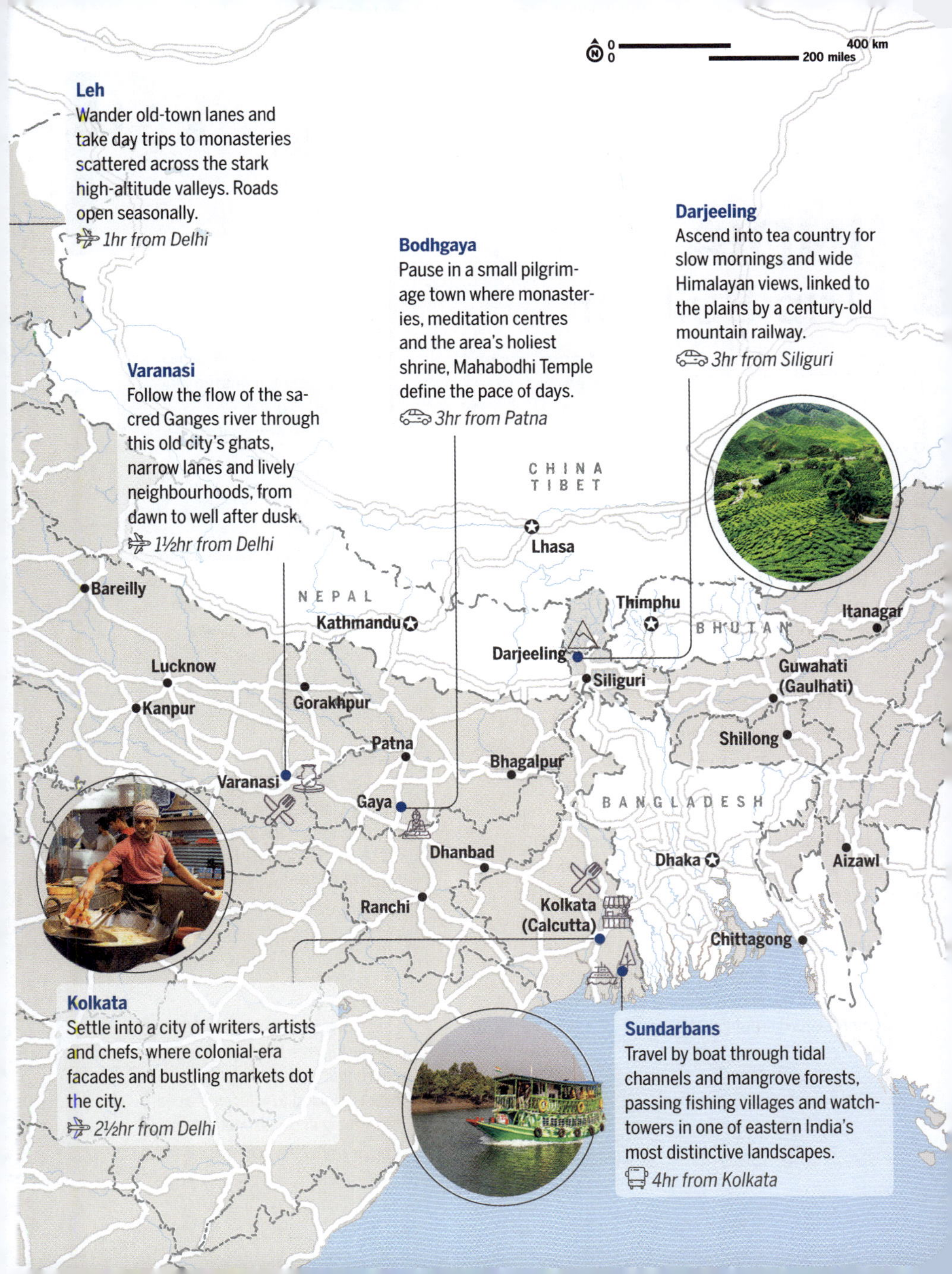

Leh

Wander old-town lanes and take day trips to monasteries scattered across the stark high-altitude valleys. Roads open seasonally.

1hr from Delhi

Bodhgaya

Pause in a small pilgrimage town where monasteries, meditation centres and the area's holiest shrine, Mahabodhi Temple define the pace of days.

3hr from Patna

Darjeeling

Ascend into tea country for slow mornings and wide Himalayan views, linked to the plains by a century-old mountain railway.

3hr from Siliguri

Varanasi

Follow the flow of the sacred Ganges river through this old city's ghats, narrow lanes and lively neighbourhoods, from dawn to well after dusk.

1½hr from Delhi

Kolkata

Settle into a city of writers, artists and chefs, where colonial-era facades and bustling markets dot the city.

2½hr from Delhi

Sundarbans

Travel by boat through tidal channels and mangrove forests, passing fishing villages and watchtowers in one of eastern India's most distinctive landscapes.

4hr from Kolkata

NORTHERN & WESTERN INDIA

Trip Builder

TAKE YOUR PICK OF MUST-SEES AND HIDDEN GEMS

From the Himalayas to the Arabian Sea, Northern and Western India combine mountain travel, historic cities and coastal life. Highlights range from high passes and temple towns to craft regions, vineyards and port cities, best explored by focusing on one connected route at a time.

Trip Notes

Hub towns Delhi and Mumbai are primary international gateways. Chandigarh, Lucknow, Ahmedabad and Panaji are key regional hubs.

How long Allow 10 days for a focused north or west loop; 2 weeks to combine the two.

Getting around Trains work well between major cities. Flights save time between distant regions.

Tips Weather dictates pace. Summers bring crowds to the hills; winter fog in the north; monsoons disrupt coastal life.

CLOCKWISE FROM TOP LEFT: CHETANSONI/SHUTTERSTOCK, SAIKO3P/SHUTTERSTOCK, PRADEEPGAURS/SHUTTERSTOCK

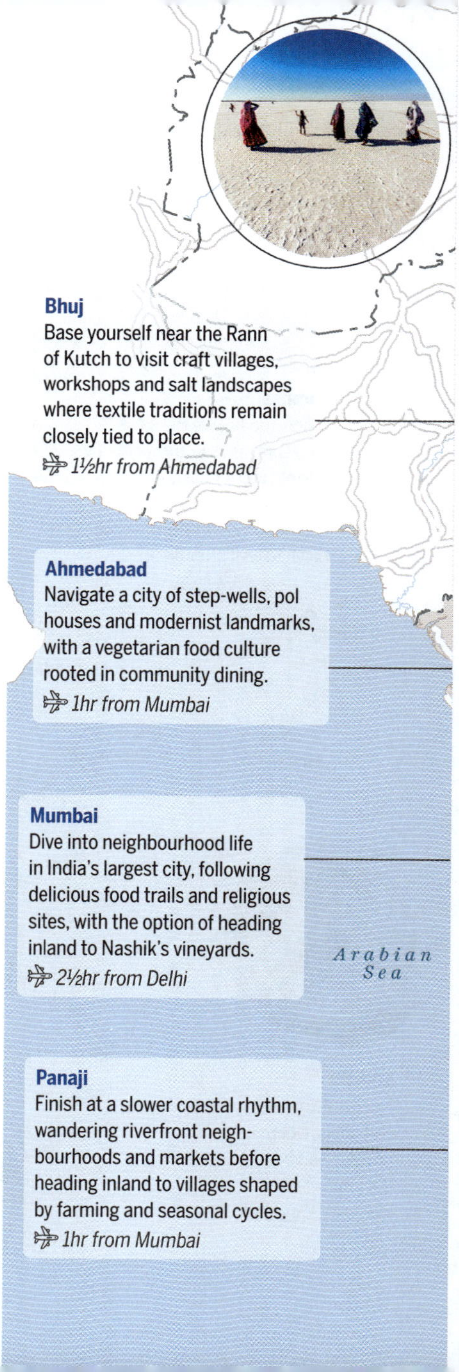

Bhuj
Base yourself near the Rann of Kutch to visit craft villages, workshops and salt landscapes where textile traditions remain closely tied to place.
1½hr from Ahmedabad

Ahmedabad
Navigate a city of step-wells, pol houses and modernist landmarks, with a vegetarian food culture rooted in community dining.
1hr from Mumbai

Mumbai
Dive into neighbourhood life in India's largest city, following delicious food trails and religious sites, with the option of heading inland to Nashik's vineyards.
2½hr from Delhi

Panaji
Finish at a slower coastal rhythm, wandering riverfront neighbourhoods and markets before heading inland to villages shaped by farming and seasonal cycles.
1hr from Mumbai

Chandigarh

Walk a planned Indian city, where modernist architectwure and Hollywod film locations (Sector 15 market) offer a clear contrast to historic north India.

3hr from Delhi

Himachal Pradesh

Walk through former British-era cantonments where bakeries, clubs, churches and forest paths shape daily life. These quiet hill-station villages reveal a nice, slow pace of life.

6hr from Delhi

Lucknow

Eat your way through a city shaped by Awadhi culture and slow cooking, where neighbourhood markets, old houses and everyday Urdu inflect daily life beyond monuments.

7hr from Delhi

7 Things to Know About INDIA

INSIDER TIPS TO HIT THE GROUND RUNNING

1 Money Matters

Many monuments and metros now accept only digital Unified Payments Interface (UPI) transactions using apps like GooglePay, PhonePe and Paytm, not cash or foreign cards. To bypass this restriction, book tickets online or use an authorised travel agent. While having small notes for tips and street food is a good idea, you can expect credit cards to be accepted in airports, hotels, large restaurants and supermarkets.

▶ See more about money on p245

2 Tipping Culture

Tip guides ₹500 to ₹1000 per day, drivers ₹200 to ₹500 for full-day hires and porters ₹50 to ₹100 per bag. In restaurants with or without a service charge, rounding up or leaving around 5–10% is standard.

▶ See more about tipping on p245

3 Food is Regional

Indian food changes dramatically from one region to the next, so let the region influence what you order. In the north, meals lean on wheat-based breads, buttery dhal and slow-cooked meats. Along the West Coast, seafood and coconut-rich curries dominate. Kitchens in the south turn out crisp dosas, savoury rice dishes like biryani and spice-driven gravies. Central India favours millets, lentils and earthy curries. Ordering a local thali is the way to go.

▶ See more about food on p44, p92, p116, p204, p226

4 Temple Etiquette

Shoes are removed at places of worship – wearing socks protects your feet from the hot stone floors. Always dress modestly, covering your shoulders and knees.

▶ See more about etiquette on p250

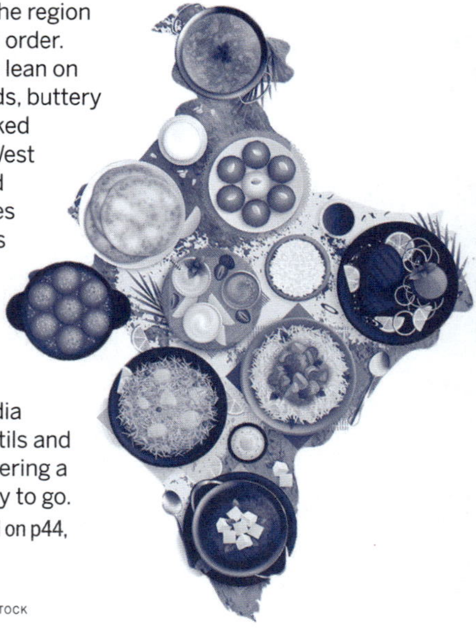

2.FARBAI/SHUTTERSTOCK, 3.MACROVECTOR/SHUTTERSTOCK,
5.IMAGE V/SHUTTERSTOCK, 6.PAPER TRIDENT/SHUTTERSTOCK, 7.KATE GARYUK/SHUTTERSTOCK

5 Festivals Change Everything

Festivals can transform your travel plans overnight. During Diwali, Holi or other major regional festivals such as Dussehra (Durga Puja) and Onam, expect packed trains, road closures, long temple queues and sold-out accommodation. Check local calendars, book transportation in advance and build flexibility into your itinerary – plans can often shift and that's part of the experience of travelling in India.

▶ See more about festivals on p18

6 Tips for Solo Women Travellers

Being aware of your surroundings when travelling solo as a woman in India is key. While contemporary Western fashion is common in larger cities, wearing loose, breathable and modest clothing by local standards makes movement simpler, especially when using public transport or in small towns. Hotel-arranged drivers and rideshare apps like Uber and Ola are widely used and reliable, and arriving in a new city during the day gives you time to orient yourself. Curiosity towards foreigners is common – questions, conversations and sometimes more attention – and while it isn't automatically hostile, it's always optional for you to engage. You don't owe anyone politeness. Festivals, markets and temple visits bring dense crowds and compressed personal space. Move deliberately: stay in places with staff on hand, check in with your accommodation hosts and take cues from local women about where to linger and when to leave.

▶ See more about women travellers on p251

7 Drinking Water

Stick to bottled or filtered water for drinking and brushing your teeth. Avoid ice unless you're confident it's made with purified water. Most hotels and airports provide safe refills. Carry a reusable bottle and top up where filtration is clearly marked. When unsure, choose sealed bottles from reputable vendors.

▶ See more about drinking water on p250

Read, Listen, Watch & Follow

READ

Heart Lamp (Banu Mushtaq; 2025) Short stories on gender and faith; International Booker Prize winner.

Azadi (Arundhati Roy; 2020) Essays on nationalism and freedom in contemporary India.

Gods, Guns and Missionaries (Manu S Pillai; 2024) How colonial encounters shaped modern Hindu politics.

The Covenant of Water (Abraham Verghese; 2023) Generational epic tracing medicine, migration and faith in South India.

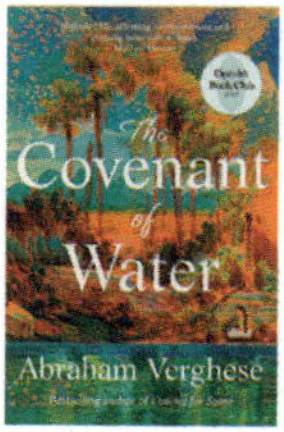

LISTEN

The Seen and the Unseen (2017) Podcast hosted by journalist Amit Varma unpacking Indian politics, economics and everyday life.

Desi Crime Podcast (Aishwarya Singh and Aryaan Misra; 2020) True-crime stories that offer real insights into India's social realities and justice gaps.

The History of India Podcast (Kit Patrick; 2015) A chronological guide to India's long, complex history from 600 BCE onwards.

Guide (Lata Mangeshkar; 1965) Mangeshkar's definitive soundtrack to the film *Guide*, while at her peak, with songs that many Indians still know by heart.

MATT JELONEK/GETTY IMAGES

Big Dawgs (Hanumankind; 2024; pictured) A breakout rap hit whose viral video marked the rapper's arrival beyond India's homegrown hip-hop scene.

WATCH

Boatcast (2025) Artist Zahir Mirza's YouTube series exploring Kerala's history with historians, creatives and scholars.

Cactus Pears (2025) Sundance-winning film about grief, gay love and rural Maharashtra life.

Piku (2015) Wry, intimate look at family, relationships and independence in middle-class urban India.

All We Imagine As Light (2024; pictured top right) Cannes Grand Prix-winning drama tracing the lives of three women in modern Mumbai.

Monkey Man (2024; pictured bottom right) Gritty action film channeling contemporary Indian politics through myth and street-level violence.

COLLECTION CHRISTOPHEL/ALAMY

COLLECTION CHRISTOPHEL/ALAMY

FOLLOW

The Swaddle (*theswaddle.com*) Reporting on culture shaping modern India.

Luru (*lurumagazine.com*) Stories about Bengaluru's creative communities.

@thathyderabadiboy Street food, local history and city life in Hyderabad.

@indialostandfound Visual archive of lesser-known places across India.

Goya Journal (*goya.in*) Long-form essays on food and culture across India.

DELHI

IMMENSE | HISTORIC | CAPTIVATING

RESEARCHED BY MARGOT BIGG

SAHIL GHOSH/SHUTTERSTOCK

DELHI
Trip Builder

There's never a dull moment in Delhi. Whether you've come to learn about the past, check out the architecture or just do a bit of shopping and eating, India's buzzing capital is the perfect place to choose your own adventure.

SADAR BAZAAR
Southern Ridge Forest
Talkatora Gardens
Nehru Park
Hauz Khas Deer Park
Aurobindo Marg

Break bread with the Sikh community at the *langar* (dining hall; pictured left) at **Gurdwara Bangla Sahib** (p48).
20min from Connaught Place

Shop for crafts from across the country at **Dilli Haat** (p53).
Next to Dilli Haat–INA metro station

CLOCKWISE FROM BOTTOM LEFT: RITU MANOJ JETHANI/SHUTTERSTOCK, PRADEEPGAURS/SHUTTERSTOCK.SOUMEN 21/SHUTTERSTOCK. AVIJIT BOURI/SHUTTERSTOCK

See Old Delhi's Mughal masterpieces: **Red Fort** (p50) and **Jama Masjid** (p48).
Red Fort is next to Lal Quila metro station and Jama Masjid is next to Jama Masjid metro station
Learn about Vedic history and see a fountain show at the **Akshardham Temple** (p48).
6min from Akshardham metro station
Stroll through massive gardens dotted with plants and Mughal monuments at **Sunder Nursery** (pictured; p47).
9min from India Gate
Listen to *qawwali*, an ancient type of Sufi devotional music, at the **Nizamuddin Dargah** (p46).
15min from India Gate
Browse the chic boutiques and bookshops of **Khan Market** (p53).
5min from Khan Market metro station
Sample tangy-sweet-spicy-crunchy-watery ***pani puri*** (p45) at Prince Chaat.
8min from Kailash Colony metro station
OLD DELHI
Netaji Subhash Park
Central Park
Indraprastha Marg
Firoz Shah Rd
PRAGATI MAIDAN
National Stadium
Boating Lake
NEW DELHI
Ring Rd (MG Rd)
Hapur Bypass
Yamuna River
Subramaniam Bharti Rd
Delhi Golf Course
Sunder Nursery
Lodi Gardens
Lodi Rd
August Kranti Marg
Astha Kunj Park
Hauz Khas Forest
0
2 km
0
1 mile

Practicalities

OLIVER FOERSTNER/SHUTTERSTOCK

ARRIVING

Indira Gandhi International Airport (pictured) is Delhi's main gateway for domestic and international flights. To get into town, hire a fixed-price taxi from the Delhi Police-run prepaid taxi stand or take the Airport Express line of the Delhi metro.

New Delhi Railway Station, one of the three main train stations in Delhi (the other two are **Delhi Junction**, aka Old Delhi Railway Station, and **Nizamuddin Railway Station**), has direct metro connections to key spots around town, including the airport.

HOW MUCH FOR A

Cup of roadside chai
₹20

One-litre bottle of water
₹20

Serving of aloo tikki
₹50

WHEN TO GO

OCT-DEC
Pleasant temperatures but off-the-charts pollution for the months following Diwali.

JAN-MAR
Foggy and chilly weather that begins to warm up by March.

APR-JUN
Temperatures can soar past 45°C, heralding in hot winds and mango season.

JUL-SEP
Muggy monsoon season, with intermittent periods of serious showers.

GETTING AROUND

Taxi The most convenient, comfortable and expensive way to get around the city. It's not easy to hail them off the street; instead, use the Ola Cabs or Uber app for a fixed-price ride, or even a day hire (travel agents and hotel desks can also help with this).

Metro Delhi's air-conditioned metro system is reliable and extensive, with 10 lines and over 250 stations, but it can get crowded. A dedicated women's carriage is available on every train.

Autorickshaw Great for short rides and getting around quickly, these (usually) green-and-yellow carts are piloted by experts at weaving through traffic. Negotiate fares before you set out.

EATING & DRINKING

Delhi is known for its snacky street food, or *chaat* (p44), which is available in abundance both at roadside stalls and in *chaat*-themed restaurants. While you could easily fill up on samosas and other goodies without ever sitting down at a restaurant, it's worth saving room to fill up on rich local favourites, such as butter chicken (a Delhi invention; pictured top right) and *rajma chawal* (red beans and rice; pictured bottom right). The fine-dining scene is excellent, too, with many spots putting creative twists on Indian classics.

Must-try butter chicken Moti Mahal (p56)

Best soya chaap Canvas V (p56)

WHERE TO STAY

Delhi is huge and somewhat spread out, which is amplified by its notorious traffic jams. If you plan to take the metro, choose accommodation within walking distance of a station.

Place	Pros/Cons
Paharganj	Backpacker enclave with loads of budget options. Crowded and tout-filled.
Connaught Place	Central location with great dining and metro choices. On the pricier side.
Chandni Chowk	Conveniently close to Old Delhi highlights. Crowded and noisy.
Majnu-ka-Tilla	Quiet Tibetan neighbourhood with good food. Far from some attractions.
Hauz Khas Village	Hip area near a massive park. Can get hectic with partiers at night.
Aerocity	Well-maintained hotels with easy airport access. Far from the city centre.

CONNECT & FIND YOUR WAY

Connectivity While some cafes will give you their wi-fi password, you're better off getting a local SIM card or, if you don't have a phone with a physical SIM slot, an international data plan from your home country.

Navigation Google Maps works fairly well in Delhi. Download offline maps to protect yourself from potential data drops in narrow-laned areas.

AIR QUALITY

Delhi's air quality can reach toxic levels, especially in the winters. Check the air quality index (AQI), pack face masks and seek out accommodation with air purifiers

MONEY

A growing number of restaurants and shops accept credit cards, but carry cash for autorickshaws, small shops and tips. Change is in short supply, so try to have smaller notes.

01 Serious CHAAT

FOOD | SNACKS | SPICE

There's no denying that Delhi is a city that's obsessed with food. You'll find every type, including many fine-dining restaurants with fancy spins on Indian classics, but the capital is best known for its own brand of street-food snacks, collectively known as *Dilli-ki-Chaat*. Just make sure to pace yourself – there's a lot to try.

How to

Getting there You'll find loads of street-food vendors across the city: just walk to the nearest market to see what's on offer.

When to go Many restaurants open early and stay open late for meals, while late afternoon to early evening is when many Delhiites go out for a pre-dinner snack.

Tea time Nothing beats a cup of masala chai – just don't call it 'chai tea' (which is akin to saying the equivalent of 'tea tea').

Quintessential eats
Delhiites take street food seriously, which means loads of unmissable dishes are available across the city. *Aloo tikki*, a mashed potato patty fried in oil or ghee and usually smothered with some combo of chutney, yogurt, pomegranate seeds or chickpeas, is a filling must-try, as is *papri chaat*, crisp fried wafers (often flavoured with cumin) covered in sweetened yogurt, coriander-mint-and-tamarind chutney, and *sev* (tiny chickpea-flour noodles). Although originally a Tibetan snack, *momo* (dumplings stuffed with veg or meat) are also ubiquitous – while they're traditionally served with a chilli sauce, mayonnaise has become an increasingly popular accompaniment in recent years.

Stews and skewers Very popular with meat lovers, *nihari* is a slow-cooked goat stew with Mughal origins that's typically served for breakfast, especially in Old Delhi. Kebabs are another must; the seekh kebabs at **Ghalib Kabab Corner** in

PRADEEPGAURS/SHUTTERSTOCK

the **Nizamuddin** area are particularly beloved.

Play it safe If you're nervous about eating from street-food vendors, you have options. **Prince Chaat** in South Delhi's posh GK-1 neighbourhood is a reliable favourite, as are chain restaurants such as **Haldiram's** and **Bikanervala**; both have branches all over, including in Chandni Chowk and Connaught Place. Such spots put a premium on hygiene and use purified water for classics such as *pani puri* (aka *golgappa*), crisp fried puffs stuffed with a potato-onion-chickpea mix, drenched with tamarind chutney, dunked in a vat of cool spiced water, and then consumed in one explosively flavourful bite.

At the Chef's Table

Parathas at **Pandit Ji Parantha Hut** are a mix of nostalgia and pure deliciousness. They have several fillings, but for me, the classic potato-and-onion paratha cooked in ghee is the best.

Doda Barfi Treacle Tart Served at **Indian Accent** this Punjabi, fudge-like, sticky dessert is elevated to another level.

Chhole Bhature at **Embassy Restaurant** are exceptionally fluffy and taste oil-free despite being fried. These football-sized breads, eaten with spicy chickpeas and onions, will take you all the way to heaven in 1st class.

Malleshwaram 18th Cross Dosa at **Carnatic Café** are a thicker-than-usual dosa, smothered with butter and chilli powder.

Ritu Dalmia, *celebrity chef, restaurateur and cookbook author. @ritudal*

Above Street food vendors, Delhi

02 Echoes in STONE

HISTORY | CULTURE | GARDENS

Anchored by Humayun's Tomb, the first UNESCO World Heritage Site in Delhi and the inspiration for the Taj Mahal, the Nizamuddin heritage precinct offers an immersive look into life in the city under the Delhi sultanate and early Mughal empire. Come here to explore beautifully preserved tombs, shrines and gardens, with a stop in a 'sunken' museum for a glimpse into the past.

YAMASK/SHUTTERSTOCK

Trip Notes

Getting here The easiest way to get here is by taxi or autorickshaw; the JLN Stadium metro station is a 20-minute walk away.

When to go Humayun's Tomb and Sunder Nursery are open daily. The museum is closed Mondays.

Combo ticket Cost- and time-saving combo tickets allow you to pass directly from Humayun's Tomb into the museum or vice versa.

Souvenir stop Drop by the museum shop for books and gift items.

ROY JOHNSON/ALAMY

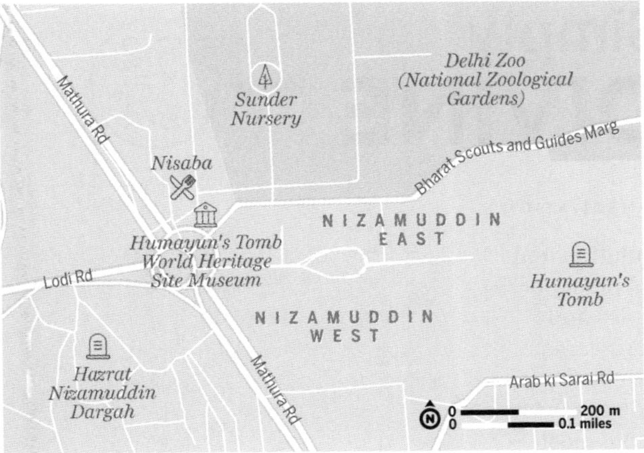

Top left Humayun's Tomb
Bottom left Nizamuddin dargah

A Historic Trio

Start with a morning visit to **Humayun's Tomb**, which opens at sunrise. Dating to 1570, it was the first garden tomb on the subcontinent and is considered the first true example of Mughal architecture. This masterpiece in stone features a blend of white marble and red sandstone, with its design based on principles of Islamic architecture. It's the star attraction of a larger tomb garden that includes several other Mughal tombs, including the blue-domed **Nila Gumbad** and the **Nai-ka-Gumbad**, or 'Barber's Tomb,' rumoured to be the final resting place of the emperor's hairdresser.

Once you've finished at the tomb, descend into the adjacent **Humayun's Tomb World Heritage Site Museum**. This underground complex tells the story of the area from the 13th century to the modern day through exhibits on everything from Humayun's extensive travels to the works of poet-minister Rahim.

Exit the museum from the side opposite where you came in. If you're feeling peckish, stop by fine-dining restaurant **Nisaba** in a courtyard near the museum gate. Otherwise, follow signs to **Sunder Nursery**, a 90-acre expanse of trees, plants, birds and butterflies. A large network of pathways crisscrosses the park, connecting picnic areas and lush gardens with public art installations and beautifully restored Mughal monuments. Highlights include pavilions, platforms and dome-topped tombs as well as a lotus pond that's both shaped like a lotus and filled with floating lotuses.

Nizamuddin Basti

On the opposite side of Mathura Rd from the tombs and gardens, Nizamuddin is a predominantly Muslim neighbourhood that's best known for two things: the 14th-century **dargah** (shrine) of Sufi saint Hazrat Nizamuddin and its rich Mughlai food. The shrine is the main draw for many (it's said that Humayun himself wanted to be buried near the energy of the medieval saint), and people of all faiths come here on Thursday nights to listen to *qawwali* (devotional music) performances. If you can't make it in the evening, it's still worth visiting for a kebab stop at the famous **Ghalib Kabab Corner**.

03 Simply DIVINE

TEMPLES | SPIRITUALITY | MEDITATION

Delhi's diverse population and sheer size mean that it has plenty of spiritual sites. Hindu temples and mosques abound, as do gurdwaras, Buddhist temples and churches. You don't have to be a spiritual seeker to enjoy the city's spiritual side; most spots welcome all visitors, from spiritually minded solace seekers to architecture enthusiasts.

How to

Getting here Many top temples are near major metro lines, including the Akshardham Temple (Blue Line), Chhatarpur Mandir (Yellow Line), Gurudwara Bangla Sahib (Orange Line/Airport Express) and the Lotus Temple (Violet Line).

When to go Check individual timings. Many Hindu temples close for a few hours in the afternoon.

Shoe in Be prepared to remove footwear before entering temples; you should also cover your head.

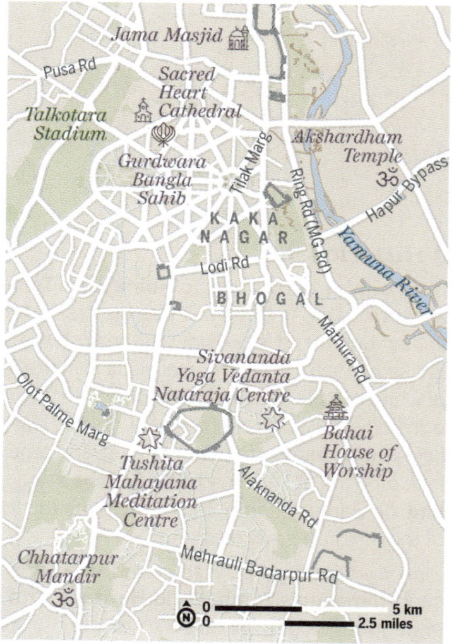

Hindu mandirs Delhi's largest Hindu temple, or mandir, is **Akshardham Temple**, a massive complex full of intricately carved domes, canopies and courtyards. While admission is free, it's worth splurging for the three-attraction exhibition ticket, for access to a film, an animatronic display and a narrated boat ride extolling the virtues of Hindu civilisation. Stay till sunset for a colourful water light-and-water show. In Delhi's southern outskirts, Chhatarpur Mandir Rd is lined with temples, including the sprawling **Chhatarpur Mandir**, which blends North and South Indian architectural styles.

Many faiths Delhi's other famous holy spots include the **Jama Masjid** in Old Delhi and the Catholic **Sacred Heart Cathedral**. Around the corner from the cathedral, **Gurdwara Bangla Sahib** is Delhi's most prominent Sikh temple. This white-marble spot draws people of all faiths to pay their respects

Yoga & Meditation

Not far from the Lotus Temple, in the leafy Kailash Colony neighbourhood, the **Sivananda Yoga Vedanta Nataraja Centre** offers introductory and advanced courses in yoga asana (postures), pranayama (breath control) and meditation. Courses are taught entirely in English, with free beginner-friendly intro classes on Sunday mornings.

Tushita Mahayana Meditation Centre in South Delhi's Hauz Khas neighbourhood offers half-hour-long analytical and mindfulness meditations on weekday mornings at 9am, as well as a regular schedule of debate classes and dharma (Hindu-Buddhist moral code) lectures. The centre's teachings are based on the Tibetan Mahayana traditions of Buddhism.

and meditate. It's worth stopping to dine, or even volunteer, at the langar, a free community kitchen that's open to all. Best known as the Lotus Temple, the flower-shaped **Bahai House of Worship** welcomes small batches of visitors inside to pray or meditate.

Above Akshardham Temple
Left Gurdwara Bangla Sahib

04 Turn Back TIME

HISTORY | ARCHITECTURE | LIVELINESS

If you like history, or intensity, you'll love Old Delhi. Here you'll find a mix of massive Mughal monuments and historic temples, all packed tightly together with street-food vendors and markets selling everything from nose-tingling spices to bedazzling attire fit for an Indian wedding.

STEVE ESTVANIK/ SHUTTERSTOCK

How to

Getting here Take the metro to the Chandni Chowk or Chawri Bazar station on the Yellow Line or the Lal Qila station on the Violet Line.

When to go Visit on a midweek morning to avoid crowds. Note that Red Fort is closed on Mondays.

Dress the part Wear clothes that cover your knees and shoulders and bring a head covering for visiting mosques and gurdwaras.

Living History

Shri Digamber Jain Naya Mandir is a historic Jain temple housing ancient Tirthankara idols.

Haveli Dharampura is a 200-year-old *haveli* (residence), restored with exceptional sensitivity.

Khari Baoli (pictured left) is Asia's largest wholesale spice market, famous for its vibrant lanes filled with spices and teas.

Vidyun Goel, *director, Haveli Dharampura. @haveli dharampura*

02 Dating to the 18th century, **Gurudwara Sisganj Sahib** honours the ninth Sikh Guru, Tegh Bahadur, who was beheaded at this spot more than a century earlier at the command of Mughal emperor Aurangzeb.

03 Commissioned by Shah Jahan (the man behind the Taj Mahal), the UNESCO-listed **Red Fort** served as the emperor's residence for centuries.

01 Right off bustling Chandni Chowk, **Paranthe Wali Gali** is a narrow lane that's locally beloved (by brave eaters) for its greasy, deep-fried jalebi, a popular breakfast food.

04 Another Shah Jahan creation, **Jama Masjid** (pictured above) is among the largest mosques in India; a beautiful example of Mughal architecture with two towering minarets (one of which you can ascend).

05 Tucked down a maze of winding lanes, **Razia Sultan's Tomb** is the humble resting place of the only woman ruler of the Delhi sultanate.

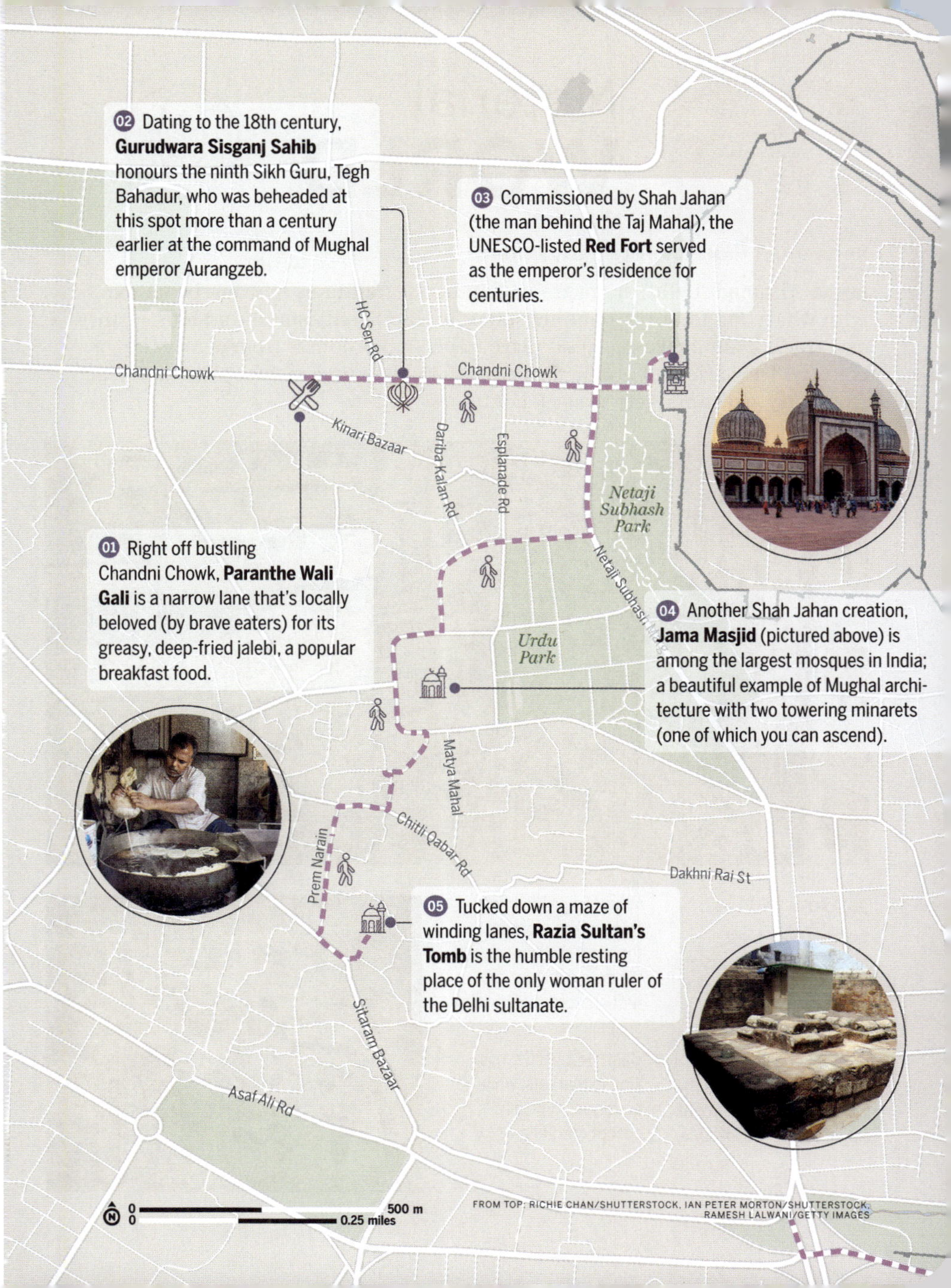

FROM TOP: RICHIE CHAN/SHUTTERSTOCK, IAN PETER MORTON/SHUTTERSTOCK, RAMESH LALWANI/GETTY IMAGES

05 Material WORLD

SHOPPING | HANDICRAFTS | SOUVENIRS

Although Delhi's homegrown handicraft traditions may not be on par with what's found in surrounding states, its capital-city status and long history as a trading hub make it a great place to pick up products from across the country. The variety of products is rivalled by the range of shopping experiences, from busy street markets to sleek boutiques.

HADYNYAH/GETTY IMAGES

How to

Getting here Most major shopping areas are accessible by metro. For Paharganj, take the Blue Line to RK Ashram Marg. Janpath and Khan Market both have stations on the Violet Line, while Sarojini Nagar is on the Pink Line.

When to go Visit first thing in the morning for great deals: many vendors consider the first customer of the day auspicious.

Cash or card Cash is king in markets, while boutiques typically accept credit cards.

IMAGEDB.COM/SHUTTERSTOCK

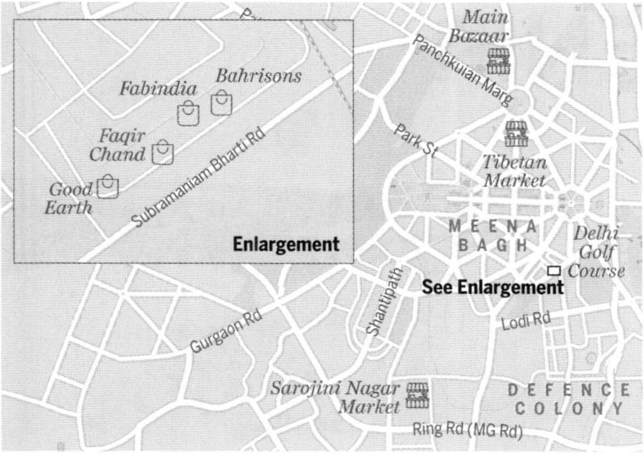

Bargain hunters Across from the New Delhi Railway Station, the **Main Bazaar** in the backpacker enclave of Paharganj offers primo deals on everything from *pashmina* shawls to brass door handles. Sure, the quality might not be the best, but the prices certainly are – shopkeepers here are typically fluent in English and masters of bargaining, so be prepared for convivial hustling.

Nearby on Janpath, just off Connaught Place, the **Tibetan Market** is the place to go for souvenir trinkets and costume jewellery. Fashionistas who don't mind sorting through piles of clothes can find serious steals at South Delhi's **Sarojini Nagar Market**, where slightly flawed factory seconds from global high-street brands go to get one last chance at a forever home. A bit of Hindi can help here, but most everyone will understand English numbers.

Boutique finds If you're looking for quality gifts that will last, head to Khan Market, an upscale spot favoured by posh Delhiites and embassy employees. For elegant tablecloths, quilts and clothes, head to **Anokhi**, a Jaipur brand that's been a major force in preserving and promoting the tradition of hand-block printing. **Good Earth** is full of treasures from the home, including gorgeous table settings, but they cost a premium.

There are also two branches of ubiquitous **Fabindia**, one specialising in clothes and the other in home goods. For books, hit up **Bahrisons** or oft-Instagrammed **Faqir Chand**.

Top Left Main Bazaar
Bottom Left Religious statues, Tibetan Market

Gifts from Across India

For handicrafts from across the country, sans shouting and heavy sales pressure, it's well worth paying the ₹100 fee to enter **Dilli Haat** in South Delhi. This government-managed market showcases a rotation of vendors from across the country, which means on any given day you're as likely to encounter a vendor selling Gujarat's famously colourful Kachchh embroidery as you are to find silk *kasavu* saris from Kerala. While handicrafts are a big draw for visitors, Delhiites frequently come to the market to visit the outdoor food court, which features over a dozen state-specific food booths dishing up regional specialties.

SOUVENIR
Checklist

01

02

03

04

05

01 Jewellery
Shimmering glass bangles, bell-shaped jhumka earrings, enamelled meenakari and polki (uncut diamond) jewellery are among the many treasures available in Delhi.

02 Incense
Used in India for prayer, home fragrance and even as insect repellent, incense sticks and cones make a low-cost and easy-to-pack gift.

03 Sweets
A traditional gift for auspicious occasions, sugary *ladoos* (sweet gram-flour balls) and *barfi* (a fudge-like sweet) are quintessential sweets to take home.

04 Musical instruments
From sitars and veenas to twin-drum tablas, Delhi is the place for Hindustani and Carnatic instruments.

05 Textiles
Fabrics from across India are sold as tablecloths, bed linens and clothes across the capital. Rajasthan's hand-block prints are particularly popular.

06

07

08

09

10

06 Shawls and Scarves
Cosy *pashmina* shawls from Kashmir and lightweight cotton scarves that are perfect for warmer weather make great, easy-to-pack gifts.

07 Books
India's English-language publishing industry is massive, which translates to loads of incredible titles.

08 Spices
Fragrant spices are the quintessential culinary souvenir and are available in bulk or by the box. Chai masala mixes are popular.

09 Ayurvedic Products
From herbal supplements to nourishing soaps containing ingredients such as neem and tulsi, Ayurvedic products are ideal for natural self-care.

10 Indian Cookware
Must-have cookware for preparing North Indian food includes *tawas* (round griddles for flatbreads) and *kadais* (multipurpose pots).

01 ATUL996/SHUTTERSTOCK, 02 PIXEL-SHOT/SHUTTERSTOCK, 03 STOCKIMAGEFACTORY.COM/SHUTTERSTOCK, 04 TILT PHOTOGRAPHY/SHUTTERSTOCK, 05 SNEHIT PHOTO/SHUTTERSTOCK, 06 RADAR_MARK/SHUTTERSTOCK, 07 RAHUL SAPRA/SHUTTERSTOCK, 08 ALEX EROFEENKOV/SHUTTERSTOCK, 09 STOCKIMAGEFACTORY.COM/SHUTTERSTOCK, 10 NITEENRK/SHUTTERSTOCK

Listings

BEST OF THE REST

North Indian Classics

Chor Bizarre ₹₹

If you can't make it to Kashmir, you can still enjoy many of the region's most famous meat-heavy dishes at this Old Delhi favourite.

Kwality ₹₹

This old-timey spot in the heart of Connaught Place has been drawing crowds with its gargantuan *chhole bhature* (deep-fried puris with spicy chickpea curry) since 1940.

Moti Mahal ₹₹

Said to be the birthplace of Delhi's most famous dish, butter chicken, this longstanding favourite has locations all around the city.

Canvas V ₹₹

Fill up on plant-based takes on rich Mughlai and Punjabi specialties, including dal *makhani* and soya *chaap,* along with innovative fusion fare.

South Indian Delights

Carnatic Café ₹₹

Famous for its wide variety of dosas, this popular spot with locations across Delhi specialises in the cuisine of Karnataka.

Coast Café ₹₹₹

The culinary traditions of the Malabar Coast are highlighted at this sunny spot, serving seafood curry and rich coconutty veg stews.

Naivedyam ₹₹

In this beautiful, fresco-adorned spot near the entrance of hipsterish Hauz Khas Village, waiters dressed in traditional South Indian attire serve tasty thali and massive dosas.

Saravana Bhawan ₹₹

Giant dosas, spongey *idli* rice cakes and frothy South Indian filter coffee have Delhiites and visitors alike queueing up for this perpetually busy Connaught Place superstar.

Cute Cafes

Latitude 28 ₹₹₹

Above the Good Earth home-decor shop in Khan Market, this lovely spot with a sunny atrium serves continental fare and delicious desserts along with wine, spritzers and espresso drinks.

Café Lota ₹₹

This semi-outdoor restaurant at the National Crafts Museum & Hastkala Academy is worth stopping by for its inventive interpretations of regional dishes, even if you aren't visiting the museum.

Cha Bar ₹₹

Stop for a cuppa at this tea shop in Connaught Place's Oxford Bookstore, which features hundreds of types of tea and a solid selection of finger food.

Cafe Stone ₹₹

Overlooking a lake in Mehrauli Archaeological Park, this leafy garden cafe offers tasty burgers, sandwiches and coffee drinks with spectacular Qutb Minar views.

Greenery Galore

Deer Park

This sprawling green space in South Delhi features a massive lake, 14th-century ruins and a spacious enclosure with its own resident deer.

Lodhi Garden

Popular among picnickers, joggers and canoodling youngsters, this massive park in the heart of the city preserves a series of beautiful tombs from the Lodi and Sayyid dynasties.

Nehru Park

Set among the imposing embassies of the Chanakyapuri diplomatic enclave, this massive park and playground draws in walkers, joggers and families in equal measure.

Garden of the Five Senses

This 20-acre expanse features flowers, topiary and artistic installations designed to stimulate all five of the senses.

Historic Havens

Agrasen ki Baoli

Tucked down a lane near Connaught Place, this photogenic 14th-century *baoli* (stepwell) was once used to collect rainwater for times of drought. Today, it's a popular spot for a bit of inner-city calm and pigeon-watching.

Jantar Mantar

One of several observatories commissioned by Maharaja Jai Singh II of Jaipur in the early 18th century, this quirky complex is full of gargantuan astronomical instruments designed to track the placement of stars and planets.

Qutb Minar

Dating to the 12th century, this 73m minaret is the oldest of Delhi's three UNESCO World Heritage Sites (Red Fort and Humayun's Tomb are the other two). The same complex also houses the first mosque built in the country.

Mehrauli Archaeological Park

Not far from the Qutb Minar, Mehrauli Archaeological Park preserves hundreds of monuments in a forested expanse, including tombs, mosques and stepwells.

SAIKO3P/SHUTTERSTOCK

Qutb Minar

Safdarjung's Tomb

Escape the crowds at this oft-overlooked 18th-century tomb finished in red sandstone; it was inspired by Humayun's Tomb.

Must-See Museums

National Crafts Museum & Hastkala Academy

India's artistic traditions are celebrated at this indoor-outdoor museum, with a special focus on textiles. There's also an outdoor section with reproductions of traditional architecture.

National Gallery of Modern Art (NGMA)

Art fans won't want to miss the massive collection at the NGMA, an excellent introduction ot India's modern-art scene. Free curator-led tours are held a few times a day.

National Museum

For an immersive introduction to Indian history, head to this government museum, which showcases a massive collection of items of historic significance from the past five millennia.

Sulabh International Museum of Toilets

As gimmicky as it may sound, this free nonprofit-run museum does a stellar job of educating people about the importance of sanitation through educational displays.

AGRA

HISTORY | ARCHITECTURE | CRAFT

RESEARCHED BY PUNEETINDER KAUR SIDHU

WAJ/SHUTTERSTOCK

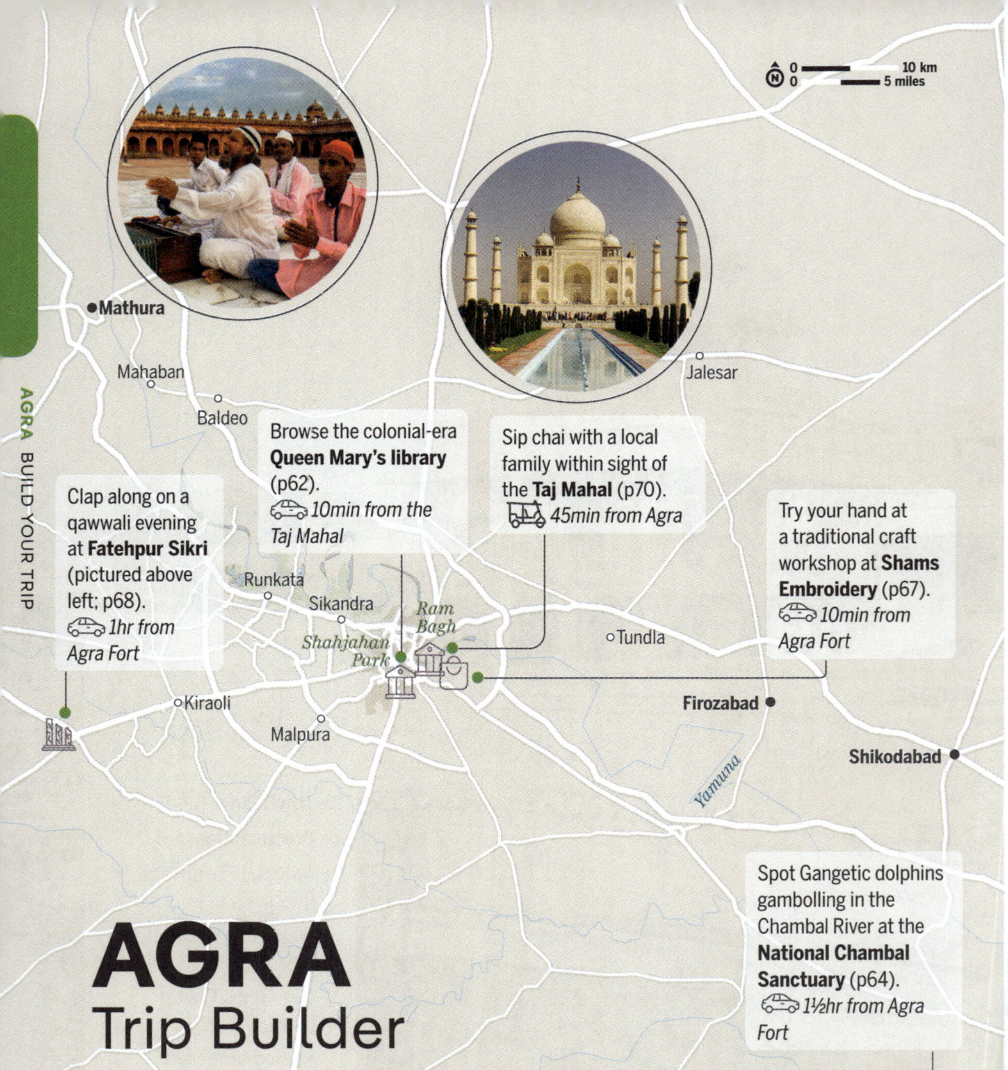

AGRA
Trip Builder

Agra is a sensory feast steeped in history and romance, from the dazzling centrepiece, the Taj Mahal, to grand forts, sprawling riverside gardens, stunning tombs, busy streets, buzzing bazaars and a vibrant food scene ranging from the heirloom to the contemporary.

CLOCKWISE FROM TOP LEFT: GODONG/ALAMY, KATERYNA NEGODA/GETTY IMAGES

Practicalities

ARRIVING

Agra Cantt, the main railway station, has an express service to Delhi; it's also the closest station to the Taj Mahal. Kheria Airport, serving domestic flights only, is 30 minutes away.

FIND YOUR WAY

The **UP Tourism office** on Taj Road has English-speaking staff and offers useful information and literature, including maps.

MONEY

Keep cash handy to avoid high ATM transaction fees. Use big bills at shops and restaurants, and small ones for local transportation.

WHERE TO STAY

Place	Pros/Cons
Tajganj	Crowded area near the Taj, teeming with budget, backpacker accommodation.
Fatehabad Rd	Prime location dotted with premium hotels, malls, fine-dining restaurants and shopping centres.
Mela Kothi Chambal Safari Lodge	An ecolodge close to natural attractions and lesser-known Shiva and Sufi shrines, an hour from Agra.

GETTING AROUND

Rickshaws Cycle-rickshaws are convenient for exploring old-city neighbourhoods; powered autorickshaws are best for short distances around the rest of the city.

Taxi The best way to explore attractions on the outskirts and beyond the city.

TOP: MEDIAWORKSTUDIO/SHUTTERSTOCK
BOTTOM: ANUJA SHARMA/SHUTTERSTOCK

EATING & DRINKING

Join locals at Deviram Sweets and sample a *bedai-aloo-jalebi* breakfast. Tuck into Chimman Lal's *puri-rasa* in the old city, not far from Abdul Sattar Nashte Wale's French toast, and other classics in the vicinity: *nihari* at Haji Mukhtaro and Munna Lal Agarwal's *petha* sweet. Sadar-Fatehabad Rd area is the epicentre of Agra's contemporary food scene.

Best thirst-quencher Craft beer at Folks (p75)

Must-try *mithai* Petha (p73)

JAN–MAR	APR–JUN	JUL–SEP	OCT–DEC
Chilly days segue into sunny spring, peak time for travellers.	Days can be anything from warm to sweltering.	Rejuvenating monsoon rains, humid and green everywhere.	Sunny and warm, but temperatures drop in the evening.

06 COLONIAL Footprints

ARCHITECTURE | WALKS | HERITAGE

Look beyond Agra's Mughal monuments to discover its prominence as a British stronghold in the 19th century. Throughout Agra, in particular in the cantonment and Civil Lines, you'll stumble upon atmospheric bungalows, bazaars, colleges, churches and cemeteries from this era, blending Victorian, neoclassical and Indo-Saracenic influences. Taking a tonga ride (two-wheeled horse carriage) back in time with knowledgeable storytellers can be extra insightful and instructive.

FLORENT MARTIN/GETTY IMAGES

Trip Notes

Getting here You can take a cab or autorickshaw to reach the starting point of the walk or tour.

When to go Winter afternoons are a good time to explore these buildings. Some offices, colleges and churches may discourage visits during business hours, so it's best to opt for an organised tour.

Take a tour The expert-led tours by **Colonial Walks Agra** (colonialwalkagra.com) reveal delightful historical nuggets.

A Slice of History

Agra's colonial-era heritage is best embodied by its cantonment. The Golf Course in the backdrop of the fort, the **Agra Club**, the recently renovated **Queen Mary's Library**, the palatial **post office** and the **Sadar Bazar** (pictured left) are all treasures evoking both pathos and sepia-tinted times.

Anu Dhillon, *Indian National Trust for Art and Cultural Heritage member, co-owner @chambalsafari*

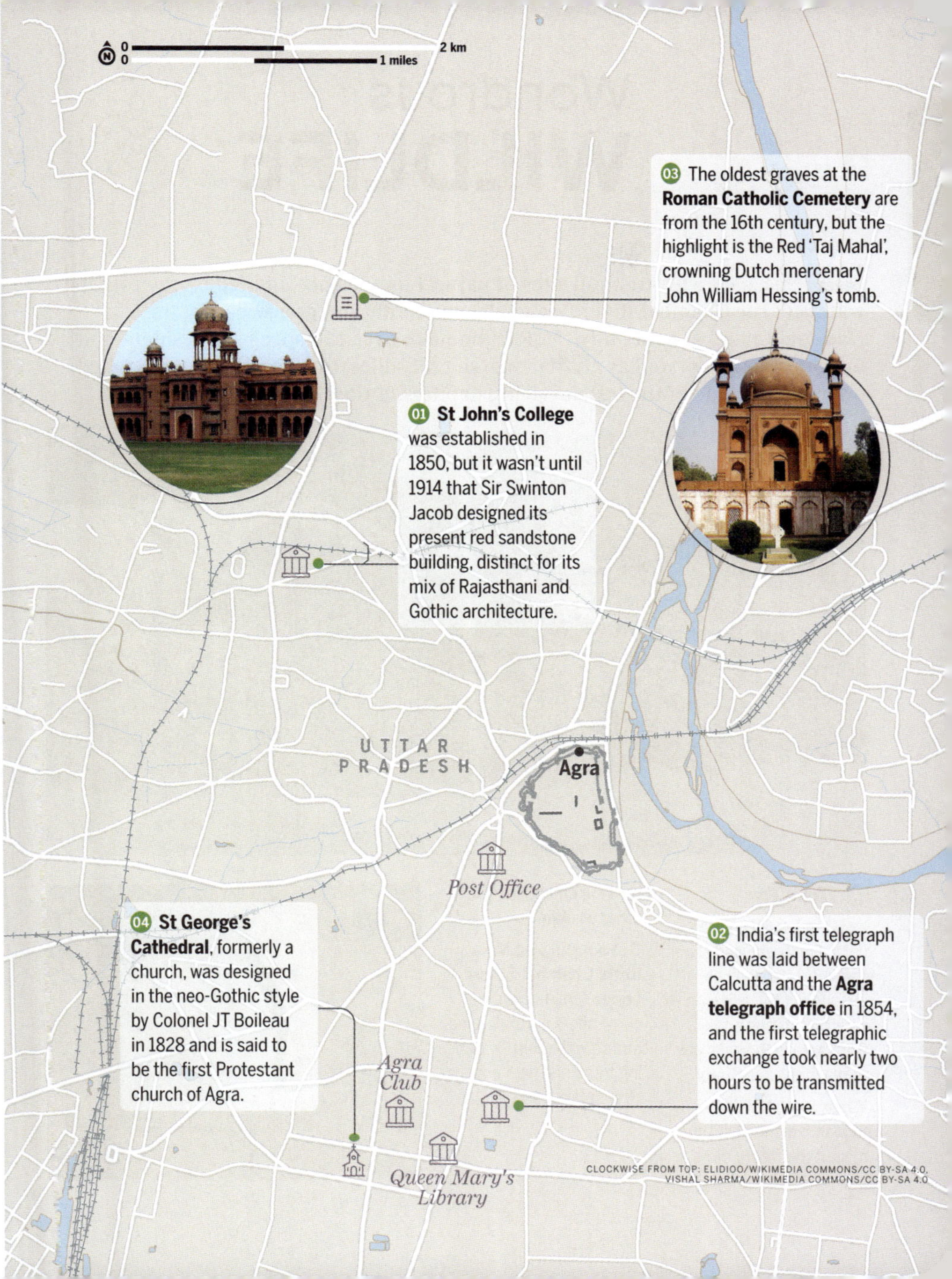

01 **St John's College** was established in 1850, but it wasn't until 1914 that Sir Swinton Jacob designed its present red sandstone building, distinct for its mix of Rajasthani and Gothic architecture.

02 India's first telegraph line was laid between Calcutta and the **Agra telegraph office** in 1854, and the first telegraphic exchange took nearly two hours to be transmitted down the wire.

03 The oldest graves at the **Roman Catholic Cemetery** are from the 16th century, but the highlight is the Red 'Taj Mahal', crowning Dutch mercenary John William Hessing's tomb.

04 **St George's Cathedral**, formerly a church, was designed in the neo-Gothic style by Colonel JT Boileau in 1828 and is said to be the first Protestant church of Agra.

07 Wondrous WILDLIFE

BIRDS | RIVERS | RAVINES

Speckled with tranquil sites of natural importance and fed by the pristine waters of the Chambal River flanked by mud cliffs and grassy banks, the National Chambal Sanctuary (NCS) is home to over 330 species of resident and migratory birds as well as gharial, marsh crocodiles, turtles and smooth-coated otters, and is one of the last surviving habitats of the Gangetic dolphin.

SURAJEET 96/SHUTTERSTOCK

How To

Getting here If you're part of an organised tour, transportation will be included. If travelling on your own, hiring a taxi from Agra is the best way to reach the sanctuary.

When to go November to March is the best time to spot migratory birds, basking crocodiles and other wildlife.

Get a naturalist **Mela Kothi Chambal Safari Lodge** (chambalsafari.com) offers naturalist-led nature walks, bird-watching tours and jeep and river safaris.

STEVE MIDGLEY/SHUTTERSTOCK

Top left Gharials
Bottom left Indian skimmers

Gliding on water The calm and gentle waters of **Chambal River** are best explored by eco-friendly boats helmed by trained boatmen. You'll glide past sandbanks rife with sunbathing gharial and mugger crocodiles, motionless one moment, swiftly splashing into the water the next. The National Chambal Sanctuary is a favourite with bird-watchers for sightings of Indian skimmers, black-bellied terns and herons. You'll see turtles along the banks, hares scuttling up the slopes and blue bulls watching from the dramatic ravines. Enlisting a naturalist will not only give you an insight into the sanctuary's flora and fauna but also ensure you have ample opportunities to spot and photograph wildlife, as well as the spectacular landscape.

Juddering over land Hopping onto a 4WD for a bumpy ride into the undulating ravines of the NCS will reward you with excellent sightings of blackbuck deer and birds like the Indian courser. You'll drive into remote villages and habitations and walk through lush green farmland. Be sure to keep a sharp look out for non-riverine wildlife, as there is every chance you'll be playing hide-and-seek with striped hyenas, jackals and foxes. From here, you'll want to drive further afield, away from the buffer zone of the NCS, for the wetlands of **Etawah's Sarus Crane Conservation Reserve**, breeding ground to India's largest congregation of the species. It's best to do this with a trained naturalist guide.

River & Ravines

Chambal River, known as Charmanyavati (meaning 'river of hides') in ancient Indian texts, is said to have originated from the blood of cows sacrificed by an Aryan king called Rantideva. In all likelihood, this not-so-holy beginning contributed to the river's survival, and it has remained untouched and unpolluted through the centuries. Today, Chambal is one of India's most pristine rivers. Its treacherous ravines, on the other hand, have served as inaccessible hideouts for the outlawed since British rule. With the last of the infamous dacoits (bandits) flushed out by the police in the 2000s, the ravines are now largely peaceful.

08 Get Arty & CRAFTY

ARTISANS | PERFORMANCES | CREATIVITY

A day in Agra is all you need to realise you're surrounded by incredible handicrafts – the marble-inlay coaster or miniature painting in your hotel room, the beautifully embroidered outfits in display windows, the eye-catching backpacks spilling out of Sadar Bazar shops or a hand-knotted rug you can picture in your home. Learn how to create some of these artefacts yourself.

ANDERS BLOMQVIST/GETTY IMAGES

How To

How to book Contact the company directly, or book ahead through your travel company, so you're sure of getting a place.

How long Most courses take half a day, and may include a meal. In some instances, you'll need to return later to pick up your handiwork.

What to wear Don't wear your best clothes, and carry an apron, as you're likely to get dusty or splash yourself with paint.

RHONDA GUTENBERG/GETTY IMAGES

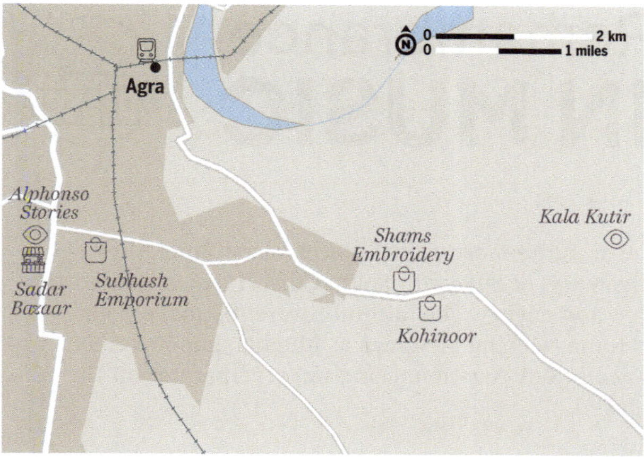

Designs on you If you've been awestruck by the exquisite pietra dura marble inlays embellishing the Taj Mahal, this is your chance to give it a go yourself. Head over to **Sadar Bazaar**, where the master craftsmen at **Subhash Emporium** (subhashemporium.com) will show you how to chisel, cut, inlay and polish these timeless pieces of art. They specialise in both the delicate Persian *parchin kari* and the more flamboyant Florentine version, and you can try your hand at either. **Shams Embroidery** (instagram.com/shams_zardozi) has half-day courses run by master *kaarigar* (artisans) skilled in their distinct three-dimensional embroideries, on display at the **Kohinoor** museum (kohinoorjewellers.com) on Fatehabad Rd. If it's miniature paintings that interest you, you can get a hands-on experience at **Alphonso Stories** (alphonsostories.com), where an art historian introduces you to the intricacies of the art and teaches a traditional Mughal motif.

Creative corners Head over to Budhana village, where the art-led residency **Kala Kutir** (instagram.com/_kalakutir) brings together art, nature and community to inspire dialogue and creativity. Visit during the Agra Arts Festival (October to November) to be treated to open-air performances, poetry recitals, enriching panel discussions and animated storytelling sessions. Be sure to find a spot on the mattresses strewn across the grounds or a comfy cane *murrah* (woven stool) if sitting cross-legged proves challenging. You will also want to walk over to the food stalls and relish home-style dishes prepared by local women.

Top left Inlaid marble
Bottom left Materials for creating inlaid marble

Celebrating Creativity

Kala Kutir was conceptualised out of a simple absence as Agra had no informal, accessible space where artists could gather, exchange ideas and showcase work beyond institutional or commercial settings. Kala Kutir has since emerged as a community-led cultural centre rooted in collaboration and conversation, and the Agra Arts Festival grew from this impulse to reclaim the city as a living cultural site, where art, food, music and community come together through participation, slowness and shared human connection. Our other initiatives include Taj ke Saat Rang, a queer heritage festival; *qawwali* evenings; and Grameen Bhojanam, a village food experience.

Kaleem Isovi Ahmed *is a cultural curator and founder of @_kalakutir*

09 Remembrance IN MUSIC

CULTURE | FAITH | MUSIC

Fatehpur Sikri is one of Agra's most visited places year-round, but it's during the *urs* (death anniversary) of Sufi saint Salim Chishti that it transforms into a place of deep emotion and energy. The faithful reverently make their offerings at the Sufi saint's tomb, seeking blessings as Mughal emperor Akbar did centuries ago, and *qawwali* (Sufi devotional singing) reverberates off the sandstone walls of Jama Masjid.

ARUN SAMBHU MISHRA/SHUTTERSTOCK

How To

Getting here Electric buses leave Agra's Idgah Bus Stand every half-hour, but you can save time by hiring a taxi.

When to go The date of the *urs* changes each year, calculated according to the Islamic calendar, but is always around Ramadan. Keep a lookout for updates on social-media sites.

What to wear Fatehpur Sikri is a place of worship and spiritual significance, which mandates dressing modestly; avoid shorts and revealing outfits.

NITHID/SHUTTERSTOCK

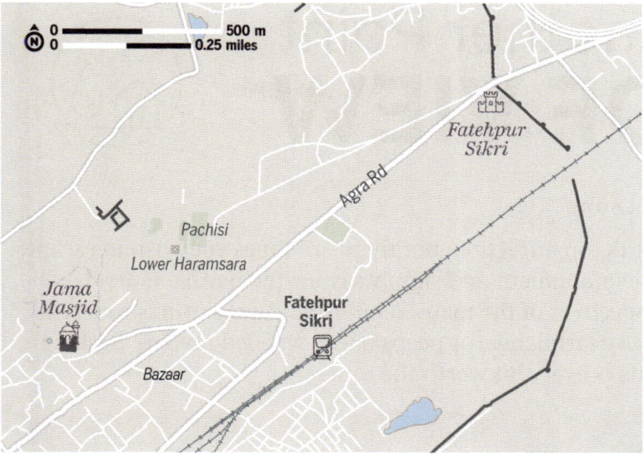

Top left Tomb of Sufi saint Salim Chishti, Jama Masjid
Bottom left Fatehpur Sikri

Commemorating a saint Be sure to plan a visit around the *urs,* when **Fatehpur Sikri** exudes a whole different kind of energy for three days, almost fair-like in its vibe. You'll witness its transformation into a functional place of devotion with rituals and gatherings, a meaningful alternative to royal architecture for those seeking spirituality, music and lived tradition. Walking around the colourfully illuminated mausoleum, watching children enjoy rides or food vendors trying to match endless demands for kebabs and biryani is an enlivening and unforgettable experience. Finding a quiet corner to sit down and listen to uninterrupted *qawwali* can be spiritually rewarding.

Qawwali nights Linger on past sunset and reward yourself with a soulful *qawwali* performance by local musicians at Fatehpur Sikri's **Jama Masjid**. For extra-special renditions, come on a Thursday evening when the sun's last rays dramatically deepen the shades of the red-sandstone walls of Buland Darwaza. The place vibrates with the evening call to prayer, vendors and touts wind up for the day, the mosque gradually empties of visitors, and full-throated, mellifluous voices belt out one Sufi *qalam* after another in front of Chishti's dargah (mausoleum). Observing a musician's fingers effortlessly run over the keys of a harmonium is as hypnotic as the clapping that accompanies it.

Beyond the Palace

Fatehpur Sikri reveals itself to those who look beyond the palace precincts. In the surrounding villages lie prehistoric rock shelters with cave paintings dating back to the 2nd to 6th centuries BCE. An elaborate water system, anchored by the Tehra Mori dam, stepped wells, aqueducts and water-lifting devices once sustained the imperial capital. Its many *hammams* (public baths) reflect a refined urban culture, while the *qasba* (town) still holds *havelis* (mansions) and royal *karkhanas* (workshops), such as the Farrash Khana, where carpet-weaving survives today in handwoven *chindi* (fabric-waste) durries.

Shahena Khan, *heritage conservation architect and co-founder of @trikonestays*

10 Another Point OF VIEW

NATURE | ADVENTURE | VILLAGES

The Taj Mahal is Agra's top attraction, but there are times you wish to escape the awestruck throngs at the monument and simply savour the marble marvel from afar. Find special perspectives of the mausoleum from rural settings, where it backdrops villages, rises above farmlands, or peeps out of wooded ravines. Seeking out these vantage viewpoints is every bit worth the time.

TAHIR AHMED/SOUL WALKS

How to

Getting around Whether you're cycling, driving, or on a horse, a certain amount of walking in villages and ravines is expected. Wear sturdy shoes and comfortable, outdoorsy clothes.

When to go The best time is early morning to watch it gleam at sunrise or suffused in the dramatic hues of a setting sun.

Grab a bite Enjoy an alfresco meal amidst the ravines with **Ekaa Villa**'s Secret Taj High Tea (ekaahotels.com).

EQROY/SHUTTERSTOCK

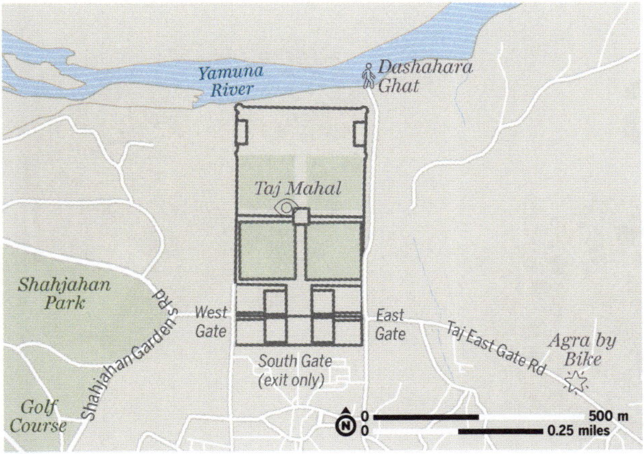

On wheels Be sure to explore Agra's bucolic outskirts and village life, a startling change from its urban chaos, even if it means spending a couple of hours bumping along winding country roads on a battery-operated tuk-tuk tour with **Agra Beat** (agrabeat.in). Interacting with friendly locals, sipping chai with them, learning about the roles and responsibilities of women, or visiting a village school are deeply rewarding and insightful forms of cultural immersion. Another enjoyable way to get to the wonderful viewpoints is cycling through the countryside with specialists **Agra By Bike**, combining nature and heritage with a fun activity, followed by high tea at an undisclosed viewpoint. For those with less time, hiring a taxi to drive you around is a good option, though this may require some longer walks in places where navigating on four wheels is difficult.

On hooves Wondering what 16th-century travel to Agra looked and felt like? Finding an answer means saddling up for a few hours of equestrian exploration and summoning a great amount of imagination! Trotting along on a guided horseriding tour with **Soul Walks** (soulwalks.org), and passing through sandy ravines, sleepy villages and fecund farmlands could well be the closest experience to a visit from centuries ago. You'll want to dismount from the horse periodically to walk around historic spots, little-known mosques and mausoleums of Sufi saints along the way, before ending your day with a much-needed high tea.

Top left View of the Taj Mahal on a horse riding tour
Bottom left Tuk-tuk, Agra

Witness Living Culture

It is Agra's little-known traditions that I love experiencing myself and would like most of all to introduce to visitors. During Mughal emperor Shah Jahan's *urs* observances at Taj Mahal, for instance, the atmosphere shifts from sightseeing to remembrance. It becomes less about taking photos and more about witnessing living culture. Similarly, kabootar bazi (pigeon flying) is deeply embedded in the culture of the old city. An early morning rooftop ritual with the Taj as a backdrop resonates with calls, whistles, spinning flocks and chai. Another favourite is idling riverside at **Dashahara Ghat** near the Taj and simply letting time pass by.

Tahir Ahmed Qureshi, *story-teller and founder of @soul_walks_india*

AGRA ICONS

01

02

05

03

04

01 Soapstone Souvenirs
Intricately carved and pierced figures, trinket boxes and coaster sets that don't bust the bank.

02 Marble Inlay
Carry back exquisite pietra dura coasters, figures, tabletops and panels that reflect the matchless design legacy of the Taj.

03 Handmade Rugs & Carpets
Woven on wooden looms, these brightly coloured rugs and elegant carpets blend Persian motifs with centuries-old weaving traditions.

04 Zardozi Textiles
Agra produces the finest of this delicate gold-and-silver-thread embroidery.

05 Leather Accessories
Agra's supple leather bags and backpacks, jackets, belts and shoes blend durability with a long-standing artisanal tradition.

06

07

08

10

09

06 Glass Bangles
A clinking, colourful and dazzling spillover from nearby Firozabad, known for its glass-making since the 16th century.

07 Jewellery
Round off your glittery souvenirs with a gem-studded pendant, ring, necklace or pair of earrings in gold or silver.

08 Petha
This chewy ash gourd *mithai* (sweet) is synonymous with Agra and is said to be inspired by the white of the Taj Mahal.

09 Dal Moth
A crunchy and tangy whole-lentil savoury snack best enjoyed alongside a cup of tea or as a spicy salad topping.

10 Gajak
Popular energy- and nutrient-packed winter treat featuring sesame, jaggery, ghee and dried fruits.

Listings

BEST OF THE REST

The Other Sufis

Dargah Hazrat Amir Abul Ullah

Be sure to swing by this 17th century Sufi's mausoleum on the outskirts of the city. If possible, come around the *urs* observance for this major figure from the Naqshbandi order.

Bukhari Shrines

Sufi brothers Sheikh Jalal Bukhari and Sheikh Ahmed Bukhari were contemporaries of Mughal emperor Shah Jahan, and their dargahs, located west of the Taj Mahal, are said to safeguard the monument.

Live Like a Local

Morning Miles Club

Feel included in the city's everyday life by joining in for a run with the local community, an energising, low-cost chance to discover new spaces and exchange stories over chai.

Cycling Groups

Pedal your way into friendly fitness communities like **Agra Elite Cyclists** and **Agra Cycling Club** to explore local spots.

Agra Jamming Club

Get acquainted with Agra's contemporary youth culture at a jam session where youngsters gather to play, sing and let down their hair. It's also a great chance to meet locals.

Bazm-e-Maikash

This cultural space in the ancestral *haveli* (traditional residence) of celebrated poet Maikash Akbarabadi, hosts *mushaira* (poetry readings), *qawwali* evenings, and the Sufi Basant festival; and also awards individuals promoting Urdu language and culture.

Agra with Insiders

Trocals

Knowledgeable guides and expert storytellers unravel an Agra far beyond the Taj and otherwise hidden from view. You'd do well to join the Agra Village Walk or Photography Tour.

Breakaway

Long-standing specialists in immersive craft and textile experiences, Breakway offers bespoke walks and tours to artisan clusters, as well as workshops centred on traditional handmade crafts like *zardozi* embroidery and marble inlay.

Cafes & Microbreweries

Bungalow ₹₹

Enjoy an alfresco coffee and bite in the courtyard of this restored house, re-imagined as a cozy cafe. Better still, come for breakfast and stay for the burnt Basque cheesecake.

Greens & Beans ₹₹

Stop by at this snug little cafe, Agra's first specialty coffee shop, for a well-brewed

Dargah Hazrat Amir Abul Ullah

cuppa. Pair it with a garlic mushroom cheese sandwich, or tuck into a smoothie bowl.

Sheroes Hangout Café ₹

This is a meaningful, pay-what-you-like place run by acid-attack survivors rebuilding their lives. Purchase local crafts or get henna-ed while you wait for your paneer *makhani* or *hakka* noodles.

Folks Pub & Brewery ₹₹

This brewpub's laid-back and moody vibe makes it the perfect hangout for an unhurried evening nursing a freshly brewed IPA or Vienna lager; you're not here for the food.

Top-End Restaurants & Bars

Esphahan ₹₹₹

Enjoy a delectable Mughlai meal at this fine-dining restaurant at Oberoi Amarvilas, while live traditional music plays on. Reservations required; dress code is smart casual.

Peshawari ₹₹₹

Another go-to for Mughlai and Frontier food is this premium restaurant at ITC Mughal. Try the *murg malai kebabs* (barbecued chicken chunks) and round off with some *phirni* (sweet rice pudding) or *kulfi faluda* (ice cream with cornstarch noodles).

Mughal Bar ₹₹₹

Experience luxury and timeless allure in opulent surroundings with vantage views of Agra's most iconic landmark as you sit back to nurse a Speyside single malt or fine French wine.

Retail Therapy

Amar Lok

Spend an unhurried afternoon at this unique cultural-cum-retail hub housed in shipping containers featuring cafes, live music and art, built with an eye on sustainable design and community building.

PRABHJIT S. KALSI/SHUTTERSTOCK

Phirni (sweet rice pudding)

Sadar Bazar

This lively market is famous for handicrafts, textiles and leather goods, notably shoes and bags, and street food. Come evening, it transforms into foodie haven for *chaat* and *mithai* lovers.

Kinari Bazar

Agra's go-to for wedding items, the colourful lanes of this historic market near Jama Masjid brim with textiles, embroidery and traditional jewellery shops, giving shoppers an Old World retail experience.

Subhash Emporium

This museum-like shop brims with exquisite pietra dura, from the intricate Persian *parchin kari* to its more flamboyant Florentine predecessor. You can also observe skilled artisans create these incredible masterpieces.

Kalra's Cottage Industry

Drop in to observe weavers shape the most beautiful hand-knotted silk and wool carpets with Persian designs. Give in to temptation; treat your home to a statement floor covering.

RAJASTHAN

DESERTS | FORTS | RAJPUT PALACES

RESEARCHED BY JOE BINDLOSS

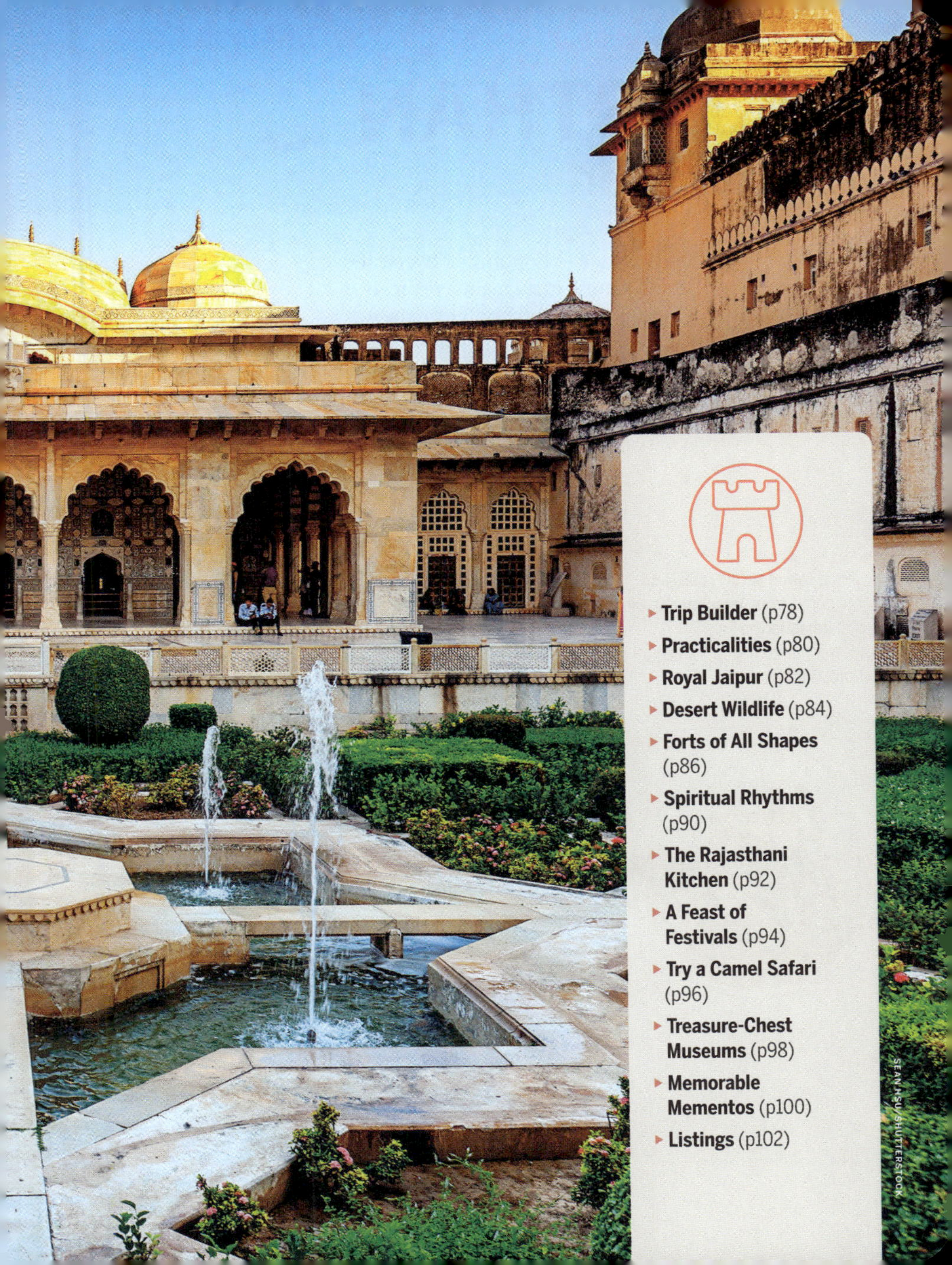

SEAN HSU/SHUTTERSTOCK

RAJASTHAN
Trip Builder

Visiting Rajasthan means hopping between the former capitals of India's most extravagant princely states. Drop into towering forts and opulent palaces, explore temple towns and buzzing medieval bazaars, ride camels through the dunes and scan the jungle for tigers on 4WD safaris.

Join a **camel safari** (p96) into the dunes from **Jaisalmer's** still-inhabited fort.
from half a day to 3 days from Jaisalmer

Take a cooking course with spice masters **Mohanlal Verhomal** (MV; p93) Spices in Jodhpur.
20min from Jodhpur Junction Station

Marvel at the **Mehrangarh** (p88), Jodhpur's cliff-ringed palace-fortress.
20min from Jodhpur Junction Station

CLOCKWISE FROM BOTTOM RIGHT: JORISVO/SHUTTERSTOCK, PHUONG D. NGUYEN/SHUTTERSTOCK

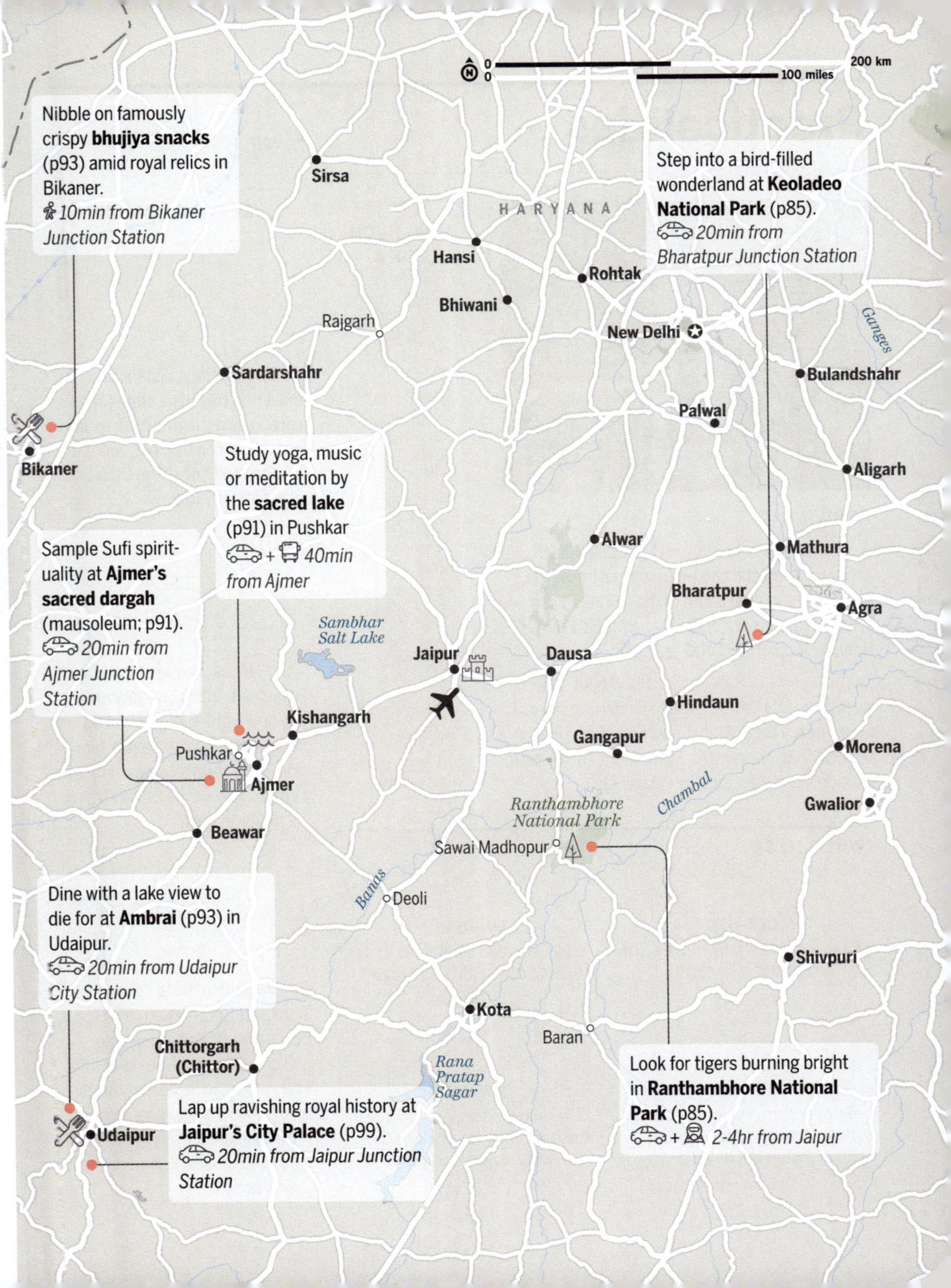

0 200 km
0 100 miles
Nibble on famously crispy **bhujiya snacks** (p93) amid royal relics in Bikaner.
10min from Bikaner Junction Station
Step into a bird-filled wonderland at **Keoladeo National Park** (p85).
20min from Bharatpur Junction Station
Study yoga, music or meditation by the **sacred lake** (p91) in Pushkar
+ 40min from Ajmer
Sample Sufi spirituality at **Ajmer's sacred dargah** (mausoleum; p91).
20min from Ajmer Junction Station
Dine with a lake view to die for at **Ambrai** (p93) in Udaipur.
20min from Udaipur City Station
Lap up ravishing royal history at **Jaipur's City Palace** (p99).
20min from Jaipur Junction Station
Look for tigers burning bright in **Ranthambhore National Park** (p85).
+ 2-4hr from Jaipur
Sirsa
HARYANA
Hansi
Rohtak
Bhiwani
Rajgarh
New Delhi
Ganges
Sardarshahr
Bulandshahr
Palwal
Bikaner
Aligarh
Alwar
Mathura
Bharatpur
Agra
Sambhar Salt Lake
Jaipur
Dausa
Hindaun
Kishangarh
Gangapur
Morena
Pushkar
Ajmer
Chambal
Gwalior
Ranthambhore National Park
Beawar
Sawai Madhopur
Banas
Deoli
Shivpuri
Kota
Baran
Chittorgarh (Chittor)
Rana Pratap Sagar
Udaipur

Practicalities

SNEHIT PHOTO/SHUTTERSTOCK

ARRIVING

Jaipur International Airport (pictured) With separate domestic and international terminals, 13km (30 minutes) south of the centre. Reach town by Uber or Ola or arrange a prepaid taxi or hotel pick-up; from ₹400 to ₹800.

Jaipur Junction Railway Station About 4km west of the City Palace, close to Sindhi Camp bus stand. Reach the Old City by autorickshaw, Uber or Ola (₹100-200), or on the Jaipur metro (disembark at Badi Chaupar for the City Palace; ₹15).

HOW MUCH FOR A

Kachori or samosa from ₹15

Meal of dhal bhatti churma from ₹150

Bottled beer in a restaurant from ₹400

WHEN TO GO

OCT–DEC
Peak season; warm, mostly dry days and mild nights.

JAN–MAR
Clear weather continues, but expect cool nights and foggy mornings.

APR–MAY
Temperatures spike ahead of the monsoon; uncomfortably hot in the desert.

JUN–SEP
The monsoon brings colour to the landscape, but also flooding and transport disruption.

GETTING AROUND

Air To cover long distances quickly in this huge state (at a carbon cost), flights buzz to Jaipur, Jaisalmer, Udaipur, Jodhpur, Bikaner and Kota from Delhi and other Indian hubs.

Train The backbone of travel in Rajasthan. Trains go everywhere, day and night, but seats fill up fast so book in advance. Jaipur Junction is the state's central hub; use comfortable Vande Bharat trains for daytime trips.

Bus Rajasthan State Road Transport Corporation (RSRTC) buses and more comfortable and convenient private buses go everywhere, with sleeper buses on overnight trips. Always check the departure and arrival point for private buses; it may not be in the centre.

EATING & DRINKING

Rajasthani cuisine is rich, with lots of vegetarian options based on pulses and millet (often used to make chapatis). Snack foods such as *pakora* (veg fritters), *kachori* (fried stuffed pastries; pictured top right) and *mirchi bada* (potato-stuffed battered chillies) are found everywhere. At sit-down restaurants, seek out royal dishes such as *laal maas* (pictured bottom right) – a rich, red meat curry flavoured with red chilli. Dhal *bhatti churma* (lentil soup with ground wheat with sugar and ghee) is a popular alternative to the standard Indian thali.

Best Rajasthani meal Suvarna Mahal (p83)

Best dinner view Indique (p93)

CONNECT & FIND YOUR WAY

Mobile phones Signals are reliable almost everywhere; get online easily with a local data SIM package (Airtel has good coverage).

Wi-fi Common in hotels and restaurants, but connections can be slow; use a local phone data SIM as a back up.

Navigation Google Maps is invaluable for checking progress on train journeys and navigating tangled bazaars – another reason to get a local data SIM.

ELECTRIC VEHICLES

Many of Rajasthan's autorickshaws are battery-powered, but these vehicles can struggle on steep slopes. Use petrol-powered autorickshaws to reach hilltop forts and temples.

WHERE TO STAY

Rajasthan has accommodation for all budgets, from backpacker hostels to lavish rooms in former royal palace. Book ahead as demand can be heavy; most hotels are on booking.com and agoda.com.

Place	Pros/Cons
Jaipur	Allow several days for the sights; most hotels are outside the Old City.
Jaisalmer	Hotels sprawl around the central fort; stay outside the fort walls to help preserve this ancient site.
Jodhpur	Hotels and friendly guesthouses dot the lanes south of the Mehrangarh fort.
Pushkar	A hippie vibe endures, meaning plenty of inexpensive hotels and guesthouses.
Udaipur	Lots of hotels around Lal Ghat and Hanuman Ghat, beside Lake Pichola.

MONEY

ATMs are everywhere but carry cash as a backup. Some hotels, shops and restaurants accept cards. Break large bills in shops, restaurants and hotels to pay for rickshaw rides.

11 Royal JAIPUR

ROYAL GRANDEUR | HUMBLING HISTORY | VIEWS

The royal capital of Maharaja Sawai Ram Singh II (1835–80) and the proud Kachhwaha dynasty, Jaipur is known as the Pink City, after its ruler had the streets redecorated in salmon pink to honour the visiting Prince of Wales. Admire the royal monuments dotted around the Old City and sprawling over nearby hilltops for a time-travel trip deep into Rajput royal life.

MUKESH KUMAR JWALA/SHUTTERSTOCK

How to

When to go Royal Jaipur is impressive at any time of day or year, but best experienced in the morning, before the crowds gather, or at sunset for the views.

Getting there Zip across Jaipur by taxi, autorickshaw or the metro, then explore on foot.

Best street-food recharge Drop by the Lala Ji Pakodi Wale food stand near the Hawa Mahal for tasty fried snacks.

SAIKO3P/SHUTTERSTOCK

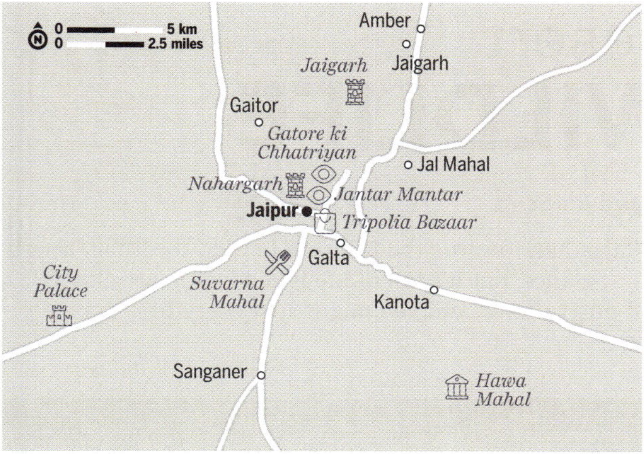

Top left City Palace
Bottom left Jantar Mantar

An urban maharaja Start at the magnificent, still-occupied **City Palace** (citypalace.org) of Maharaja Jai Singh II (1699–1727). As you weave through opulent palace buildings and audience rooms, you'll see bristling weaponry, royal portraits and photos taken by the maharaja, a famous early tech adopter.

A giant 18th-century sundial Beside the City Palace, the **Jantar Mantar** (tourism.rajasthan.gov.in) was the astronomical observatory of the scientifically curious Jai Singh II. Contemplate the purpose of these curious crescents and stairs to nowhere that calculate the movements of the spheres. If it's sunny, the Laghu Samrat Yantra will measure the time, accurate to within 20 seconds.

Queen's view of Jaipur To see Jaipur the way it was viewed by its queens, peek through the perforated *jali* screens of the **Hawa Mahal** (obms-tourist.rajasthan.gov.in), where royal women observed a city they ruled but could rarely enter.

Retreats with a view Jaipur's maharajas balanced lavish palaces with practical boltholes to escape to in times of trouble. Take in dizzying Jaipur views from **Nahargarh** (tourism.rajasthan.gov.in), a battle-ready summer house, or explore eerie, impregnable **Jaigarh** (citypalace.org) – linked to Amber Palace by a secret passage, and guarded by the world's largest wheeled canon.

A regal exit End your tour, as the maharajas did, at the city's royal cenotaphs. The elegant marble *chhatri* (tombs) of the Kachwaha maharajas rise dramatically at the **Gatore ki Chhatriyan**. Maharanis are honoured at a separate complex closer to Amber.

Live Like a Maharaja

You can kit yourself out with treasures to make a maharaja jealous in the streets of Jaipur's Old City. Glittering, low-cost costume jewellery and bangles are sold along **Tripolia Bazar** and **Maniharon ka Rasta,** but for the real deal, try the gem workshops of **Pahar Ganj**, or the fancy jewellers, goldsmiths and silversmiths of the **Johari Bazaar**.

Suitably adorned, book a table for dinner at **Suvarna Mahal** (tajhotels.com) inside the opulent Rambagh Palace hotel, or stop for a drink at the hotel's elegant **Polo Bar**. Alternatively, dress to impress at the baroque **Bar Palladio** inside the similarly lavish **Narain Niwas Palace Hotel** (hotelnarainniwas.com).

12 Desert WILDLIFE

TIGERS | CAMELS | MIGRATING BIRDLIFE

Spilling west from Rajasthan towards the Pakistan border, the Thar Desert seems arid and empty at first glance, but it's full of life if you look more closely. Head into the dry hills and dusty dunes, and you might spot everything from tigers to demoiselle cranes.

SHUBHROJYOTI/SHUTTERSTOCK

Tips for Birders

November to February is the very best time to visit Keoladeo. Try to come early in the morning, when the birds come out for their first feed of the day. This applies to birds of prey too – when their food is active, so are they!

Mohan Singh Solanki, *birding guide at Keoladeo National Park. @mohan.solanki.161*

Trip Notes

Getting around Ranthambhore and Bharatpur (for Keoladeo) are easily reached by train from Delhi, Agra and Jaipur. Onward connections link Bikaner to Phalodi (for Kichan) and Jodhpur.

When to go The dry late-winter months bring wildlife into the open; migratory birds gather from November to February.

Getting closer to the wildlife Birdlife can be viewed on foot at Keoladeo, Rao Jodha and Kichan; seek tigers by 4WD and desert fauna on camel-back safaris in Bikaner.

01 Start the wildlife adventure on safari in **Ranthambhore National Park**. Scan the undergrowth at dawn or dusk for tigers loping through the jungle, as well as sambar, spotted deer and nilgai antelope.

02 Bharatpur is the gateway to **Keoladeo National Park**, where walking trails provide access to serene, seasonal wetlands alive with kingfishers (pictured far left), cranes (pictured above), spoonbills, eagles and other migrating birdlife.

03 Jaipur's urban sprawl hides two of the best places to see leopards (pictured above) in India: the **Jhalana Leopard Reserve** and **Amargarh Leopard Reserve**. Be blown away by big cats stalking the city fringes.

04 Slip into the desert from **Bikaner** on a camel-back safari to quiet corners where desert foxes (pictured right), antelopes and myriad bird species thrive, then drop into the **National Research Centre on Camels**.

05 Continue west via **Kichan**, mobbed by a chorus line of demoiselle cranes every winter, to **Jodhpur**, where the waterfowl-filled pools of **Rao Jodha Desert Rock Park** spill north from the Mehrangarh fort.

FROM TOP: ROHIT BENIWAL/SHUTTERSTOCK, SOURABH BHARTI/SHUTTERSTOCK, SOURABH BHARTI/SHUTTERSTOCK

13

Forts of All SHAPES

HISTORY | PALACES | STORIES

Medieval Rajasthan was a dangerous place to be a maharaja. With rival rulers and colonial invaders on the prowl, sensible royals surrounded their luxurious pleasure palaces with sturdy battlements. From elegant Amber to nostalgic Bundi, Rajasthan's fortified palaces blend opulence, romance and tragedy.

KK1HB/SHUTTERSTOCK

How to

Getting around Buses, trains and planes connect all of Rajasthan's royal capitals, but book travel in advance.

When to go Fort hopping is most fun during the mild winter (Oct to Mar). Expect sweaty sightseeing from April to May and during the June to September monsoon.

Go with a guide Get more from Rajasthan's forts with an official guide, who can point out secret spots such as the ancient water-haulage mechanism inside Amber Fort.

ZIGGYSOFI/SHUTTERSTOCK

Top and bottom left Amber Fort **Above** Mural, Bundi Palace

EFIRED/SHUTTERSTOCK

Get Lost in a Maze of Wonders

If one fort sums up Rajasthan's royal balancing act between opulence and self-defence, it's **Amber Fort** (obms-tourist.rajasthan.gov.in) near Jaipur. Formidable on the outside, adorned with filigree flourishes within, the former capital of the Kachawa dynasty is linked to the even more impregnable **Jaigarh** fortress by a hidden passage straight out of *Game of Thrones*.

Drift between the fort's successive courtyards, each representing a greater level of exclusivity. Ordinary citizens were permitted to enter Jaleb Chowk to view spoils of war; behind the Ganesh Pol gate, the Diwan-i-Am was reserved for invited courtiers and dignitaries.

Bundi's Royal Heritage

My forefathers were prime ministers for the Maharaja of Bundi, and I grew up watching the walls of **Bundi Palace** lit up by flickering lamps. The palace and **Taragarh** fort look over streets with a living connection to royalty.

Mukesh Mehta, *owner of Bundi's Haveli Braj Bhushanjee hotel. kiplingsbundi.com*

Walk in the footsteps of the top tier of Rajasthani society in the Jai Mandir hall, then get lost in the maze-like *hammam* and the *zenana* (women's quarters), designed so the maharaja could visit his wives and concubines at will.

Design-Magazine Palace Chic

The rust-coloured walls of the **Mehrangarh** (mehrangarh.org), Jodhpur's landmark fortress, rise over the bottle-blue streets like a living extension of the desert. Inside, cliff-sheer battlements hide palaces of astonishing elegance. Enter by the Jai Pol gate, noting the anti-elephant spikes and cannonball damage, beneath carved windows of fairytale whimsy. Beyond, find mirror mosaics in the Sheesh Mahal, painted bouquets in the Phool Mahal, and spaces illuminated by rainbow shafts of light in the Moti Mahal's Durbar Hall.

Exit via the Fateh Pol gate into the lanes of **Navchokiya**, famed for its indigo-blue homes. Trace the mural-lined **Blue Corridor** below the fort walls to watch black kites swooping in the thermals.

Weapons Fit for Royalty

Rajasthan's forts were forged in an age when alliances were created by conquest, sustained by force and terminated with the thrust of a *katar* dagger. Accordingly, the state's royal armouries were stacked to the rafters with formidable weaponry. Expect to see horse and elephant armour, chainmail, spears and polearms, battle axes, maces, *katar* punch daggers, talwar swords, flintlock guns and battle-axes with hidden guns, daggers with secret back-up daggers, and other blood-thirsty tools of war. Most of them are lavishly engraved, belying their grisly purpose. Drop into Jodhpur's **Mehrangarh** to see the personal sword of the Mughal emperor Akbar, with Persian inscriptions inlaid in gold on the blade.

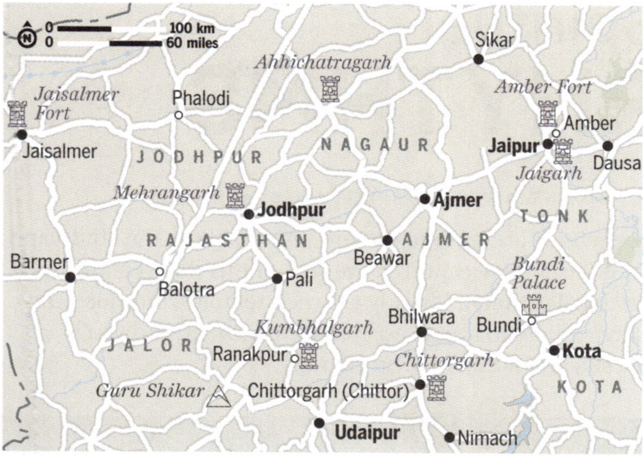

Left Lion-headed sword, Mehrangarh Fort **Below** Jaisalmer Fort

See Silent Splendour

The evocative magic of Rajasthan's forts is amplified by silence. You might be the only visitor wandering the sun-scorched courtyards of Nagaur's **Ahhichatragarh** (mehrangarh.org), whose name translates to 'Fort of the Hooded Cobra'.

Hidden in Udaipur's Aravalli Hills, **Kumbhalgarh** (tourism.rajasthan.gov.in) spins evocative tales of medieval India. Beyond the austere palace of Rana Fateh Singh, follow whisper-quiet paths past scattered step-wells and temples recalling the fort's 15th-century golden age.

Conquered or Undefeated?

The crumbling palaces of **Chittorgarh** (tourism.rajasthan.gov.in), India's largest fort, swim with ancient tragedy. Ramble around shattered ruins and contemplate the three times that residents staged mass suicides rather than face the dishonour of defeat to invading armies.

Not every fort was vanquished. Head across the state to never-conquered **Jaisalmer Fort**, one of the only forts in India still inhabited by ordinary people. Amid its maze of tangled lanes, you'll stumble across tightly packed homes and shops, and mesmerising Jain and Hindu temples.

FROM LEFT: AKASHG6/SHUTTERSTOCK, DINESH HUKMANI/SHUTTERSTOCK

14 Spiritual RHYTHMS

ARCHITECTURAL MARVELS | MOVING RITUALS | SPIRITUAL SURPRISES

Rajasthan's spiritual rhythms are as timeless and immutable as the landscape itself. Myriad faiths, sects and gurus have captured the soul of this desert state, and every city has its own rich collection of lavishly adorned temples, mosques and shrines. Visit respectfully, paying note to areas reserved for believers, and you'll witness India's religious tapestry unfolding in vivid colour.

PAUL PANAYIOTOU/GETTY IMAGES

How to

When to go Festivals take place year-round at Rajasthan's temples and shrines. Check if any ceremonies are planned when you visit.

Getting around To find the state's sacred sites, look for people moving with purpose through the streets, carrying offerings.

Temple etiquette When visiting religious sites, remove shoes, cover your head if asked, and respect restrictions on non-believers. Many Jain sites ban leather, food, drink, phones and cameras, and do not admit menstruating women.

ABHISHEKMITTAL/SHUTTERSTOCK

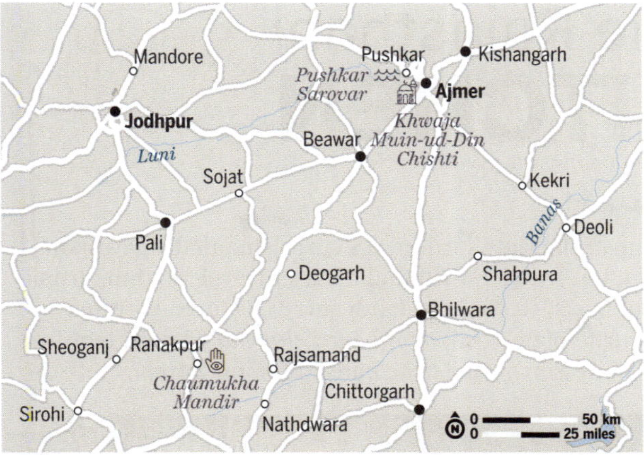

Top left Chaumukha Mandir
Bottom left Hindu evening ritual, Pushkar Sarovar

Writhing spirituality If you suffer from musophobia – the fear of rats – then the Karni Mata Temple at Deshnok near Bikaner is not for you. Here, you'll walk barefoot while thousands of squeaking rodents skitter across the floor – worshipped as the reincarnated children of the Hindu goddess Karni Mata.

Sounds of Sufism While the Mughals were militarily ruthless, they drew spiritual guidance from the broad-minded teachers of Sufism (mystical Islam). Feel the intensity of Sufi belief at the dargah (tomb) of **Khwaja Muin-ud-Din Chishti** in Ajmer, where you'll be carried along by a human tide of pilgrims chanting *qawwali* (devotional hymns).

Find the heavens on Earth Rajasthan was a major centre for Jainism, a faith focused on non-violence and reflection. At Ranakpur near Udaipur, the 15th-century **Chaumukha Mandir** was a white-marble recreation of a wealthy merchant's dream of heaven. Look up to see stone clouds floating with deities, five-bodied demons symbolising the negative passions and carvings that conjure up fractal patterns and passion flowers.

Experience lakeshore spirituality Indian and Western interpretations of spirituality mingle in the hippie hangout of **Pushkar Sarovar**, where Hindu pilgrims perform prayers on the shores of a sacred lake, while travellers study yoga, meditation and Indian classical dance and music in search of higher meaning. The experience of joining devotees at dawn or dusk on the lakeshore is sublime.

Rajasthan's Divine Royals

Not content with being kings and queens of all they surveyed, Rajasthan's royal families also claimed direct lineage from the gods. The Mewar rulers of Udaipur and Chittorgarh trace their family back to Surya, the Sun God; they declined to take the title 'maharaja', regarding themselves instead as caretaker custodians on behalf of Lord Shiva. The maharajas of Jaisalmer, meanwhile, track their lineage to Krishna, and Jaipur's Kachhwaha rulers claim descent from Kusha, the son of Rama and prince of Ayodhya. Look out for the divine family trees proudly displayed in the state's royal palaces.

15 The Rajasthani KITCHEN

SPICY | SURPRISING | PORTABLE

Considering the fame of the state's rulers, it's surprising that Rajasthani cuisine is not better known, but travelers will find dishes to rival anything from Kerala or Punjab. From laal maas – a complex lamb curry flavoured with red chillies – to the state's favourite plate meal, *dhal bhatti churma* (stewed lentils with wheat rolls and a sweet dessert), your taste buds are in for a treat.

DENIS.VOSTRIKOV/SHUTTERSTOCK

How to

When to go Time a foodie trip around seasonal ingredients. Winter is the time for custard apples and berries, sweet carrot *halwa* and *pyaaz ki* kachori (fried onion pastries). During the monsoon, seek out veg dishes made with gourd, green leaves and desert mushrooms.

Getting around Explore Rajasthan's towns and cities on foot to maximise street-food-grazing opportunities.

Meal timing *Dhal bhatti churma* is often only served at lunchtime, between noon and 2pm.

STOCKIMAGEFACTORY.COM/SHUTTERSTOCK

Rajasthan's sweet tooth From the state-favourite *churma* (flour mixed with ghee and jaggery) to sugary sweets found in every village, Rajasthan has a famously sweet tooth. To sample, hit the many *misthan bhandars* (sweet shops) – try *malpua* (syrup-steeped pancakes) in Pushkar, honeycomb-like *ghewar* in Jodhpur and Jaipur, and Ajmer's fudge-like *sohan halwa*.

City of snacks Few cities are as strongly associated with a single food as **Bikaner**, birthplace of bhujiya – peppery, crispy noodles made from dew-bean flour. Some 2.5 million people work to produce this protected-origin snack. Stroll between the station and Kote Gate and see which of the many snack shops serves the best version.

Learn Rajasthan's spice lexicon Where better to learn about Rajasthan's rich, varied spice palate than in a cooking class run by the daughters of a famous Jodhpur spice merchant? South of Sardar Bazaar, **Mohanlal Verhomal (MV) Spices** (mvspices.com) runs classes that immerse you in the spices of the Rajasthani kitchen.

Memorable meals You'll eat like a maharaja in Rajasthan's royal cities. Udaipur scores highly with fans of dinner with a view – try **Upré** or **Ambrai** (ambrairestaurant.com) for lavish meals overlooking Lake Pichola and the City Palace. Then there's **Indique** (palhaveli.com) in Jodphur, gazing towards the Mehrangarh from its rooftop perch, or fort-facing **1st Gate Home Fusion** (1stgate.in) in Jaisalmer. In Jaipur, dine in style at **Peacock** (hotelpearlpalace.com), **Suvarna Mahal** or veg-masters **Johri** (thejohrijaipur.com).

Far left Street vendor, Bikaner
Bottom left *Dhal bhatti churma*

Jodhpur Treats

Cooking is my passion from childhood, and I've worked at Jaipur's Rambagh Palace and Jodhpur's Umaid Bhawan Palace. There's great food in Jodhpur – the city is famous for its *pyaz ki kachori* (fried pastries stuffed with onion), *mirchi bada* (chillies stuffed with potato in gram-flour batter), and *dhal bhatti* (stewed lentils with bread rolls). If you like sweets, Jodhpur's *ghewar* (honeycomb-like rings) and *gulab jamun* (dough balls in syrup) are the must-tries. Lal maas (lamb with ground red chilli) is a personal favourite Rajasthani dish; my family often prepares it for guests at **Pushp Guest House**.

Nikhil Mathur, *manager of Bristows Haveli, Jodhpur. bristowsindia.com*

16 A Feast of FESTIVALS

CAMELS | RITUAL | PARTY VIBES

Rajasthan's festival calendar is packed year-round, and your trip may well coincide with music, dancing, colourful religious rituals and festival food. Celebrations for Hindus, Jains and Muslims are joined by events marking the changing seasons and fairs celebrating desert culture. In winter, expect exuberant wedding processions filling the streets; bring your dancing shoes!

NOMAD1988/SHUTTERSTOCK

How to

When to go Autumn and winter are particularly busy with Diwali, the Pushkar Camel Fair, Jaipur's Literature Festival and Uttarayan. Spring brings flying colours for Holi and Udaipur's Mewar Festival.

Getting around Public transport can be swamped at festival times; overcrowding is common and advance booking is essential.

Know the calendar Dates of religious festivals change annually relative to the Gregorian calendar. Check the current year's dates before booking a festival-focused trip.

ZZVET/GETTY IMAGES

NURPHOTO/GETTY IMAGES

Far top left Camels, Desert Festival
Far bottom left Bagpiper, Camel Festival
Left Dancers, Mewar Festival

Camels for all Fancy mingling with tightrope walkers, snake charmers, sadhus (holy men) and thousands of camels? Head for Pushkar's legendary **Camel Fair** (tourism.rajasthan.gov.in) in October or November. Part livestock market, part sacred ceremony, part cultural spectacular, this is the place to see moustache contests, ritual bathing and competitions to pick Rajasthan's most beautiful camel.

Meet Mr Desert You've heard of Miss World? Now meet Mr Desert! Every January or February, Jaisalmer pulls out all the stops for the **Desert Festival** (desertfestivaljaisalmer.com), a fun-filled romp through desert culture. Cheer on camel races, camel polo, turban-tying competitions and the contest to find the most unmistakably Rajasthani gentleman in the state.

Read a book, fly a kite Jaipur hosts some of the highlights of the cultural calendar. Every January, bookworms and wordsmiths gather for the **Jaipur Literature Festival** (jaipurliteraturefestival.org) to hear readings from the likes of William Dalrymple and Kiran Desai. In the same month, **Uttarayan** fills the skies over Jaipur with bobbing kites; grab a ₹5 paper kite from a Kishanpole Bazaar kite vendor and get flying!

Mewar magic The Maharanas of Mewar used to weigh themselves in Udaipur's **City Palace** and distribute their weight in treasure to the masses. Today, their largesse is manifested in the **Mewar Festival** in March or April, coinciding with the Hindu festival of Gangaur. Expect singing, dancing, fireworks, a royal boat flotilla and women parading effigies of Shiva and his wife Gauri around Lake Pichola.

Islamic Rajasthan

Islamic festivals are focused on family, prayer and reflection, but visit at the end of Ramadan, the Muslim month of fasting, and you can join families wolfing down treats such as biryani, kebabs, *nihari* (richly spiced stewed lamb) and *haleem* (a thick meat, wheat and lentil stew) for the **Eid al-Fitr** feast. Offering a window onto the traditions of Mughal India, the streets around the Sufi dargahs (mausoleums) in Ajmer, Nagaur and Jhunjhunu are great spots to join the celebrations. **Urs ceremonies**, honouring Sufi saints such as Ajmer's Khwaja Muin-ud-Din Chishti, are also top times to feel Islam's spiritual rhythms.

17 Try a Camel SAFARI

CAMELS | DESERT SUNSETS | STARGAZING

Romantics are drawn to Rajasthan by visions of camel caravans tramping across the desert, laden with silk, spices and opium, and camel drivers in desert outposts across the state are happy to bring the dream to life (minus the opium). Camel safaris lasting anywhere from half a day to a week or more embark daily, offering an evocative taste of Rajasthani desert life.

MUBARAK_KHAN/SHUTTERSTOCK

How to

When to go Winter brings mild days, cool nights and clear skies for stargazing. Wise camel trekkers avoid the damp monsoon and the energy-sapping heat of April and May.

Getting there Short camel safaris can be arranged on arrival in Jaisalmer, Bikaner or Osian; give operators several days' notice for multiday trips.

Camel safari essentials Carry lots of water, sunscreen, a hat, insect repellent and a warm layer for cold desert nights.

SCOTT BIALES DITCHTHEMAP/SHUTTERSTOCK

SOMIL K. MAKADIA/SHUTTERSTOCK

Far top and bottom left Camel safaris
Left Desert fox

Choosing a Safari

Choosing a safari The most famous hubs for camel safaris in Rajasthan are **Jaisalmer** and **Bikaner**, but silence and serenity isn't guaranteed. Take a short camel safari to **Sam** and **Khuri** near Jaisalmer or **Osian** near Jodhpur and you'll find a party on the dunes, with music, dance shows and themed desert camps. Seek out multiday 'non-touristic' camel safaris, which roam deeper into the desert, starting the trip by 4WD to escape the crowds.

Meet the desert locals As you wobble out into a landscape of thorn trees, scattered villages and dunes, you'll encounter plenty of desert dwellers. On safaris from Jaisalmer with operators such as **Trotters** (trottersjaisalmer.net) and **Sahara Travels** (saharatravelsjaisalmer.com), expect encounters with excited village children and turbaned farmers, and perhaps glimpses of desert foxes, black buck and bustards, particularly around **Desert National Park**. Around **Bikaner**, the birdlife is spectacular, and wildlife is easier to spot away from the crowds. Arrange safaris with a birding focus through **Vinayak Guest House** (vinayakguesthouse@gmail.com), or roam the desert in the company of the charming **Vijay Singh Rathore**, the Camel Man (camelman.com).

Midnight at the oasis One of the highlights of a camel safari is spending a night under the stars. After a campfire dinner, you'll slip into a camp bed on the dunes beneath a light-pollution-free canopy of stars, with the star-dotted Milky Way clearly in view.

Camel Safari

For me, the best length of safari is three days and two nights, because you'll start understanding your camel's riding style and you'll have time to see wildlife such as antelopes and desert foxes and pause for activities such as cooking lessons and visits to village homes. My favourite experience is sleeping outside under the stars – it's wonderful because there's no pollution and the sky is so clear. It's like another world. The atmosphere is so peaceful that you almost don't want to go back to the noise of the city!

Hiteshwar Rathore, *camel- and cycling-tour leader at Camel Man. camelman.com*

18 Treasure-Chest MUSEUMS

HEIRLOOMS | CULTURE | FOLK HISTORY

Rajasthan's rulers lived lives of extraordinary luxury, so it's not surprising that the state's museums are jam-packed with royal treasures and trinkets. From glittering jewels to miniature paintings and armouries full of inlaid weaponry, Rajasthan's royal collections offer a window onto the gilded existence of the state's most powerful dynasties. Dig in to some of India's best museums.

IMAGESOFINDIA/SHUTTERSTOCK

How To

When to go Look out for seasonal events at the big palace museums, such as the Holi bonfires at Udaipur's City Palace.

Getting there Rajasthan's royal cities typically grew around their royal palaces, so the top museums are right in the centre. Explore Shekhawati's painted mansions by chartered taxi.

Composite tickets When visiting Rajasthan's museums and monuments, look out for 'composite tickets' offering cheaper entry to multiple sights.

RADIOKAFKA/SHUTTERSTOCK

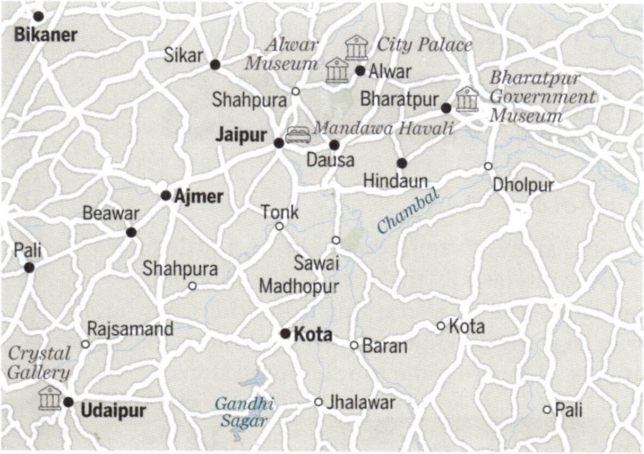

Heirlooms of Udaipur Arguably Rajasthan's best museum, the **City Palace** (citypalacemuseum.org) in Udaipur rises like a carved block of ivory beside Lake Pichola. Seek home-decor tips in chequerboard courtyards and chambers crammed with glinting weapons and palanquins, and eye-popping spaces like the turquoise Bhim Vilas, which could take pride of place in any interior-design magazine. In the flanking Fateh Prakash Palace hotel, the **Crystal Gallery** displays a vast collection of British crystal trinkets, ordered by a maharaja who died before they were delivered. Then there's the royal car collection, awash with vintage prestige motors.

Treasures of small kingdoms Don't overlook Rajasthan's smaller princely states. In **Alwar**, royal capital of Jai Singh Prabhakar, discover a treasure-stuffed **museum** balanced over government offices in the reclaimed City Palace. In nearby **Bharatpur**, enter the elegant palace of the Sinsinwar maharajas, with its treasure-filled **government museum**.

Painted Shekhawait Shekhawati, northwest of Jaipur, is a living museum of painted *haveli* – elegant homes built by wealthy merchants in the 19th and 20th centuries. From **Jhunjhunu**, take a visual journey through Indian history in the grand houses of nearby **Mandawa**, **Nawalgarh** and **Fatehpur**, visiting mansions painted from floor to ceiling with deities, ancestors and modern innovations such as trains, planes and automobiles, which were arriving in India for the first time. Nawalgarh's **Yunus Khan** (9414491281) is an expert guide.

Top left City Palace, Udaipur
Bottom left Mansion, Nawalgarh

Royal Architecture 101

Visit a few Rajasthani palaces and you'll soon spot architectural features that crop up in almost every royal residence. Royal rule was a delicate balancing act between projecting power and personal protection, so meetings with the ordinary public were conducted under armed guard in the *diwan-i-am* ('hall of public audiences'). Only approved dignitaries were admitted to the *diwan-i-khas* ('hall of private audiences') deeper inside the compound. Chambers beyond were reserved exclusively for the royal family; reflecting the gender divisions of the time, women of the royal household were cocooned in the *zenana* (women's quarters) and only permitted to observe palace meetings through perforated screens.

19 Memorable MEMENTOS

ARTISTRY | FOLK ARTS | VIVID COLOUR

With so much colour on display, it's tempting to bring a little of Rajasthan's rainbow home with you. Luckily the state is one enormous emporium, with bazaars and stores selling everything from iridescent saris and handwoven *khadi* fabrics to intricate gold and silver jewellery, *lac* (resin) bangles and traditional puppets. Here are some top shopping stops.

JOCELYN BAUN/ALAMY

How to

Getting around Go shopping in Rajasthan on foot, so you can duck into promising-looking shops and hone your haggling skills at intriguing street markets.

When to go Rajasthan's shops open late, at around 10am, but stay open into the evening, closing around 7pm or 8pm.

Cash or card Unless prices are marked, some gentle haggling is normal when buying souvenirs. Only upmarket stores take cards; elsewhere, cash is king.

HEMIS/ALAMY

Top left Bangles, Manikaron ka Rasta
Bottom left Johari Bazaar

Jaipur's sampling pot Looking for a reminder of Jaipur's kaleidoscopic bazaars? Start in **Rajasthali** (instagram.com/rajasthali_emporium) on MI Rd, a government-run emporium selling everything from embroidered patchwork wall hangings to deity images. For classy gifts curated with the modern home in mind, head to **Anokhi** (anokhi.com) on Prithviraj Marg or **Agora** (agorajaipur.com) on Hawa Mahal Rd. **Manikaron ka Rasta** specialises in vividly colourful *lac* (resin) bangles; try **Johari Bazaar** for gold and silver. Not a jewellery fan? Head west to **Khajane Kalon ka Rasta**, where masons whittle snow-coloured marble into statues.

Grab a Bikaner miniature At **Bikaner Miniature Arts** (bikanerminiaturearts.com) you can buy some of the most detailed miniature paintings imaginable, from Mughal court scenes to intricate depictions of wildlife, painted with brushes as thin as a human hair. Before you buy, artists from the Swami family will show you preparation of pigments and the application of real gold to miniatures.

Udaipur's fine arts Head to Bhattiyani Chotta for ornate picture frames inlaid with shell and camel bone. Close to the City Palace, **University of Arts** is stacked with traditional Rajasthani puppets, crafted by a master puppeteer. For a truly one-off memento, book a miniature-painting class and produce your own artwork. Respected art schools include **Ashoka Arts** (ashokaarts.co.in) and **Pacific Art** (pacificartudaipur.com).

Portable Prosperity

India has a centuries-old tradition of storing wealth in the form of jewellery – often lavish wedding jewellery adorned with glinting precious stones. In unpredictable times, jewellery was easily hidden, highly portable and easily resold. Some 35,000 tonnes of gold is locked up in family jewellery collections in India – 7.5 times greater than the gold reserves in Fort Knox! Jaipur is India's national hub for polishing and cutting precious stones, with hundreds of gem workshops (and testing labs to confirm stones are real). Across Rajasthan, look out for *johari* (jewel) bazaars, lined with silversmiths and goldsmiths selling jewellery, deity images for home shrines and *meenakari* (enamelwork).

Listings

BEST OF THE REST

Sights with Insight

Govind Dev Ji Temple

Founded by Maharaja Jai Singh II, Jaipur's spiritual heart buzzes with energy; leave flowers as an offering, then drop into **Govindam** for sweet treats.

Central Museum

Drop into this eccentric government museum in Jaipur, designed by a Brit commissioned by a maharaja, to see the kleptomaniac way Raj architects borrowed motifs from Indian architecture.

Chand Baori

Visit this mammoth step-well in Abhaneri, 95km east of Jaipur, for its monumental scale. But pause to consider its desecration by Mahmud of Ghazni, who hacked the face off every deity at the Harshat Mata Temple.

Palace of Suraj Mal

This overlooked palace near Bharatpur shows the maharajas at their most playful. In the Keshav Bhavan, hidden mechanisms and rolling boulders recreated artificial thunder and monsoon showers.

Soniji Ki Nasiyan Temple

Explore this rust-red temple in Ajmer to learn the life story of Rishabhadeva (Adinath), the first *tirthankar* (teacher) of Jainism, through glinting dioramas coated in real gold.

Raniji-ki-Baori

This Mines of Moria-worthy step-well plunges south of Bundi's bazaars. Peer into more portal-like wells nearby at Nagar Kund, Sagar Kund and Dabhai Kund.

Delwara Temples

At these amazing Jain mandirs (dilwarajain-temple.org) at Mt Abu in Rajasthan's only hill station, deities and demons float in a cosmic paradise carved from milky marble.

Toorji Ka Jhalra

This Jodhpur Old City step-well still functions as a vibrant hub for Jodhpur social life – a reminder of the role played by step-wells across India in times past.

Mandore Gardens

This green bower in Jodhpur was the seat of the Marwar dynasty until 1459; its great leaders are marked by towering cenotaphs that pay homage to Jain and Hindu temples.

Jain temples in Jaisalmer

Seven lavish Jain temples (tourism.rajasthan.gov.in) in Jaisalmer Fort tell the story of Jainism's great *tirthankars* (teachers) in a riot of buttery stone embellishments.

Patwa-ki-Haveli

A group of Jaisalmer *haveli* mansions that conjure up past desert grandeur – compare antiquities-stuffed **Kothari's Patwa-ki-Haveli Museum** to the eerily empty but elegant **government museum**.

Junagarh

Two palace museums combined in Bikaner, with heirlooms from a camel-riding maharaja and tragic memorials to brides who died on their husband's funeral pyres.

Artful Activities

Cyclin' Jaipur

Let the sociable guides of Cyclin' Jaipur (cyclinjaipur.com) lead you on a pedal tour of the Old City's intoxicating bazaars, stopping at local haunts for street food snacks.

Anokhi Museum of Hand Printing

Wander past Amber Fort, the **Sri Jagat Shiromani Ji Temple** and **Panna Meena** step-well to this intriguing museum (anokhimuseum.com) where you can block-print your own scarf, bag or T-shirt.

Palace on Wheels

India's most famous luxury train (palaceonwheels.in) reproduces the lavish carriages of the maharajas, offering a whirlwind tour around temples, forts, palaces and tiger reserves.

Saraswati Music & Dance School

At this respected Pushkar school, take Indian music lessons with Birju, dance classes with Hemant or **Rajasthani cooking** classes with Deepa.

Dharohar

Get a taste of traditional Rajasthani dance, music and puppetry through colour-swirling performances in the courtyard at the Bagore-ki-Haveli, Udaipur (dharoharfolkdance.org).

Mount Abu Trekking

Wander Mt Abu's scenic viewpoints and wildlife-filled forests in search of crocodiles, leopards, bears and birds with expert Mahendra 'Charles' Dan (mountabutrekking.co.in).

Flying Fox

Zoom over the battlements of the Mehrangarh fort and its garden of rocky outcrops on this spiderweb of six interconnected ziplines (flyingfox.asia).

Meals to Inspire Memories

Lassiwala ₹

Surrounded by imitators, this celebrity lassi shop at 312 MI Rd, Jaipur, lures a constant tide of customers with rich, creamy lassis served in clay cups.

V DRONE/SHUTTERSTOCK

Cabin, Palace on Wheels

New Bungli Restaurant ₹₹

After boggling at kaleidoscopic murals in Nawalgarh's painted *haveli,* call ahead (9414491281) for a lunch of delicious Rajasthani home-cooking.

Bundi Vilas ₹₹₹

Clamber to the top floor of this stylish *haveli* home for an exclusive Rajasthani dinner overlooking *Lord of the Rings*-esque Bundi Palace.

Millets of Mewar ₹₹

Discover the richness of Rajasthani cooking at this stalwart restaurant near Lal Ghat, Udaipur, where millet-infused veg dishes feature prominently on the menu.

Stepwell Cafe ₹₹

Enjoy coffee, cakes and light lunchables (or a glass of wine) overlooking the striking depths of Jodhpur's most stunning stepwell.

Saffron ₹₹

Perched above one of Jaisalmer's most characterful courtyard mansions, doling out quality meals with views across the golden rooftops.

NORTHERN INDIA

MOUNTAINS | ADVENTURE | CULTURE

RESEARCHED BY PUNEETINDER KAUR SIDHU

NITINSHARMA/SHUTTERSTOCK

NORTHERN INDIA
Trip Builder

From natural beauty, cultural complexity and metropolitan highs to centuries-old craft traditions and splendid dining, Northern India has it all. Rugged mountains, gushing rivers and wildlife-filled jungles offer adventure; historical towns enthral with ruins; and big cities get the party going.

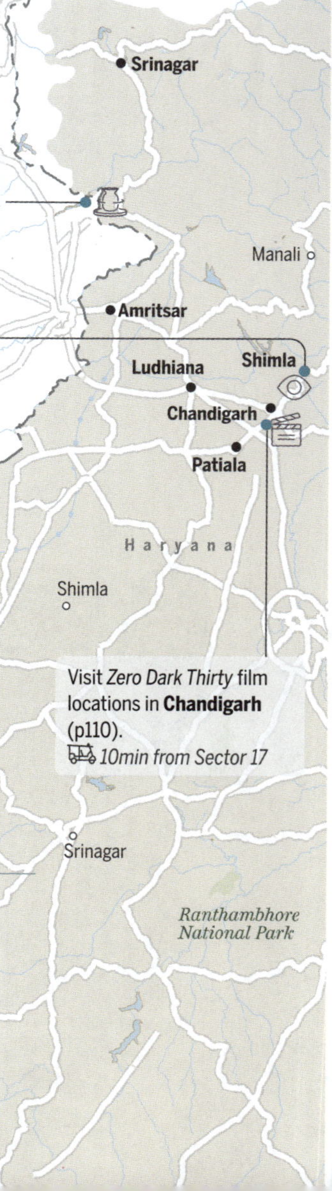

Try your hand at weaving a durrie carpet in **Balwaar Khurd** (p118).
1hr from Patiala

Count tunnels and bridges on the **Kalka–Shimla toy-train route** (p114).
40min from Chandigarh

Visit *Zero Dark Thirty* film locations in **Chandigarh** (p110).
10min from Sector 17

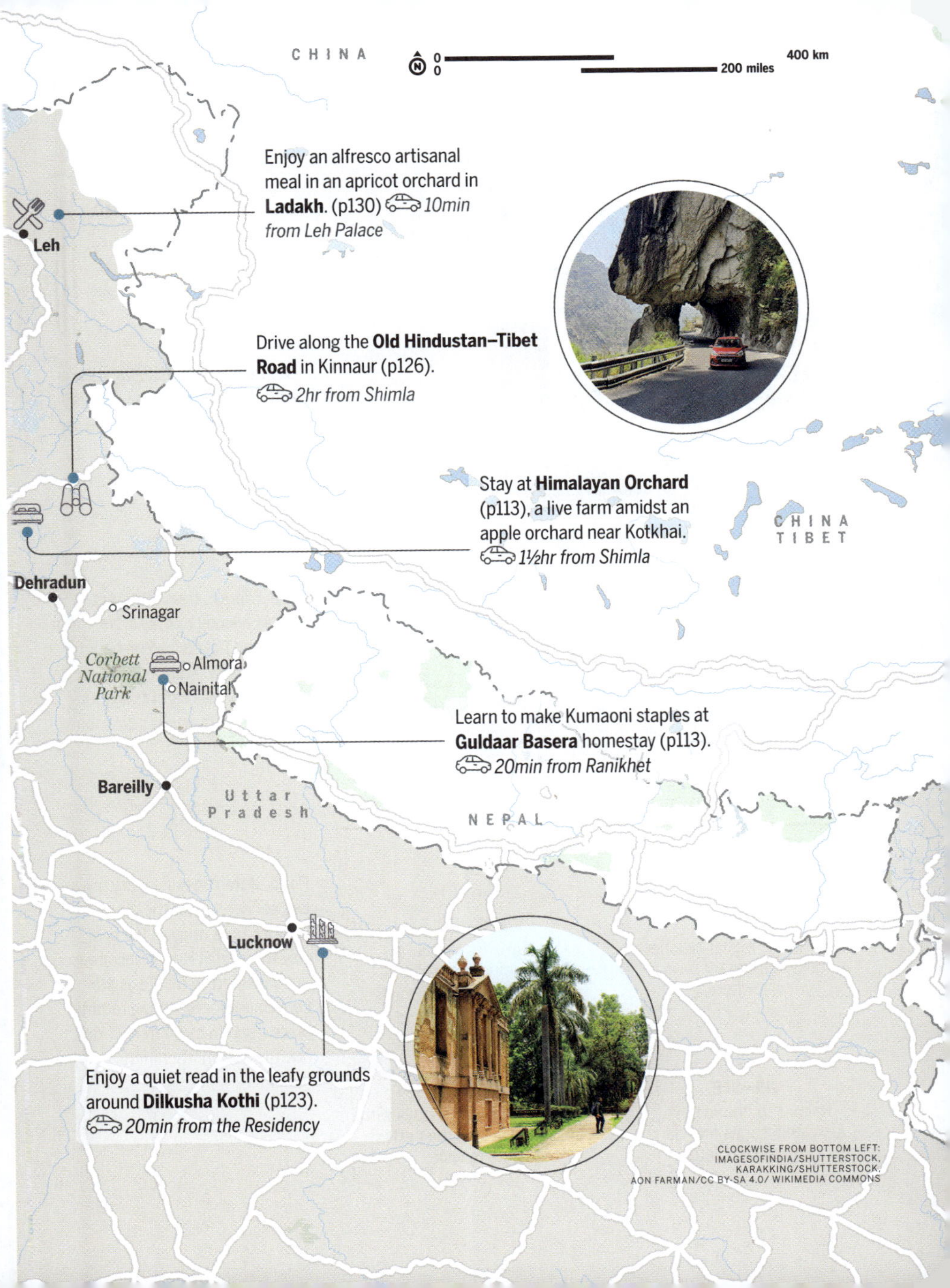

CLOCKWISE FROM BOTTOM LEFT: IMAGESOFINDIA/SHUTTERSTOCK, KARAKKING/SHUTTERSTOCK, AON FARMAN/CC BY-SA 4.0/ WIKIMEDIA COMMONS

Practicalities

MATYAS REHAK/SHUTTERSTOCK

ARRIVING

Shaheed Bhagat Singh Airport (Chandigarh) is served by limited flights from the Middle East, while **Sri Guru Ram Das Jee Airport** (Amritsar; pictured) is served by flights from cities in the Middle East, Southeast Asia and the United Kingdom. Lucknow's **Chaudhury Charan Singh Airport** and Varanasi's **Lal Bahadur Shastri Airport** are served by flights from Bangkok and Dubai.

HOW MUCH FOR A

Samosa
₹10-100

Masala chai
₹20-200

Taxi per day
₹3500-5000

GETTING AROUND

Air Intercity domestic flights are the quickest, but not necessarily the cheapest, way to traverse the region.

Train Express trains connect almost all major cities in Northern India, and tickets can be bought online. Long distances are best covered by overnight train journeys which (mostly!) save money and time.

TAXI

Road State-run and luxury private bus services cover the region. Besides taxis, they're the best way to travel in Himalayan areas unconnected by rail. Taxis are convenient for exploring remote places, and to move freely from one town to another in the flatlands.

WHEN TO GO

JAN–MAR
Snow in the higher reaches; cold to pleasant days elsewhere.

APR–JUN
Peak time for Himalayas, coinciding with school holidays.

JUL–SEP
Rainy and humid days; lush landscapes for hiking enthusiasts later.

OCT–DEC
Warm to mild winter days with vibrant festivals; the perfect time to visit.

EATING & DRINKING

Northern India is blessed with regional cuisine, featuring Tibetan staples like meaty broths and *momo* (savoury dumplings; pictured top right) from the trans-Himalayas, the *siddu* (steamed buns filled with lentils or jaggery) of Himachal Pradesh, Uttarkhand's *aloo ke gutke* (spicy potato) and *bhatt ki churkani* (black soybean dhal) and the comforting *rajma-chawal* (kidney-bean rice; pictured bottom right) and stuffed *paratha* (fried flatbreads) of Punjab. Lucknow's *dum* biryani and *shami* kebabs are legendary.

Best cocktails with a twist Ikk Panjab (p117)

Must-try siddu Himalayan Orchard (p113)

CONNECT & FIND YOUR WAY

Wi-fi is widely available with multiple providers servicing urban areas, though remote hinterlands can experience patchy to no service. Before hitting the road, get a local SIM card for navigation and the use of travel apps. They are easy to obtain through official phone company offices found downtown. Also get paper maps from the local tourism information centre.

CERTIFIED GUIDES

Secure a government-certified local guide wherever you go to avoid touts and misinformation. It's best to agree on a price in advance.

WHERE TO STAY

There is no shortage of accommodation in Northern India, from backpacker hostels and budget guesthouses, to homestays, farmstays and glamping, plus boutique, heritage and luxury hotels.

Place	Pros/Cons
Leh	Busy, crowded central hub in Ladakh; a springboard for trans-Himalayan adventures.
Kotkhai-Kotgarh-Thanedar	Quiet homestays in apple country. The gateway to Kinnaur, away from busy Shimla.
Ranikhet	Less action than Naintal, but easily accessible with great views of Himalayan peaks.
Chandigarh	Hip and lively; less than an hour from the luxuriant countryside of Punjab and Haryana.
Lucknow	Transport hub, central for day trips to Ayodhya and Kannauj.
Varanasi	Touristy with busy streets, but lots of eating and sleeping options.

MONEY

Always carry some cash on you. Taxis, smaller shops and street stalls don't take credit cards. Use big bills at shops and restaurants, small ones for local transportation and snacks.

20 Behind the SCENES

FILMS | PHOTOGRAPHY | LANDSCAPE

Northern India's stunning trans-Himalayan terrain, dusty flatlands, busy cities and sleepy villages have lured many a film crew. They caught the imagination of director Jean-Jacques Annaud, who filmed *Seven Years in Tibet* in Ladakh; Chandigarh markets masqueraded as a Pakistani town in Katheryn Bigelow's *Zero Dark Thirty,* while princely Pataudi featured in Ryan Murphy's *Eat Pray Love.*

DANG NHAT VU/SHUTTERSTOCK

Mass Tourism

Stunning visuals notwithstanding, filming in untouched natural locations comes with a host of challenges and drawbacks. The environmental impact is the most significant, as popular locations can attract hordes of curious visitors, as Pangong Tso (pictured), a lake in Ladakh, found to its detriment after featuring in Bollywood's satirical comedy *Three Idiots*.

Trip Notes

Getting around Chandigarh is well connected to Delhi by air, train, and bus, with a daily flight to Leh, and Pataudi is a five-hour bus ride away.

When to go Other than snowbound areas, locations can be seen year-round, though it's better to explore the Himalayas in summer and flatlands in cooler months.

Top tip If you wish to find the exact location of a film, you'll want to bring a snapshot from a scene.

04 The Shyok River near **Diskit Gompa** (pictured below) in Nubra Valley and some of the outlying parts of Leh form the backdrop in several scenes of *Seven Years in Tibet*.

03 **Baralacha Pass** (pictured below) which connects Himachal Pradesh's Lahaul with Ladakh also makes a brief appearance in *Seven Years in Tibet* and is a popular viewpoint between Manali and Leh.

02 With a few artfully and strategically placed signs and shop names in Urdu, the busy **Sector 15** market in Chandigarh easily passed for a Pakistani town in *Zero Dark Thirty*.

01 The Ashram Hari Mandir in **Pataudi**, Haryana, features prominently in director Ryan Murphy's romantic biopic *Eat Pray Love*. Protagonist and author Elizabeth Gilbert, played by Julia Roberts, is seen practising meditation here.

FROM TOP: JOHN NOBLE, RAHUL D'SILVAI/SHUTTERSTOCK

21 Escape the CITY

FARM LIFE | ORCHARDS | FOOD

There are times when metro madness overtakes you, and you just have to get out of the city for some downtime. Luckily, many Northern India cities are within an hour's drive from lush fields, organic farms and fruit-dripping orchards, all of them dotted with hospitable homestays promising short hikes, nature trails and foraging and cooking options.

RUPENDRA SINGH RAWAT/SHUTTERSTOCK

How To

Getting around The best way to reach these places is by car. Most are connected by local and state-run buses, but those in the mountains have infrequent service.

When to go It is better to explore Himalayan destinations in the summer months, and the other areas in cooler months.

Take directions Call ahead for detailed directions, Google Maps may not be up to date and networks can be patchy in places.

DUSHI82/SHUTTERSTOCK

Top left Anti-hail nets on fruit trees, Himachal Pradesh
Bottom left Dairy farming, Shimla

Around the bend Head across to apple country over the winding, tree-flanked country roads from Shimla. Be sure to experience life at **Himalayan Orchard** during harvest season, when hillsides heave with protective-net-covered, fruit-heavy trees – a delightful sight. Lending a hand picking the apples is a great way to stay fit on holiday, and you can see apples being graded and packed if you're curious about the process. Peeling, pitting or chopping up the excess bounty for jams, chutneys and juices is another deliciously rewarding activity. Should you be in Uttarakhand, enjoy the rural settings of Ranikhet, stroll along pine-lined paths and terraced vegetable patches, try making *aloo ke gutke* (spicy potato) with some hand-holding from your host at the **Guldaar Basera** homestay.

In the dusty plains Wake up to birdsong and the sight of Punjab's luxuriant, bucolic countryside. Hopping onto a tractor ploughing fields, milking buffaloes and sun-drying garlands of winter vegetables at **Hansali Organic Farm** adds a whole new perspective to agrarian lifestyles. Be sure to forage for mustard spinach and observe its time-gobbling transformation into an appetizing *saag*. A hugely enjoyable way to factor in some exercise, and observe local communities going about daily life, is cycling around farmlands amid sandy ravines along the Chambal River in Uttar Pradesh. Another way to get a taste of the farming life is signing up for hands-on activities at farmstays, like **My Mom's Village** in Ayodhya and **Planter's Bungalow** in Prayagraj.

A Sustainable Lifestyle

Long before sustainable practices entered everyday language, agrarian communities lived by its principles out of necessity and understanding. For us, this continues much as it always has. Food is grown in season and surplus preserved. The orchard is tended, dead trees are used for fire wood, rainwater is harvested, kitchen and animal waste is composted and returned to the soil. Work follows daylight and weather, not the clock. These practices are not ideological – they rely on practicality and observation of the land and seasons, restraint, economy and continuity. A received way of life, wisdom passed through daily work and directing daily choices.

Devanshe Chauhan, *environmentalist and owner of @himalayanorchard*

22 All Aboard the TOY TRAIN

ENGINEERING | VIADUCTS | TUNNELS

Hop aboard the UNESCO World Heritage Kalka–Shimla narrow-gauge train (pictured) for the ride of a lifetime through pine-clad ridges and over arched bridges. It chugs up the Shivalik range and toots through 102 tunnels on one of north India's most scenic train journeys.

DINESH HUKMANI/SHUTTERSTOCK

Trip Notes

Getting around Indian Railways (irctc.co.in) operates three daily services: the early morning Shivalik Deluxe Express, a single-coach Rail Motor and the Himalayan Queen, which connects with other express trains.

When to go The best time to go is from March to June and September to December, the heavy rains in July and August can affect visibility and result in delays.

Top tip Book early as tickets sell out quickly.

A Cinematic Icon

The train's quaint wooden interiors, louvered windows and vintage charm have featured in Bollywood hits like *Jab We Met* and *Gadar – Ek Prem Katha*, making it a celluloid icon. In the 1974 film *Dost*, you can hear it tooting away in the very hummable Hindi song, 'Gaadi Bulla Rahi Hai'.

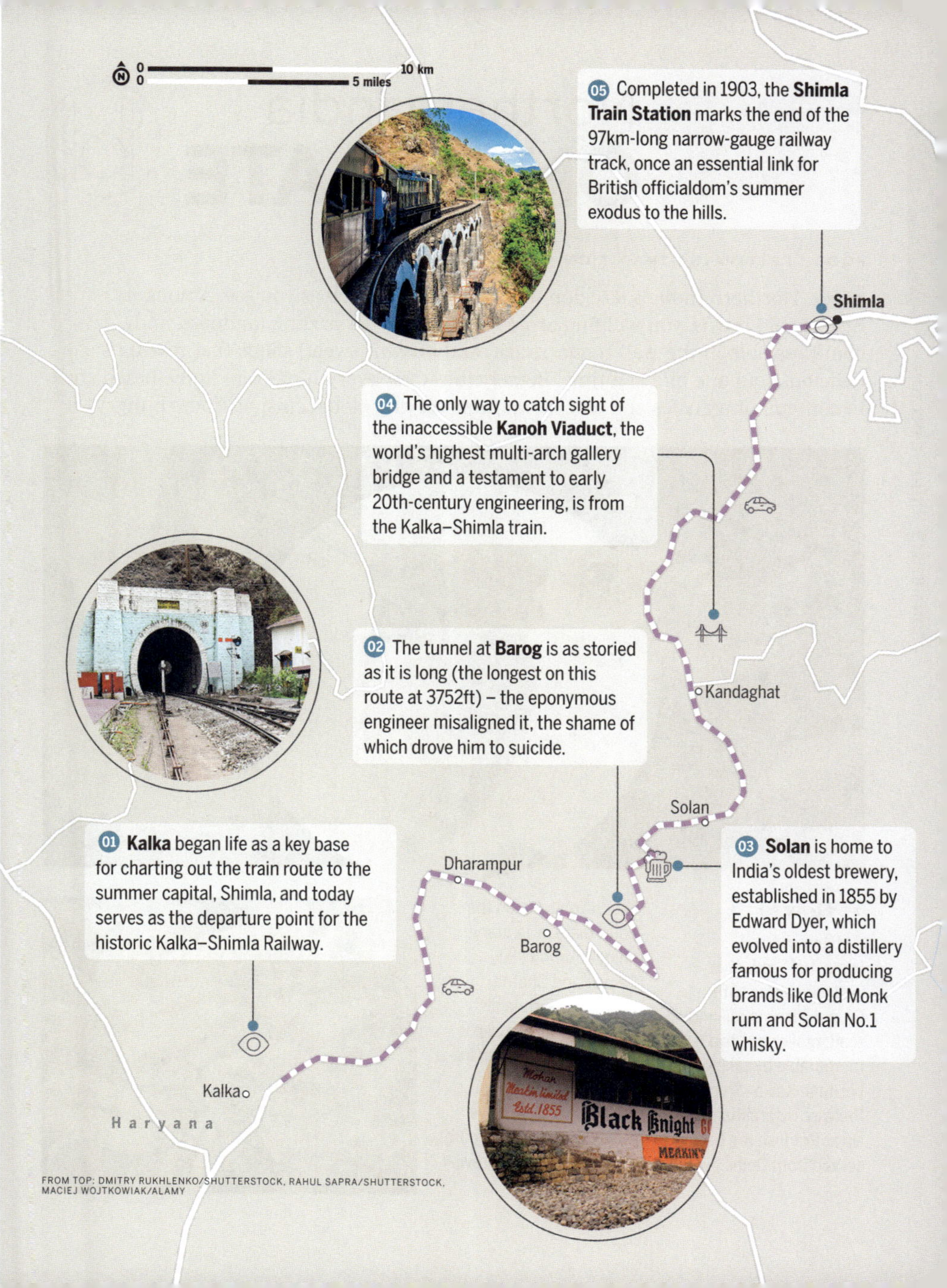

01 **Kalka** began life as a key base for charting out the train route to the summer capital, Shimla, and today serves as the departure point for the historic Kalka–Shimla Railway.

02 The tunnel at **Barog** is as storied as it is long (the longest on this route at 3752ft) – the eponymous engineer misaligned it, the shame of which drove him to suicide.

03 **Solan** is home to India's oldest brewery, established in 1855 by Edward Dyer, which evolved into a distillery famous for producing brands like Old Monk rum and Solan No.1 whisky.

04 The only way to catch sight of the inaccessible **Kanoh Viaduct**, the world's highest multi-arch gallery bridge and a testament to early 20th-century engineering, is from the Kalka–Shimla train.

05 Completed in 1903, the **Shimla Train Station** marks the end of the 97km-long narrow-gauge railway track, once an essential link for British officialdom's summer exodus to the hills.

FROM TOP: DMITRY RUKHLENKO/SHUTTERSTOCK, RAHUL SAPRA/SHUTTERSTOCK, MACIEJ WOJTKOWIAK/ALAMY

23 Northern India ON A PLATE

FOOD | FESTIVALS | TRADITION

Northern India is a region that you taste as much as you see. Among its historic old towns, you will find aromatic street foods, sizzling tandoors, and countless hole-in-the-wall *chaat* (snack) and *mithai* (sweet) shops that reveal its delicious soul one bite at a time. Bigger cities offer everything from home-based chefs to contemporary cafes and chic restaurants serving global cuisine. Come hungry.

V. ARYA/SHUTTERSTOCK

How to

Getting around Himachal Pradesh is well connected with Chandigarh via rail and road; make your trip memorable by taking the heritage Kalka–Shimla Railway. Uttarakhand and Uttar Pradesh are better served from Delhi.

When to go Catch the Lohri taste in January; enjoy Jhumroo, Ikk Panjab and Chetna Srivastava's specials through winter; make it to Himachal Pradesh in March and April.

Food tours Deep Dive India (deepdiveindia.com; from ₹5000) tours reveal local delicacies.

DINODIA PHOTOS/ALAMY

PRADEEPGAURS/SHUTTERSTOCK

Far left top *Siddu*
Far left bottom *Launglata*
Left Street food vendors, Uttarakhand

Seasonal festivities Changing seasons take on a whole new flavour across Northern India, throwing another reason to feast into the mix. Punjab emerges from deep winter to tuck into *roh di kheer,* rice pudding made with sugarcane juice, consumed a day after the winter harvest festival, ***Lohri*** (Makar Sakranti). In Uttarakhand, the festival is uniquely called Kala Kauva, when sweetened flour dumplings are worn as garlands and offered to crows. ***Lingad*** (fiddlehead fern) announces spring in Himachal Pradesh, when it's turned into a tangy pickle or eaten as a stir-fry. ***Siddu,*** a steamed bun stuffed with lentils or jaggery and eaten with ghee, is a Himachali celebratory staple. ***Launglata,*** Varanasi's favourite winter dessert, is made from flour, stuffed with dried fruits and cloves, and soaked in sugar syrup.

Carrying on tradition Concept restaurant **Jhumroo** keeps culinary culture alive with its creative millet-based repertoire, replacing rice in the creamy pudding *kheer* with mixed millets, for one. At the **Ikk Panjab** restaurant, nostalgia meets deliciousness with Sialkot's tandoori leg of lamb, and the Baluchistani sajji, a spice-coated whole chicken, invoking an undivided Punjab's culinary landscape. Lucknow-based home-chef **Chetna Srivastava**'s *mangoda* (green-lentil fritters) and *kele ki macchli* (flour-coated banana fritters) are an ode to Kayastha cuisine (deepdiveindia.com). **Avanbai Mansion** homestay, also in Lucknow, curates dining experiences around Awadhi heirloom dishes such as *lassun ki kheer,* a creamy garlic pudding.

Himalayan Cheese

North India's cheese scene is rapidly emerging, driven by artisanal producers blending European techniques with local flavours such as cumin, garlic and fresh herbs. Small fromageries prioritise grass-fed milk and sustainability while traditional yak cheese, such as *chhurpi* from Ladakh, offers a rugged, protein-rich option. Fromageries like ours, especially in the mountains, emphasise on terroir-capturing Himalayan flavours for consumers, who increasingly favour artisanal cheese for its natural ingredients and ethical sourcing, reflecting a heightened food consciousness. Urban centres like Shimla, Chandigarh, Ludhiana and Dehradun prioritise transparency and quality over mass-produced options.

Francois Laederich, *artisanal cheese-maker and founder of @amiksa cheese*

24 Meet the MAKERS

CRAFT | HERITAGE | ARTISANS

Throughout Northern India, you can watch metals being beaten, leather being tooled, potters at the wheel and weavers at the loom. Textiles are deeply rooted in north Indian culture and there are always embroiderers, dyers and block-printing artisans within reach. Meeting the makers in their home settings is an extra-special cultural immersion.

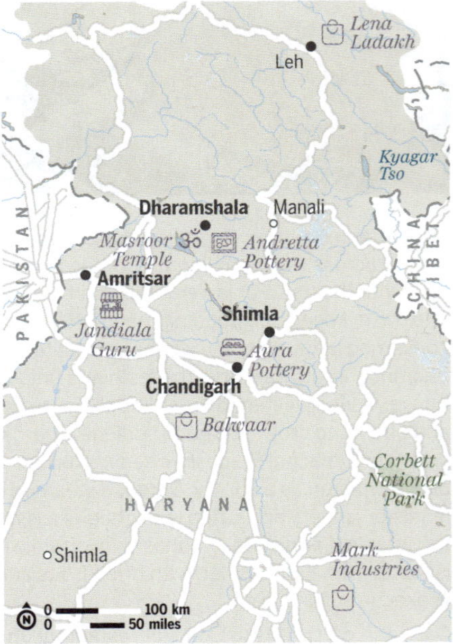

How to

Getting around Make Chandigarh your access point for road and air travel to Ladakh, Himachal Pradesh and Punjab; Khurja, Lucknow and Varanasi are more conveniently reached from Delhi by road, rail and air.

When to go Summers are best spent in the mountain destinations of Uttarakhand and Himachal; save the plains of Punjab and Uttar Pradesh for cooler months.

Book a tour Contact **Breakaway** (break-away.in; ₹6000) tour company for a well-rounded, immersive textile experience.

Threads of Northern India Hundreds of clattering looms transform silk, cotton and wool into saris, carpets and shawls across the region. At **Balwaar**, near Patiala, women artisans shape durrie carpets, and weavers artfully connect silk and creativity in the historic **Pilli Kothi** neighbourhood in Varanasi. Rural women help revive traditional wool craft at Avni in Uttarkhand, and weavers at **Lena Ladakh** fashion yak and *pashmina* wool into wearable art in the high Himalayas.

Beating into shape Skilled workers of the Thathera community hammer brass and copper into sturdy utensils in the side lanes of **Jandiala Guru**, an old town abutting Amritsar. In Moradabad, clusters of specialised artisans produce intricate brass statues, lamps and vases. The craftspeople in Lucknow's **Chowk** area hammer silver into near transparent edible foil for decorating *mithai* (sweets).

BREAKAWAY

Bespoke Craft & Textile Trails

Craft-focused tours are about moving beyond monuments and markets to the quieter places where craft truly lives – inside artisan homes, master workshops and private archives. The journeys I curate lead straight to textile heartlands: the much-coveted *pashmina* of Jigmat Couture in Ladakh; weaves at Kullvi Whims and Kilmora in the Himalayan foothills; Agra's marble-inlay traditions; and Bhairavi's renowned beaten-copper craft in Lucknow. Visiting these places is not just about what you see, but what your presence helps sustain.

Shilpa Sharma *is a craft and textile evangelist, entrepreneur and founder of tour company @letsbreakaway*

Spinning the wheel Potters are an integral part of north Indian villages, producing fterracotta items for daily use. In Uttar Pradesh's Khurja, you can observe them shape clay into objects of beauty, ready for the taking at **Mark Industries**. The classes offered by **Aura Pottery** and **Andretta Pottery** can be a grounding experience.

Poems in stone From the sandstone carvings of Kangra's rock-cut **Masroor Temple** to the exquisite soft-stone filigree work of Varanasi, Northern India boasts a rich stone carving tradition. Visit Varanasi's **Ramnagar** to observe artisans deftly cut through soapstone and create exquisite collectibles.

Above Weaver, Balwaar

25 Cantonment LIFE

HISTORY | ARCHITECTURE | WALKS

Explore Northern India's vibrant towns and hill stations that started life as strategically located cantonments and sanatoria during British rule, enclosing a host of colonial-era bungalows, mess-halls, churches, memorials and cemeteries within their sprawling, orderly and gated confines.

ARNAV PRATAP SINGH/SHUTTERSTOCK

Left Christ Church, Kasauli
Bottom left Kasauli Club

How to

Getting around Kasauli and Ambala are day trips from Chandigarh; Ferozepur and Hussainiwala demand overnights. Dehra Dun, a four-hour drive from Chandigarh, can be clubbed with Ranikhet, another eight hours by road.

When to go Winters are best for Punjab, Haryana and Uttar Pradesh; summers for Uttarakhand and Himachal Pradesh.

Top tip Parts of cantonments are no-go areas. On-the-spot permission is not granted, best to join guided tours.

Hill Stations

Kasauli in Himachal Pradesh is one of the earliest cantonments in the state and makes a convenient day-trip from Chandigarh. Should you plan a visit, look for the **Christ Church** (1853) with its beautiful stained-glass windows near the main market, and pay close attention to the gabled houses as you navigate the steep slope up to the **Kasauli Club** (1880). The tightly packed bazaar sloping down to the bus stand, always a busy area, is popular for many a school boarder's guilty pleasure, the iconic bun-samosa.

DINODIA PHOTOS/ALAMY

Another historic cantonment within driving distance of Chandigarh is Dehra Dun in neighbouring Uttarakhand. Here, walk up **Kipling's Trail** to Mussoorie through sal woodlands with lovely views of surrounding hills and valleys. Hit the peaceful hiking paths in Landour

India's First Fernery

The four-acre open-air fernery in Kalika is a must-visit for visitors to Ranikhet, especially nature lovers. Developed to conserve diverse fern species in a natural setting, it is home to 120 species, including the tree fern, a variety said to exist since the age of dinosaurs!

By Alka Kaushik, *travel writer and owner of the @guldaarbasera homestay*

further up, relax over a coffee and carrot cake at **Landour Bakehouse** or tuck into pancakes at **Char Dukan**.

Consider a road trip to the cedar-and-pine-forest-encircled Ranikhet cantonment from Dehra Dun. You'll want to stay a couple of days here. Visit the **Kumaon Regimental Centre Museum** for a century-old rare mortar displayed among their impressive collection of weapons. If you're curious about horticulture, look for the fruit-research centre in **Chaubatia Gardens**. Walk around Ranikhet's surrounding villages, many of them nearly empty because of migration to cities, and see the scores of locked *bakhali* (traditional row houses).

The Flatlands

Of the many cantonments of Punjab, the ones in Ferozepur and Ambala (now in Haryana) bookend a strategic section of the region. Head to the former to spend some time at the **Saragarhi Memorial Gurudwara**,

Gothic on the Gomti

Lucknow Cantonment is widely regarded as one of the most picturesque cantonments in North India. Its serene surroundings are home to the **All Saints' Garrison Church**, a breathtaking masterpiece of Gothic architecture. The church is a living monument that embodies a rich and diverse history, and stands as a testament to Lucknow's storied past. It was designed in the late 18th century by the British engineer Jones Ransom and has unique seating, where every bench has a niche for keeping guns, likely for soldiers on their way to or returning from duty.

Ajay Jain, *tour leader and founder of Waltz Tours & Travels.*

waltzindia.in

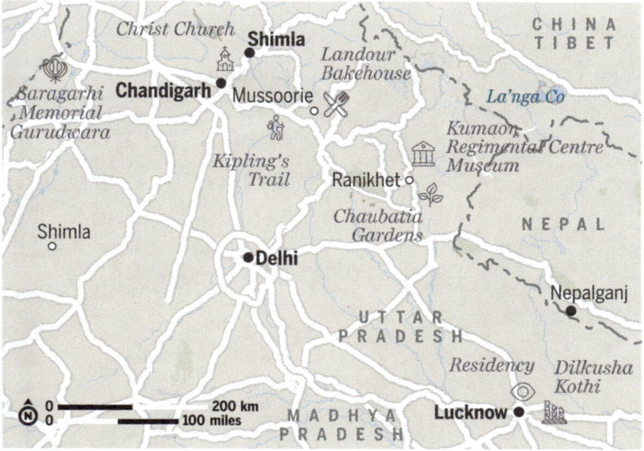

Far left All Saints' Garrison Church
Below Dilkusha Kothi

commemorating the last stand of Sikh soldiers during the Anglo-Afghan conflict. From here, drive 8km to the **National Martyrs Memorial** on the banks of the Sutlej, the natural boundary with Pakistan. Be sure to explore the curious, now defunct, railway station here, with its abruptly ending tracks.

Return to Chandigarh for a daylong exploration of the churches in Ambala cantonment (45km). Take note of the pointed arch doors and windows and exposed brick-work of the **Holy Redeemer Church**, before heading to the bombed ruins of **St Paul's Church** with its distinct Gothic revival architecture.

On a trip to Lucknow in Uttar Pradesh, visit the organised expanse of its cantonment for the atmospheric ruins of **Dilkusha Kothi**, a hunting lodge-turned-palace in the eponymous gardens. The bullet-marked **Residency**, located just outside the cantonment area, remains the most significant colonial-era site in Lucknow. Stroll to its far end to see the ruins of a church surrounded by graves of fallen soldiers.

FROM LEFT: EPHOTOCORP/GETTY IMAGES; MARTIN PAQUIN/ALAMY

26 Adventure in the High HIMALAYAS

MOUNTAINS | TREKS | EXPLORATION

The Himalayas are Northern India's premier trekking destination, and the beauty of these mountains has attracted adventurers for centuries. Today, they get their fix from road-tripping, long-distance biking, and hiking along historic trails. Add to these remote villages and hospitable people and you have the makings of a trip of a lifetime.

RAQUEL MOGADO/ALAMY

Left Trekking, Ladakh
Bottom left Ladakh's 'moonscape' terrain
Below Ladakhi people

How to

Getting around If you've booked an organised tour, you'll likely have transport included. If you're travelling independently, you'll be able to travel easily on the network of buses and shared taxis.

When to go Summers are very pleasant and very busy; spring and autumn are mild to cool, and less crowded.

Top tip Carry cash. There are no ATMs outside the bigger towns, and cards are rarely accepted in villages.

RUDRA NARAYAN MITRA/SHUTTERSTOCK

PURIPATL/GETTY IMAGES

On Foot

Hit the historic high-altitude travel paths of 19th-century travellers and be treated to the splendour of Ladakh's moonscapes and the most rugged terrain you are likely to see in these parts. Be sure to look out for elusive wildlife like the Himalayan wolf. English colonialist William Moorcroft's route will take you through arid topography, alpine grazing fields and deep valleys. The best way to experience this is an eight-day trek (bikatadventures.com) to **Digar La**, the pass connecting Indus Valley with Nubra Valley, for stunning views of the Karakoram Ranges, and experiencing Ladakhi life in remote Buddhist villages.

Blast from the Past

Of the many 19th-century explorers of the Himalayas, James Baillie Fraser (1783–1856) stands out for me. The Scottish artist, writer and later 'Great Game' spin doctor, chose the short route from Yamunotri to Gangotri in 1815, and withstood altitude sickness and frostbite in a rock shelter called Bheem ke Udar.

Michael Lidgley *is an amateur historian, tour leader and Kotkhai resident.*

Behind the Wheel

You'll need to keep your wits about you to enjoy the gobsmacking mountain and valley views along the **Old Hindustan–Tibet Road**, one of Himachal Pradesh's most dramatic roads. It connects Shimla with Shipki Pass on the India–Tibet border with overnights in Sarahan, Kalpa and Pooh, cutting through Kinnaur's stony cliffs in a series of hair-raising bends. It's only one car's width in some places and without a safety barrier in many others, on its winding way through high-altitude meadows, remote hamlets and fruit orchards. The road was built almost two centuries ago to facilitate colonial India's trade with Tibet, and in places gets washed away by rivulets, leading to time-gobbling delays. You'll need to summon all your patience and navigational skills on this weeklong 290km drive through the Sutlej Valley.

The Road Less Travelled

Rising from the Gangetic Plains, the old road to Shimla and beyond, lies largely forgotten. It follows the 19th century path that ponies and palanquins once used. Along this is **Subathu,** the cantonment that came into being at the time of the 'Gurkha Wars' of 1815–16. It has the old cemetery that also holds the last resting place of Letetia, the infant daughter of Henry Lawrence, founder of the Lawrence School in Sanawar. Further along is the village of Kunihar, once called Choti Vilayat, meaning 'Little England'. A window to a long-gone past, this remains a delightful drive that is best taken slowly.

Raaja Bhasin *is an award-winning author and columnist @raajabhasin*

Left Kunihar Valley, Shimla
Below Hiiking, Auden's Col

Follow the Artist

Easily one of the most enthralling adventures in the Western Himalayas is visiting the sites of James Baillie Fraser's collection of aquatints (metal-plate etchings), *Views in the Himala Mountains*. Starting at **Jaitak Fort** in Nahan in the foothills of Himachal Pradesh, you'll passes through pine, oak and holly forests. In places, the tour introduces steep terrain, perilous paths and high passes. After crossing alpine meadows and the massive snow-clad Bandarpunch slopes, it ends at the snowbound source of the Ganges River in Uttarkhand's Bhagirathi valley. Bring along copies of the artist's aquatints to match the exact locations of his points of view. One way of getting the most out of this is by contacting tour leader Michael Lidgley (lidgleymike@gmail.com) to customise an exciting driving and hiking trip for you.

For Mountaineering Veterans

Join a two-week expedition to **Auden's Col** (5490m) connecting the Gangotri Valley to the Kedarnath Valley in Uttarakhand and you'll be rewarded with the most magnificent panoramic, high-altitude views of the Garhwal Himalayas, including the Bhagirathi Peaks and Kedar Dome. This famously challenging and intense trek negotiates deep crevasses and crosses over daunting and dangerous glaciers, while more or less tracing the route of British geologist John Bicknell Auden, the first European to make the trek. Enlisting a highly skilled guide or certified mountaineering outfit like **Snowfox Escapes** *(snowfoxescapes.com)* will keep you on the right path and help you troubleshoot through exigent moments.

WILD
Encounters

03

01

02

04

01 Bengal Tiger
Hear it roar in the forests of Jim Corbett National Park; if luck's on your side, catch a glimpse too.

02 Leopard
Widespread, highly adaptable and found in the Himalayan foothills, particularly in Jim Corbett National Park and Binsar.

03 Snow Leopard
The 'grey ghost' inhabits high-altitude Himalayan ranges, and the best sighting spots are in Spiti, Ladakh and Kumaon.

04 Himalayan Wolf
A genetically distinct species found in the trans-Himalayan regions of Ladakh, Uttarakhand and Himachal Pradesh.

05 Himalayan Brown Bear & Asiatic Black Bear
These rare bears live in the high-altitude alpine meadows of Ladakh, Himachal Pradesh and Uttarkhand.

01 LEKSELE/SHUTTERSTOCK, 02 CLARST5/SHUTTERSTOCK, 03 GIRISH MENON/SHUTTERSTOCK, 04 SHAZIAPHOTOGHRAPHER/SHUTTERSTOCK, 05 ANAN KAEWKHAMMUL/SHUTTERSTOCK, 06 SUVOROV_ALEX/SHUTTERSTOCK, 07 LIJUANYAO/SHUTTERSTOCK, 08 ERIC ISSELEE/SHUTTERSTOCK, 09 BAISHYAJ/SHUTTERSTOCK, 10 MOHIT NAGARWAL/SHUTTERSTOCK

05

06

07

08

09

10

06 Musk Deer
An endangered species hunted for its valuable musk, these deer prefer dense, sub-alpine forests. Conservation efforts are underway in Uttarkhand.

07 Tibetan Wild Ass or Kiang
The largest species of wild ass in the world inhabits the high-altitude meadows of Ladakh bordering Tibet.

08 Gharial
A rare fish-eating crocodile, distinct for its long and slender snout, found in the National Chambal Sanctuary.

09 Gangetic Dolphins
A critically endangered freshwater species found in the Chambal River, this dolphin is recognised as the National Aquatic Animal.

10 Otters
Most likely to be spotted along the riverbanks of the Corbett and Dudhwa national parks, and in the Himalayan rivers and lakes of Ladakh.

Listings

BEST OF THE REST

Follow the Fromage

Amiksa Cheese

This manufacturer of quality artisanal cheeses located in Mashobra also curates an interactive guided session that features tastings, pairings and a hands-on experience exploring Himalayan cheese production.

Old Hill

Expect top-notch naturally aged cheeses from this small fromagerie run by village women in Mukteshwar. You'll want to stock up on that Gouda, parmesan and cheddar, among others.

Himalayan Dairy

This longstanding fromagerie, based in Jagatsukh across the river from Manali, produces high-quality cheeses including Gouda, cheddar and mozzarella using traditional techniques.

Top-End Culinary Experiences

NAAR ₹₹₹

This is a premium restaurant in Kasauli celebrated for its little-known and re-imagined Himalayan dishes, with ingredients grown and sourced locally, and a seasonal menu.

Oudhyana ₹₹

This fine-dining restaurant in Lucknow specialises in Awadhi and North Indian cuisine and is also known for its elegant old-world vibe, attentive service, and live music. Reservations required.

Where to Buy Souvenirs

Looms of Ladakh

An ethical herder-artisan-owned brand led by a women's cooperative, located in Leh's main market. It specialises in clothing accessories, including yak-, camel- and *pashmina*-wool products.

Ladakh Orchards

This Leh-based social enterprise promotes handpicked, sun-dried and chemical-free agricultural produce, and ethically sources its wares directly from Ladakhi farmers.

Namza

This designer studio in Leh is a great place to shop for rich handwoven silks and embroidered Ladakhi apparel. It also has a premium cafe.

Jigmat Couture

This small, ethical fashion brand in Leh revives, preserves and promotes Ladakhi art, craft and textiles, as well as traditional ways of life. It also curates a small textile museum.

Ekaya

Your Varanasi go-to for contemporary hand-crafted and hand-woven silks and saris, including pre-draped versions. The silk blouses and shawls are quite the rage.

TSEWANG GURMET/SHUTTERSTOCK

Ladakhi wool

Anjora

Housed in an old *haveli* (traditional residence) near Varanasi's Assi Ghat with an eye-catching display of well-priced hand-woven saris, stoles and silk fabric.

Indica Books

A bibliophile haven in Varanasi spread over two beautifully styled floors lined with wonderful collections of books of every genre possible, and countless titles about yoga, tantra and meditation.

Bhairavi

Excellent store in Lucknow for *chikankari* (traditional hand-embroidery) apparel and home linen, as well as superb renditions on block-printed and hand-woven textiles. You can even observe the products being made.

Make a Contribution

Umang

This is a collective of self-help groups and producer shareholders (umang-himalaya.com) in Uttarkhand dedicated to promoting livelihoods for the improvement of the lives of hill women and their families.

Kilmora

An artisanal produce brand of Kumaon Grameen Udyog (kilmora.in), a social enterprise working with hill communities in rural Uttarkhand, known for their herb mixes, cold-pressed oils, jams and hand-knitted accessories.

Healing Himalayas

A social enterprise (healinghimlayas.org) led by a passionate environmentalist striving to make the Himalayas garbage-free by sensitising tourists, trekkers and locals through clean-up drives and waste-management programs.

ENEZ SELVI/SHUTTERSTOCK

Gouda cheese

North

This design collective (thenorth.in) is based in Himachal Pradesh and engages in redefining eco-conscious ways of living by introducing contemporary building concepts inspired by vernacular architecture and indigenous workmanship.

Dewi Foundation

Women-led nonprofit provides training in *chikan* embroidery and other handicrafts to women from the city's surrounding villages, to empower and secure them a sustainable livelihood.

Patiala Foundation

Besides striving to revive interest in heritage through guided walks, the foundation (patialafoundation.net) also works on road safety, environmental initiatives, and promoting civic responsibility.

CENTRAL INDIA

SPIRITUALITY | INDIGENOUS CULTURE | WILD ENCOUNTERS

RESEARCHED BY JOE BINDLOSS

MEUNIERD/SHUTTERSTOCK

Ramble through the tile-covered palaces and Jain caves of **Gwalior Fort** (p143; pictured below). *20min from Gwalior Junction Station.*

Show off your photography skills snapping the wondrous carvings at **Khajuraho's temples** (p140; pictured right). *30min from Khajuraho Junction Station*

Stalk tigers in the dusty jungles of **Bandhavgarh** (p138) or **Kanha** (p139). + *3-4hr from Jabalpur*

Hear the call to prayer from the **Taj-ul-Masjid** (p141; pictured right), raised by one of Bhopal's female nawabs. *20min from Bhopal Junction Station.*

Discover Adivasi culture, customs and crafts in Chhattisgarh's **Bastar district** *(p144)*. + *30min-1hr from Jagdalpur*

CENTRAL INDIA

Trip Builder

At the heart of the nation, the Central Indian states of Madhya Pradesh and Chhattisgarh are dotted with temple towns, Adivasi (indigenous) settlements and untamed national parks that represent your best chances of spotting a tiger in the wild.

CLOCKWISE FROM BOTTOM RIGHT: OSCAR ESPINOSA/SHUTTERSTOCK, STORM IS ME/SHUTTERSTOCK, DMITRY RUKHLENKO/SHUTTERSTOCK

Practicalities

ARRIVING

Raja Bhoj Airport, Bhopal Domestic flights buzz into **Bhopal**, but you can also fly directly to **Indore**, **Khajuraho** or **Jabalpur** (for the national parks). Get around by train, bus or chartered car.

CONNECT

More expensive hotels usually provide wi-fi; a local data SIM can be more reliable. The signal is often patchy in national parks.

MONEY

ATMs are easy to find in towns and cities; elsewhere, cash rules. Confirm tiger-safari prices ahead if booking through hotels.

WHERE TO STAY

Places	Pros/Cons
Khajuraho	Rooms for all budgets, from hostel dorms to five-star palaces, but lots of demand for beds
Jabalpur	Hotels in town, plus wildlife lodges and resorts near the national parks (best reached by chartered car)
Bhopal	Abundant hotels at all price points, plus the odd heritage palace hotel

GETTING AROUND

Train Trains go to most places, but seats to Jabalpur and Khajuraho can be in heavy demand.

Bus Long-distance and local buses connect every city, town and village.

Car & Driver Chartering a car and driver is the easy way to reach Madhya Pradesh's national parks.

EATING & DRINKING

Expect northern-style thali (plate meals) that lean heavily on *sabzi* (vegetable) dishes, with more meat in the cities. Look out for Indore's *khopra* (coconut-stuffed pasties; pictured top left). *Poha* (flattened rice; pictured bottom left) is often served for breakfast with herbs and lemon juice. Try dhal *bafla* – wheat rolls, boiled, baked and served with ghee, dhal and sides.

Best Bhopal barbecues Under the Mango Tree (p146)

Bastar-style Adivasi food Bastar Heritage Cafe (p147)

OCT–DEC	JAN–MAR	APR–MAY	JUN–SEP
Busy and dry, but post-monsoon greenery can obscure wildlife.	Easier to spot animals as the undergrowth dries out.	Temperatures soar, pre-monsoon. Heat draws tigers into the open.	Cooling monsoon rains, but national parks close.

27 A Tryst WITH TIGERS

TIGERS | JUNGLE | LITERARY TALES

Teeth, tails and stripes are what visitors come to Madhya Pradesh to see. This is the best state in India to see wild tigers – Madhya Pradesh has some 785 of them, with three iconic national parks (and other lesser-known reserves) to track them down in.

SOURABH BHARTI/SHUTTERSTOCK

Left and bottom left Tigers, Bandhavgarh Tiger Reserve (p138)
Below Leopard, Pench Tiger Reserve (p139)

Trip Notes

When to go March and April offers the best chance of tiger sightings, as the hot, dry conditions draw animals into the open.

Getting around Jabalpur is the closest town to Madhya Pradesh's tiger reserves; hire a car and driver to reach the parks, or use local buses.

Maximise spotting chances Tigers are well camouflaged in the dusty jungle – take several safaris over several days to increase your chance of sightings.

SUMANKYAL/SHUTTERSTOCK

The Best Chance of Tiger Sightings

Everyone wants to see a tiger – that's a given – but there's plenty you can do to increase your chances of encountering the creature Rudyard Kipling immortalised as 'Old Stripes' in his famous *Jungle Book* stories.

Entering Madhya Pradesh's national parks on elephant-back is now discouraged because of the harm it causes to elephants, but 4WD vehicles known as gypsies and open-sided minibuses known as canters can get you close to the real-life Sher Khan.

For your best chances of sightings, go for the earliest morning safari or latest afternoon safari. Always book ahead via forest.mponline.gov.in, or through local hotels and agencies; slots open up 120 days in advance. Avoid Wednesday afternoons, when safaris skip the core zones.

HENK BOGAARD/SHUTTERSTOCK

Madhya Pradesh's Tiger Success

While some Indian tiger reserves have struggled with threats from poachers to squatter encampments, Madhya Pradesh's celebrated parks have achieved remarkable growth in tiger numbers. The 2022 census recorded 785 tigers, up from 526 in 2018 and 308 in 2014 – one of India's great wildlife success stories.

Don't expect to have the tigers to yourself. If you spot one, word will get around and other vehicles will gather. Which safari 'zone' you are assigned to depends on the luck of the draw – some are better than others, so book a few safaris to raise your odds.

Consider your sartorial choices. Stick to neutral colours, and wear long sleeves and trousers to deter mosquitoes. You'll need a warm layer for chilly morning safaris.

Max Your Tiger Tally

About 180km east of Jabalpur, **Bandhavgarh Tiger Reserve** (bandhavgarhtigerreserve.org) is the king of India's tiger habitats. The park's population of 135 tigers is concentrated in a relatively small core zone; the grassy meadow at Chakradhara and the Sukhi Patiha and Nigah Nala watering holes offer excellent chances of sightings.

Be ready for gasp-inducing moments if a tiger breaks cover and strolls into the open – or even

Tiger Tips

Of all Madhya Pradesh's national parks, Bandhavgarh is my favourite for tigers. What sets it apart is not just the density of wildlife, but the sheer quality of the viewing experience. Patience and silence are key – wildlife reveals itself when you blend into the forest rather than disrupt it. Wear neutral, earthy colours, avoid sudden movements, and keep your voice low. Going in with a single focus on seeing a tiger isn't advisable – the tiger is the cherry on the cake, but it's important to enjoy the rest of the cake too!

Indrajit Latey, *naturalist and photo guide @indrajitlatey*

Left Bengal tiger, Bandhavgarh Tiger Reserve
Below Deer, Kanha Tiger Reserve

better, issues a heart-stopping roar. Keep your eyes peeled for less-seen species such as porcupines, wolves, sloth bears and assorted hunting cats.

Find Kipling's *Jungle Book*

About 135km southeast of Jabalpur, **Kanha Tiger Reserve** (kanhatigerreserve.org) is famed for its 105 or so tigers, plus leopards, boars, deer, jackals and monkeys – and for its literary credentials. Here, you can immerse yourself in the real-life jungles that, alongside nearby Pench Tiger Reserve, inspired Rudyard Kipling's *Jungle Book*.

Tigers have more bush to hide in here; for your best chance of spotting stripes, try to get a slot in the Kanha or Mukhi zones. Tack on a side trip to the **Kipling Camp** (kiplingcamp.com), where Tara, the elephant ridden around India by writer Mark Shand, enjoys a gentle retirement.

Pench's Animal Rainbow

To meet the real-life Bagheera, seek out black panthers crouching in the dense foilage in **Pench Tiger Reserve** (penchtiger.org), the third in Madhya Pradesh's tiger trinity. Spilling into Maharashtra southwest of Jabalpur, it provides a pristine home to some 125 tigers, plus leopards, Indian wolves, sloth bears, civets, mongooses and more. You'll have to work harder for sightings here, but the comparative lack of crowds adds to the buzz of the chase.

FROM LEFT: SOURABH BHARTI/SHUTTERSTOCK, GANGAKINAREWALA/SHUTTERSTOCK

28 A Crucible OF FAITH

DEVOTION | ARCHITECTURE | RICH HISTORY

In tourism terms, Madhya Pradesh, India's second-biggest state is a slow burner compared to some of its more famous neighbours, but spirituality buzzes in its rainbow-hued bazaars and devotion fizzes in the air at its ancient sacred sites. Here, you'll find India's biggest mosque, its oldest Buddhist stupa, and temples that celebrate life and sexual liberation with unabashed enthusiasm.

PURVA JOSHI/SHUTTERSTOCK

How to

When to go Visit in February for the **Khajuraho Dance Festival**, or plan ahead for the vast **Kumbh Mela**, which returns to Ujjain in 2028.

Getting around Trains and buses link every corner of Madhya Pradesh and Chhattisgarh. You can fly directly to Indore and Bhopal from cities across India.

Khajuraho timing Allow a whole day to admire the temples, finishing with the Western Group in the late afternoon for epic sunset views.

DMITRY RUKHLENKO/SHUTTERSTOCK

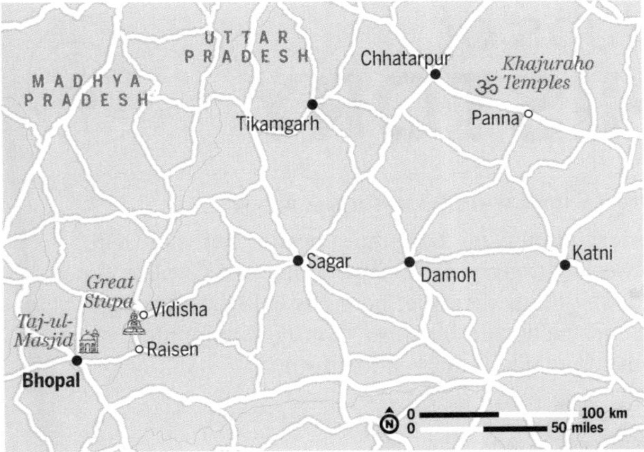

Sensual spirituality Taking centre stage in Madhya Pradesh, **Khajuraho**'s millennia-old temples bring Hinduism's sensual side vividly to life. Stay open-minded as you gaze on uninhibited carvings that include depictions of group sex, zoophilia and more. According to who you speak to, these Kamasutra-like carvings served as either a sexual manual, or an illustration of the Hindu concept of kama (desire). Don't overlook the 90% of carvings that show less risqué sides to 10th-century life.

Islamic girl power Bhopal has a devotional history to rival any of India's great capitals. It saw its golden age under four female rulers – the great Begums – who filled the city with grand Islamic monuments between 1819 and 1926. Hear the call to prayer ringing out from India's largest mosque – the **Taj-ul-Masjid**, with room for 175,000 worshippers – and you'll be sharing a soundtrack that has soared over Bhopal for centuries.

Buddhist beginnings Siddhartha Gautama, the historical Buddha, was born in Nepal, but he founded a faith that at one time rivalled Hinduism in India. The **Great Stupa** at Sanchi near Bhopal was built as a penance by Ashoka the Great, who repented of his violent ways and spread Buddhism across the subcontinent. Circle the stupa's intricately carved *torana* (gateways) clockwise, and consider that you are standing in a spot that has been sacred since the 3rd century BCE.

Top left Sculpture, Khajuraho temple
Bottom left Great Stupa, Sanchi

♀ India's Warrior Women

Male independence leaders such as Mohandas Gandhi and Jawaharlal Nehru are national heroes, but India also has a long tradition of powerful female rulers. As well as the 'four Begums' – female Muslim rulers who governed Bhopal for over a century – there was India's radical but controversial fourth prime minister, Indira Gandhi, and warrior-queen regent Rani Durgavati of Gondwana, who held back Akbar's invading armies in the 1560s. Queen Ahilyabai Holkar of Indore led the armies of Malwa on elephant-back in the 18th century, while Rani Lakshmi Bai of Jhansi was a leading figure in India's First War of Independence (Indian Uprising) in 1857.

29 Hubs of HISTORY

FABULOUS FORTS | TERRIFIC TOMBS | WHISPERING HISTORY

Central India's historic cities may not have the superstar status of Delhi, Jaipur or Agra, but the past seeps through the stonework of grand Gwalior, timeless Orchha and magical Mandu. The ruling dynasties here saw battles and conquests to rival anything in Rajasthan and the northern plains. Visit these monument-strewn outposts and discover an unsung side to India's national story.

CHETANSONI/SHUTTERSTOCK

Trip Notes

When to go: Soak up history in the dry post-monsoon months, coinciding with Gwalior's hypnotic Udbhav Utsav dance festival (October) and Tansen Samaroh music festival (December).

Getting there: Trains and buses can whisk you to every corner of central India, with Bhopal and Indore as major transit hubs.

Tomb spotting: Don't overlook the area's tremendous tombs – the mausoleums of Mohammad Ghaus and musician Mian Tansen in Gwalior are standouts.

IMAGESOFINDIA/SHUTTERSTOCK

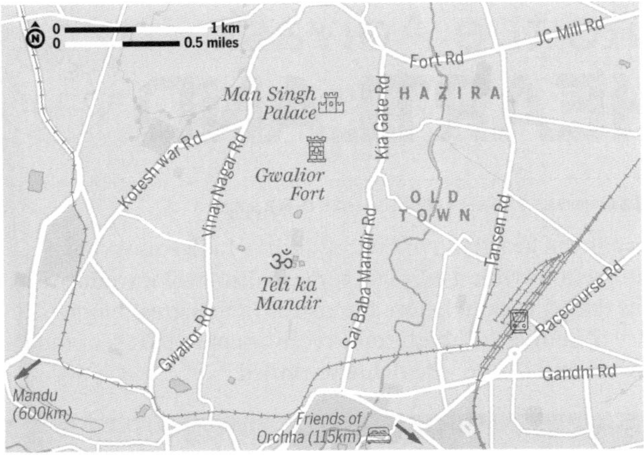

Top left Jahaz Mahal, Mandu
Bottom left Teli ka Mandir, Gwalior Fort

Tile-spotting in Gwalior Central Asian influences permeate India's Mughal-era monuments, and nowhere is this more apparent than in **Gwalior's fabulous fort**, studded with turquoise tiles of the kind more commonly associated with the grand Muslim monuments of Bukhara and Samarkand.

To see the best tilework, head for the **Man Singh Palace**, built by Raja Man Singh in a heady fusion of Hindu and Islamic styles. Nearby, float through time-scarred temples and carved caverns that conjure up the fort's Hindu and Jain past, including the 9th-century **Teli ka Mandir** – outrageously converted into a soda-water factory by the British.

Home-style history For a stay dripping with history, make for Orchha, a rural-village-turned-royal seat of power. In the 16th century, Rudra Pratap Singh filled his capital with Mughal-influenced palaces, towering temples and regal *chhatri* (cenotaphs). Get under Orchha's skin by arranging homestay accommodation through **Friends of Orchha** (orchha.org) – hosted by a local family, you'll gain an intimate introduction to local culture, customs and cuisine.

See Mandu by bike Southeast of Indore, **Mandu** is a jewel box of palaces, tombs, mosques and monuments that's listed with UNESCO. Grab a bike from Sonu Bikes in Mandu town, and take an evocative 12km pedal into the past, passing waterside palaces, elegant pavilions, and Khilji-era monuments, centered on a grand mosque, mausoleum and madrasa (Islamic school). Finish the tour at the elegant **Jahaz Mahal** palace, which rises between two ceremonial tanks.

Discover Central Asian Culture

Gwalior Fort is a mesmerising blend of Hindu, Jain and Muslim motifs. The latter can be attributed to the Turkic and Afghan rulers of the Delhi sultanate, who conquered Gwalior in the 11th century, and the Mughal Empire founded by Babur – a direct descendant of the Uzbek warlord Timur (Tamerlane) and Mongol warlord Ghenghis Khan.

Many Islamic monuments in India include Central Asian details such as Persian-style *charbagh* gardens, turquoise tilework and towering *pishtaq* gateways topped by four-centred arches. Other sites in Central India with a hint of the 'stans include the 15th-century mosque of Malik Mughith and the mausoleum of Hoshang Shah in Mandu.

30 Into the Adivasi HEARTLAND

TRIBAL CUSTOMS | CULTURAL IMMERSION | MESMERISING MARKETS

Bastar in Chhattisgarh is the heartland of Central India's Indigenous Adivasi peoples, and responsible interactions with its diverse communities will introduce you to religions and customs dating back to before the rise of India's great empires. According to India's Ministry of Tourism, Chhattisgarh receives about 0.04% of India's foreign tourists, but those who venture here are richly rewarded.

AMITRANE1975/GETTY IMAGES

How to

Getting there Jagdalpur is the gateway to Bastar, accessible by train and bus. Arrange a car and driver to visit Adivasi villages, or scoot around by local bus.

When to go Try to visit tribal villages between February and May when many local festivals take place, showcasing Adivasi beliefs, dancing and music.

Responsible photography Always ask permission before taking snaps of Adivasi people, to avoid causing offence.

SUBIR BASAK/GETTY IMAGES

Top left Bastar Dussehra, Jagdalpur
Bottom left Handmade agricultural tools, Bastar market

Dive into Bastar's markets In the **Bastar** district near Jagdalpur, weekly *haat* bazaars move from village to village as traders roam around hawking their wares, from fresh produce and spices to colourful clothing and handicrafts.

To immerse yourself in this timeless slice of traditional life, get in touch with **Ashit Dubey** (+9425246025) through the Kanker Palace Heritage Hotel (kankerpalace.com) to arrange an ethical tribal tour. Ashit has spent years building relationships with Adivasi communities, so instead of being hurried around for photo opportunities, you'll be introduced to villagers who are happy to share their customs and talk through their ancient craft traditions.

Depending on the day of the week, you might wander the vibrant Madia market at **Mardum**, shop for Ghadwa bell-metal objects at **Tokopal**, examine bison-horn crafts and terracotta pots at **Bastanar**, meet the former chieftain of the Bison-Horn Madia tribe in **Nainnar**, or join a village homestay in **Dhurwa** near Kawapal.

A very different Dussehra To experience Adivasi culture at its most exuberant, visit Jagdalpur during **Bastar Dussehra**, usually in October. Celebrations build for 75 days as local villagers honour the regional goddess Danteshwari. Try to join the party during the last 10 days, when devotees from 84 different villages descend on Jagdalpur with their deities in tow, hauling a gigantic *rath* (wooden chariot) around the streets.

Ethical Visits

The most ethical way to visit remote Adivasi villages is on a customised tour with a local guide, who understands how to interact politely with village people. This is the best way to experience *jatra* (festivals), Madai gatherings and marriages, and to interact with tribal people. One should always respect tribal culture and traditions. Rather than giving cash, buying from local markets is a better way to support local people. Your guide can arrange a meal or a dance performance, providing paid employment and helping to sustain their fast-changing culture.

Ashit Dubey and **Jai Pratap Deo**, *manager and guide at Kanker Palace Heritage. @kanker palaceheritage*

Listings

BEST OF THE REST

Special Spaces

Jai Vilas Palace

European influences infuse the 19th-century palace of the Scindias, whose love of luxury extended to a model train running around the dining table distributing wine, food and cigars.

Jehangir Mahal

Navigate an assault course of steep staircases and precipitous walkways in the 17th-century palace of Bir Singh Deo in Orchha. It's one of the high points of Indo-Islamic architecture.

Madhya Pradesh Tribal Museum

Any day except Monday is a good time to dip into Adivasi culture at this intriguing Bhopal museum full of model village houses and displays evoking sacred spaces.

Bhimbetka Rock Shelters

See just how old India's story runs at these rock-cut caverns in Bhopal, with paintings that serve as a guide to life 12,000 years ago.

Lal Bagh Palace

Much of the majesty of Indore's once powerful Holkar dynasty was lost, but you'll glimpse traces of its grandeur at this palace.

Mahakaleshwar Mandir

A sacred stop on the Kumbh Mela circuit, this Shiva temple in Ujjain is worth visiting for the air of devotion hovering around its *jyotir linga* ('self-manifested' phallic symbol).

Culinary Arts

Silver Saloon ₹₹₹

Enjoy silver service in gilded surroundings at the Taj Usha Kiran Palace hotel in Gwalior; the Maratha thali takes the plate meal to a whole new level.

S.S. Kachori Wala ₹

Feast on the food of the people at this famous Gwalior breakfast-time vendor of stuffed kachori (potato-masala) pastries and *bedai* (crispy lentil-stuffed flatbreads).

Hotel Sheesh Mahal ₹₹

A palace of a property inside Orchha Fort; feel like minor royalty as you feast from a well-rounded Indian menu, prepared with market-fresh ingredients.

Zam Zam ₹

Experience the meaty, rich cuisine of Islamic India at this beloved fast-food icon, serving Bhopal's best biryani and chicken tikka, grilled over hot coals.

Under the Mango Tree ₹₹₹

A don't-miss charmer in Bhopal that lives up to its name, serving succulent North Indian barbecue dishes in a mango-tree-flanked garden at the Jehan Numa Palace.

IMAGESOFINDIA/SHUTTERSTOCK

Jai Vilas Palace

CENTRAL INDIA REVIEWS

Sarafa Bazar & Chappan Dukan ₹

Seek out Indore's best street food at the Sarafa night market and Chappan Dukan food court; be sure to try the city's *khopra* patties (stuffed with spiced potato and coconut).

Hytte By Samrat

Toast a successful tiger-spotting safari at this buzzing Jabalpur rooftop, with cool cocktails and an encyclopaedic multi-cuisine menu.

Bastar Heritage Cafe ₹

Get your first taste of Adivasi cuisine at this artsy cafe in Jagdalpur serving locally harvested Darbha coffee and Chhattisgarh bites with views of Dalpat Sagar lake.

Memorable Perspectives

Bilal Bikes

Pop into this bike shop near the junction of Main Rd and Jain Temple Rd in Khajuraho, then pootle off on two wheels to discover the magnificent clutch of carved temples.

Narmada Ghat

Like a mini Varanasi, Maheshwar's ghats (ceremonial steps) buzz with pilgrims and holy men. Charter a boat to watch the evening *aarti* fire ceremony from the water.

Rehwa Society

Alongside leading regiments into battle, 18th-century Holkar queen Ahilyabai developed Maheshwar as a weaving hub – watch modern-day weavers at this cooperative.

Narmada Ropeway

Ride the swaying Jabalpur cable car for epic views over Dhuandhar Falls, Madhya Pradesh's 'smoke cascade', or walk close enough to the churning waters to feel the spray.

Sanjay Market

Dip into Adivasi culture every Sunday, as tribal people bring forest-sourced ingredients such as *mahua* flowers and red weaver ants (used to make chutney) to Jagdalpur's busy marketplace.

V.K.MADHAV/SHUTTERSTOCK

Chitrakote Falls

Natural Spectacles

Raneh Falls

Arrange an autorickshaw transfer from Khajuraho, then set off on foot to reach these tumbling cascades, which gush through a rainbow-hued canyon near a reserve for gharial crocodiles.

Panna Tiger Reserve

Escape tiger-tracking crowds at this often overlooked big cat sanctuary near Khajuraho, where you can combine tiger safaris with boat trips on the croc-filled Ken River.

Chitrakote Falls

Another watery wonder, the Indravati River crashes into a horseshoe-shaped basin that you can explore from the banks or by boat, inviting comparisons with Niagara.

Kotumsar Cave

Clamber into this twisting cavern in Kanger Valley National Park to explore damp, cool chambers, dripping with curtains of stalactites and forests of stalagmites.

NORTHEASTERN INDIA

WOODED LANDSCAPES | RURAL RETREATS | DIVERSE COMMUNITIES

RESEARCHED BY DR JENNY WALKER

SUMANKYAL/SHUTTERSTOCK

NORTHEASTERN INDIA

Trip Builder

Flowing down from the Himalayas, the distinct, visually stunning states of Northeastern India are difficult to reach and some require permits. This makes the perfect opportunity for authentic travel through wilderness adventure in a region of cultural complexity.

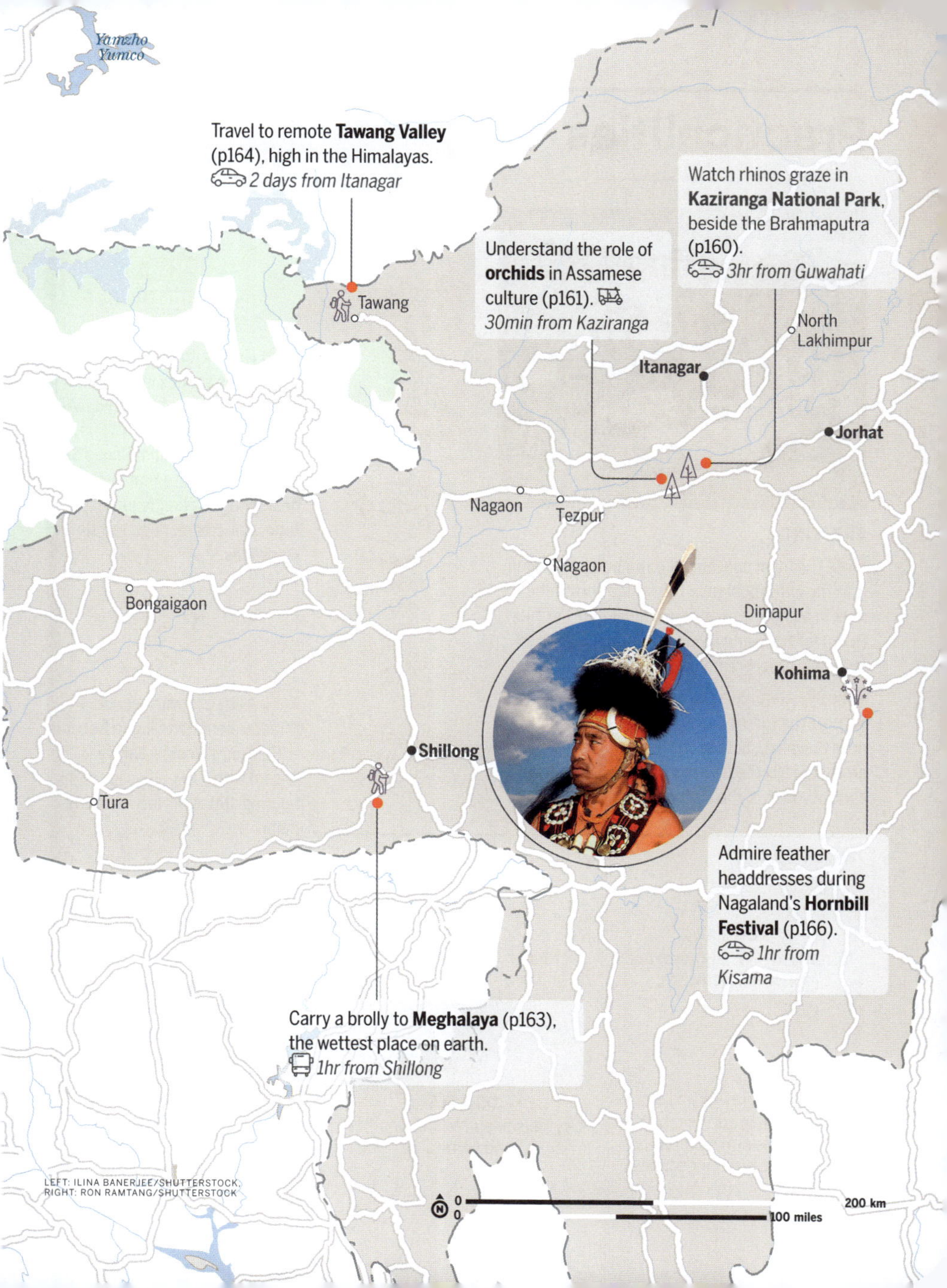

LEFT: ILINA BANERJEE/SHUTTERSTOCK,
RIGHT: RON RAMTANG/SHUTTERSTOCK

Practicalities

ALBIN RAJ/SHUTTERSTOCK

ARRIVING

Melli The most convenient entry point for Sikkim is at the checkpost near the bridge across the river in Melli. The post issues Inner Line Permits (ILPs) for travelling around the state. Sikkim's only civil airport remains closed.

Lokpriya Gopinath Bordoloi International Airport (pictured) Assam's main access point, near Guwahati, acts as a primary hub for visiting any of the Northeast Indian 'Seven Sister States', each of which is connected with Assam by road.

HOW MUCH FOR A

Arunachal Pradesh PAP permit US$50

Portion of momo ₹200

Assam national-park entry ₹650

WHEN TO GO

JAN–MAR
Snows at high altitude, good for winter activities.

APR–JUN
Perfect hiking at altitude; hot and humid pre-monsoon in lower valleys.

JUL–SEP
Heavy rains and potential landslides during summer monsoon; lush landscapes.

OCT–DEC
Dry season and hiking weather; harvest and cultural festivals.

GETTING AROUND

4WD There's no train service and limited bus service in Sikkim so most transport is by shared 4WD. Shared or private-hire 4WD is also common in the mountainous Sister States. Beware that distance bears little relation to journey times due to the rough terrain and landslides.

Train A limited train service threads along the Siliguri Corridor – 'Chicken's Neck' – linking Assam with a few cities in neighbouring states of Northeastern India.

Boat Cruises along the Brahmaputra make for a relaxing experience in Assam, connecting the capital Guwahati with the historic river island of Majuli.

EATING & DRINKING

The region encompasses many local subtleties, informed by cuisine from Myanma, Nepal and Tibet. Ubiquitous *momo* (Tibetan dumpling) and *thukpa* (Tibetan noodle soup; pictured top right) are staples in Sikkim and Arunachal, while smoked pork turns up in recipes in Nagaland, Meghalaya and Mizoram. Try fish curries (pictured bottom right) in Assam and Tripura, and cheer up a cold winter's day with *jadoh* (spicey, aromatic rice), Shillong's favourite food.

With tea estates stretching across the region, sampling tea is a must.

Best tea Elgin Nor-Khill (p167)

Must-try thalis Paradise (p167)

CONNECT & FIND YOUR WAY

Wi-fi Available throughout the region, with slower speeds in rural areas. Some free hotspots, including at most railway stations. The best way to stay connected is to buy a SIM card – if you can find one!

Navigation If hiring a bike, don't rely on navigation apps for accurate directions - hire a local guide.

MONEY

Carry cash, as card payment is not widely accepted in Sikkim and the Sister States. Digital wallets function in some areas. ATMs at major banks dispense cash with Visa or Mastercard.

WHERE TO STAY

Accommodation ranges from grand suites in luxury hotels to basic rooms in remote villages. Homestays in rural areas offer the best value for money with delicious meals and often spectacular locations.

Places	Pros/Cons
Pelling	Sikkim's main tourist hub; best to book between March and June.
Guwahati	Assam's capital with wide choice of accommodation; lacks charm of rural sleeps.
Kohima	Hosts the famous Hornbill Festival; need to book months ahead if visiting in December.
Ziro Valley	Homestays in picturesque landscapes; hard to reach, especially in monsoon months.
Shillong	Meghalaya's buzzing hill-station capital; some traffic jams in town.
Agartala	Gives access to Tripura's key sites, such as Unakoti; well off the beaten track.

PERMITS

Protected Area Permits (PAPs) are required to travel in Sikkim, Arunachal Pradesh and Mizoram and for some internal travel. Manipur is currently off-limits.

31 Superior treks in the HIMALAYAS

HIGH-ALTITUDE TREKS | BIG VIEWS | RELIGIOUS SCULPTURES

Abutting Khangchendzonga (at 8598m the world's third-highest mountain peak), Sikkim is a paradise for mountaineers and trekkers. Although summiting the sacred mountain is not permitted, there are many multiday treks in the surrounding national park. Less demanding activities include village strolls and visits to the state's giant hilltop statues – beacons on Sikkim's pilgrimage trails.

DEBARUP/SHUTTERSTOCK

How to

Permits Multiday, high-altitude treks in Sikkim must be booked through registered tour agents.

When to go Possible year-round (weather dependent). Go March to May for flowering rhododendrons; October to November for clear skies.

Booking Last-minute booking is possible in Gangtok and Yuksom, but book ahead for the best guides, drivers and porters.

Before you go Get fit! On arrival, you need time to acclimatise: low-altitude treks start above 2000m.

RUDRA NARAYAN MITRA/SHUTTERSTOCK

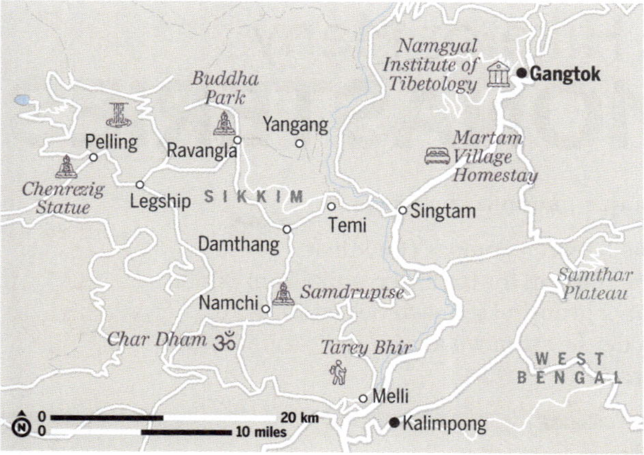

Top left Goecha La Trek
Bottom left Statue of Padmasambhava

Trekking Classics

Goecha La Trek The classic Sikkim trek, this high-altitude nine-nighter from Yuksom threads through forests, meadows and valleys to Goecha La (4950m) beside Khangchendzonga.

Uttarey to Nambu Round-Trek A stunning eight-nighter, this trek rims the India–Nepal border to Goecha La with views of Mt Everest, Khangchendzonga and peaks in between.

Village Walks

Pelling-Yuksom Hike A two-day Pelling-Khecheopalri-Yuksom hike starts with a steep descent on village trails.

Tarey Bhir Near Namchi, this 3km-path along a 3048m-line in the sky, known as 'the Cliff', is almost a nose dive into the Teesta river – don't 'selfie' too close to the edge.

Big Views from Up High

Namchi Sikkim's trend for giant religious statues began with a 45m-tall seated statue of **Padmasambhava** on Samdruptse Hill.

Ravangla The town's 41m-tall golden statue, in **Buddha Park**, surveys Sikkim's deeply incised wooded hills.

Pelling The giant, four-armed **Chenrezig** statue of the Bodhisattva of compassion stands above a town famed for superb views of Khangchendzonga.

Char Dham A 33m-tall statue of Lord Shiva is the focus of an architectural park that recreates India's greatest Hindu sites.

Gangtok In the attractive, steeply stacked state capital, a ropeway leads to **Namgyal Institute of Tibetology** with grand views over the city.

Rural Retreat

In Martam we're flanked by forests rich in birdlife and steeped in local lore, and walking our village paths amid drifting mists and choruses of crickets you'll learn about Bhutia tribal ways. Our culture is deeply shaped by faith-healing traditions, rooted in reverence for nature. In season, you can forage for edible roots, shoots and leaves, and we'll teach you to cook our favourite dishes, sip local millet brew and listen to foxes, barking deer and the squeaks of flying squirrels.

Yishey Doma, *award-winning writer of Sikkim: Soul of the Himalayas and host of Martam Village Homestay. WhatsApp: 9382012589*

32 A Hike of Many MONASTERIES

VILLAGE LIFE | WOODED TRAILS | BUDDHIST GOMPAS

This perfect day hike between gompas (Buddhist monasteries) starts in Tashiding (or, for a shorter walk, from Silnon Gompa). Punctuated by three beautiful monasteries en route to Yuksom, it passes through dense, steep woodland and rural villages with Himalayan panoramas.

TIBOR BOGNAR/ALAMY

Trip Notes

Getting here The twisting 2½-hour drive from Pelling is by shared 4WD, or hire a driver-guide through a tour agency.

When to go Possible year-round, but the short, steep climbs to each gompa are slippery in summer rains.

Length of trip For a shorter hike that allows a potter instead of a route march, visit Tashiding the day before, stay at **Silnon Homestay**, beside Silnon Gompa, and start walking from there.

Black Gold

There are two contenders for the term 'black gold' in Sikkim. One is precious, smokey-flavoured black cardamon and the other is a rare entomopathogenic fungus, *Cordyceps sinensis*, that hollows out the cocoons of ghost moths. Both are prized for alleged health-giving properties and grow well around Tashiding.

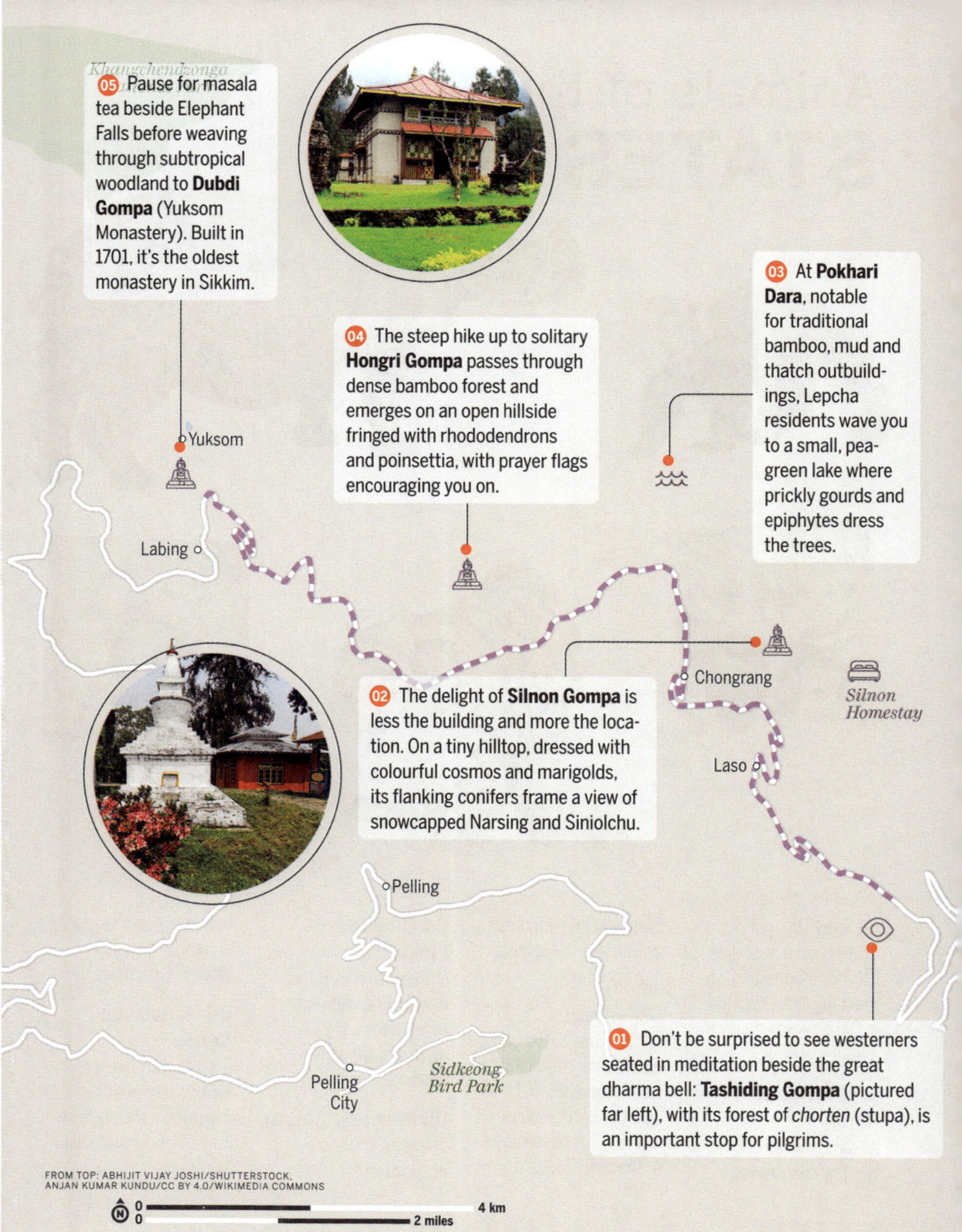

01 Don't be surprised to see westerners seated in meditation beside the great dharma bell: **Tashiding Gompa** (pictured far left), with its forest of *chorten* (stupa), is an important stop for pilgrims.

02 The delight of **Silnon Gompa** is less the building and more the location. On a tiny hilltop, dressed with colourful cosmos and marigolds, its flanking conifers frame a view of snowcapped Narsing and Siniolchu.

03 At **Pokhari Dara**, notable for traditional bamboo, mud and thatch outbuildings, Lepcha residents wave you to a small, pea-green lake where prickly gourds and epiphytes dress the trees.

04 The steep hike up to solitary **Hongri Gompa** passes through dense bamboo forest and emerges on an open hillside fringed with rhododendrons and poinsettia, with prayer flags encouraging you on.

05 Pause for masala tea beside Elephant Falls before weaving through subtropical woodland to **Dubdi Gompa** (Yuksom Monastery). Built in 1701, it's the oldest monastery in Sikkim.

FROM TOP: ABHIJIT VIJAY JOSHI/SHUTTERSTOCK, ANJAN KUMAR KUNDU/CC BY 4.0/WIKIMEDIA COMMONS

Animals of the STATES

01

02

03

05

04

01 Red Panda
State animal of Sikkim, this bamboo-eater can most easily be spotted in Gangtok's Himalayan Zoological Park.

02 One-Horned Rhino
Assam is famous for tea, the late Zubeen Garg and this gorgeous grazer, one of Assam's 'Big Five'.

03 Mithun
Dubbed the 'cattle of the mountains', this hefty, semi-domesticated beast of burden plays a role in tribal customs in Arunachal Pradesh.

04 Clouded Leopard
Unlikely to be spotted due to its camouflage, Meghalaya's shy state animal is adept at climbing trees.

05 Phayre's Langur
There's a chance of spotting the leaf monkey, Tripura's state animal, in Sepahijala Wildlife Sanctuary.

06 Himalayan Serow
It's all about the socks for this rare goat-like mammal – the state animal of thickly wooded Mizoram.

01 LOGOMAKER691/SHUTTERSTOCK, **02** WORRAKET/SHUTTERSTOCK, **03** SUPRIYO GHOSHAL/SHUTTERSTOCK, **04** ERIC ISSELEE/SHUTTERSTOCK, **05** EZAZ AHMED EVAN/SHUTTERSTOCK, **06** TENZIN AND LI PHOTOGRAPHY/SHUTTERSTOCK, **07** HENRIK KARLSSON/GETTY IMAGES, **08** LOVELY BIRD/SHUTTERSTOCK, **09** LUCK LUCKYFARM/SHUTTERSTOCK, **10** ME.KARIM1983/SHUTTERSTOCK, **11** RUDRA NARAYAN MITRA/SHUTTERSTOCK, **12** DOIKANOY/SHUTTERSTOCK, **13** RIMA_MUN19/SHUTTERSTOCK

06

07

08

09

10

11

12

13

07 Gaur
Unfamiliar with Indian bison? Manas National Park in Assam is home to large herds of these muscular giants.

08 Great Hornbill
The protected giant hornbill is honoured in an eponymous annual festival in Nagaland: new tribal feathers are now synthetic.

09 Mrs Hume's Pheasant
The state bird of Mizoram, this fabulous pheasant (with Blyth's tragopan and Sikkim's blood pheasant) graces regional highlands.

10 Green Imperial Pigeon
Pigeons receive a bad press as city nuisances, but not so this splendid splash of colour in Tripura's treetops.

11 Rhododendron Niveum
Sikkim's state plant. Travel to Khangchendzonga National Park in spring when this Himalayan shrub blooms.

12 Foxtail Orchid *(Rhynchostylis retusa)*
The Rongali Bihou (Assam's New Year's festival in April) wouldn't be Bihou without these orchids gracing women's hair.

13 Lady's Slipper Orchid *(Paphiopedilum insigne)*
Although Arunachal Pradesh, with 600 species, is the Land of Orchids, this rarity is the state flower of Meghalaya.

33 Untamed ASSAM

ASSAMESE BIG 5 | ONE-HORNED RHINOS | PARK ADVENTURES

Not many visitors make it to the Seven Sister States (and Manipur is currently off-limits), but those who do make a bee-line for Kaziranga National Park in Assam. One of India's premier sanctuaries for wildlife, it's world famous for the abundance of the one-horned rhinoceros, which can be seen grazing peacefully in this pristine park of plains, swamps and forest.

SOURAV_GANGULI/SHUTTERSTOCK

How to

Getting here Around 200km and four to five hours by road from Guwahati, the park can be reached by public bus or by tour.

When to go By and large, the dry winter season (November to April) is best for wildlife viewing.

What to pack It's cold in an open vehicle on an early-morning safari and on returning to base at sundown, particularly in winter – take a coat or blanket.

CYBERSWARUP/SHUTTERSTOCK

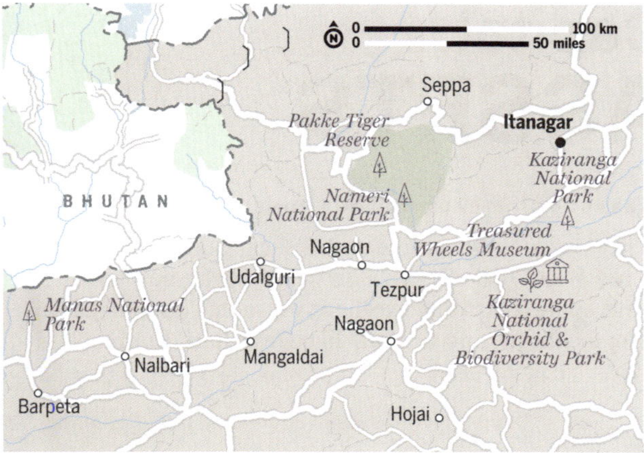

Top left One-horned rhino, Kaziranga National Park
Bottom left Orchids, Kaziranga National Orchid and Biodiversity Park

The big five Kaziranga safaris tend to focus on spotting the park's 'big five' – one-horned rhino, Bengal tiger, elephant, wild buffalo and swamp deer – and 4WDs inevitably cluster around key sightings. Ask your guide to focus on birds, including the great hornbill, or lesser-known animals, such as the black-capped langur, and you'll have parts of the park to yourself.

Orchids for every occasion Combine your safari with a trip to the **Kaziranga National Orchid and Biodiversity Park** to challenge your notion of this exotic flower. There are 2000 species of orchid and 400 of them grow wild in Assam – that represents 90% of all species found in India. Most are tiny and subtle in their beauty, but the display here includes gorgeous hybrids with remarkable striations and colour combinations.

Bihu beauties The Bihu dance, performed at Assamese New Year in April, and the precisely timed bamboo dance are two of many dances showcased in a spectacular nightly **cultural programme** (₹300; 6.30pm in winter) at the orchid park. To learn what makes the music, step into the pavilion of traditional musical instruments, also in the park grounds.

Motor mania Don't leave Kaziranga without calling in on **Treasured Wheels Museum** (₹500), which began with a red Renault 4CV and now comprises a priceless collection of heritage vehicles.

Protection Recently, Kaziranga's success in protecting its rhino population has been hotly criticised. Reports indicate that Indigenous villagers were evicted from areas of the park to expand it, while park guards have fatally shot suspected poachers.

Other Assamese Adventures

Hiking in tiger territory
It's one thing to know a tiger is present from the safety of a jeep but it's quite different on foot. At **Nameri National Park** (assamtourism.gov.in), contiguous with Arunachal Pradesh's **Pakke Tiger Reserve**, guided hikes with an armed ranger involve crossing into tiger territory on a small wooden boat.

Rafting along borders
Visit **Manas National Park** (assamtourism.gov.in) and you can raft along the Beki River, marking the boundary between Manas and Bhutan's enormous Royal Manas National Park. The border doesn't mean much to the wild water buffalo who swim across, despite the swift current.

34 Capital ASSETS

STATE MUSEUMS | BUSY BAZAARS | CONTRASTING LOCATIONS

It's probably fair to say that no one travels to the Sister States for a good night out. But rather than judge the region's cities on what they're not, go looking instead for a cultural context in some excellent museums and busy local markets. Add in outstanding locations, and capitals like Guwahati, Kohima and Aizawl are regional highlights.

RAHUL D'SILVA/SHUTTERSTOCK

How to

Getting here Flights serve many Seven Sister capitals, while modern buses link them together, often via Assam.

When to go Check state tourism websites for festivals; during these times, capital accommodation books up fast.

Top tip With the exception of Guwahati and Agartala, all the capital cities of the region are built on steep slopes, so pack comfortable shoes and be ready for near-vertical staircases.

BHASKAR GFX/SHUTTERSTOCK

Top left Ujjayanta Palace
Bottom left Assam silk

Heritage You can't travel far in Northeastern India without hearing the word 'tribe'. Each state is comprised of diverse communities whose cultures are showcased in state museums. The best of these is in Guwahati where **Assam State Museum**'s (museums.assam.gov.in) early Hindu statues are a highlight; residents of Aizawl like to tell you that **Mizoram State Museum** charts Mizoram's history from 'headhunter to the *Hallelujah* chorus'; while the award-winning **Don Bosco Museum of Indigenous Culture** in Meghalaya's capital, Shillong, describes the region's main religions. The Tripura State Museum, meanwhile, is housed in a relic from colonial-era times, the grand **Ujjayanta Palace** (1901).

Society today All the capitals in the region throng with out-of-town shoppers and joining their number is a great way to get a feel for regional customs. Look out for cultural heirlooms in the form of traditional crafts, from arrows in **Iew Duh (Bara Bazaar)** in archery-keen Meghalaya, to eri silk in **Fancy Bazaar** in Assam.

Hilltop and riverside Asked why all Mizoram towns, including the capital Aizawl, are flung across a ridgetop, Mizos will reply that it's because they're highlanders at heart. Getting lost climbing the myriad stairways, or viewing the stilted city from the **Sky Walk**, is part of a capital experience. In contrast, plains capital Guwahati swaps height for breadth with part of the city straddling the mighty river Brahmaputra.

Proud of Our Roots

We're proud to be representing our tribe: it's our opportunity to showcase our culture to the world, to revive old traditions and translate them into something of meaning for the new generation. Many things of value are being lost through modern life, including our languages. This is our chance to celebrate the connection with our rural roots. Visit our *morung* (young people's dormitories) in **Naga Heritage Village**, sample our food and drink millet beer and a warm welcome awaits.

Zayie Sodz, *Angami tribe member and participant in Nagaland's annual tribal get-together during Hornbill Festival @zayie_sodz*

35 Head for the HILLS

SPECTACULAR LANDSCAPE | DIZZYING ROADS | GEOPOLITICS

From a standing start on the plains, this classic, three-day road trip twists up through sub-tropical rain forests to a high alpine lake. With China bordering Tawang to the north, the Indian military presence forms a fascinating part of the trip.

CHATON CHOKPATARA/SHUTTERSTOCK

India-China Conflict

India went into battle with China just over 60 years ago – and won. Disputing the 890km border between the two countries, the Chinese People's Liberation Army invaded Arunachal Pradesh at Tawang in 1962 but were repulsed by an ill-equipped but outstandingly brave Indian force of just 2500 men.

Trip Notes

Getting around Tour agencies arrange Arunachal Pradesh permits, provide vehicle and driver and book accommodation.

When to go The dry season between October and April is best. Avoid the summer when landslides are common during monsoon.

Length of trip Break the journey at Dirang on the way up and Bomdila on the way back down and allow at least one day in between in Tawang .

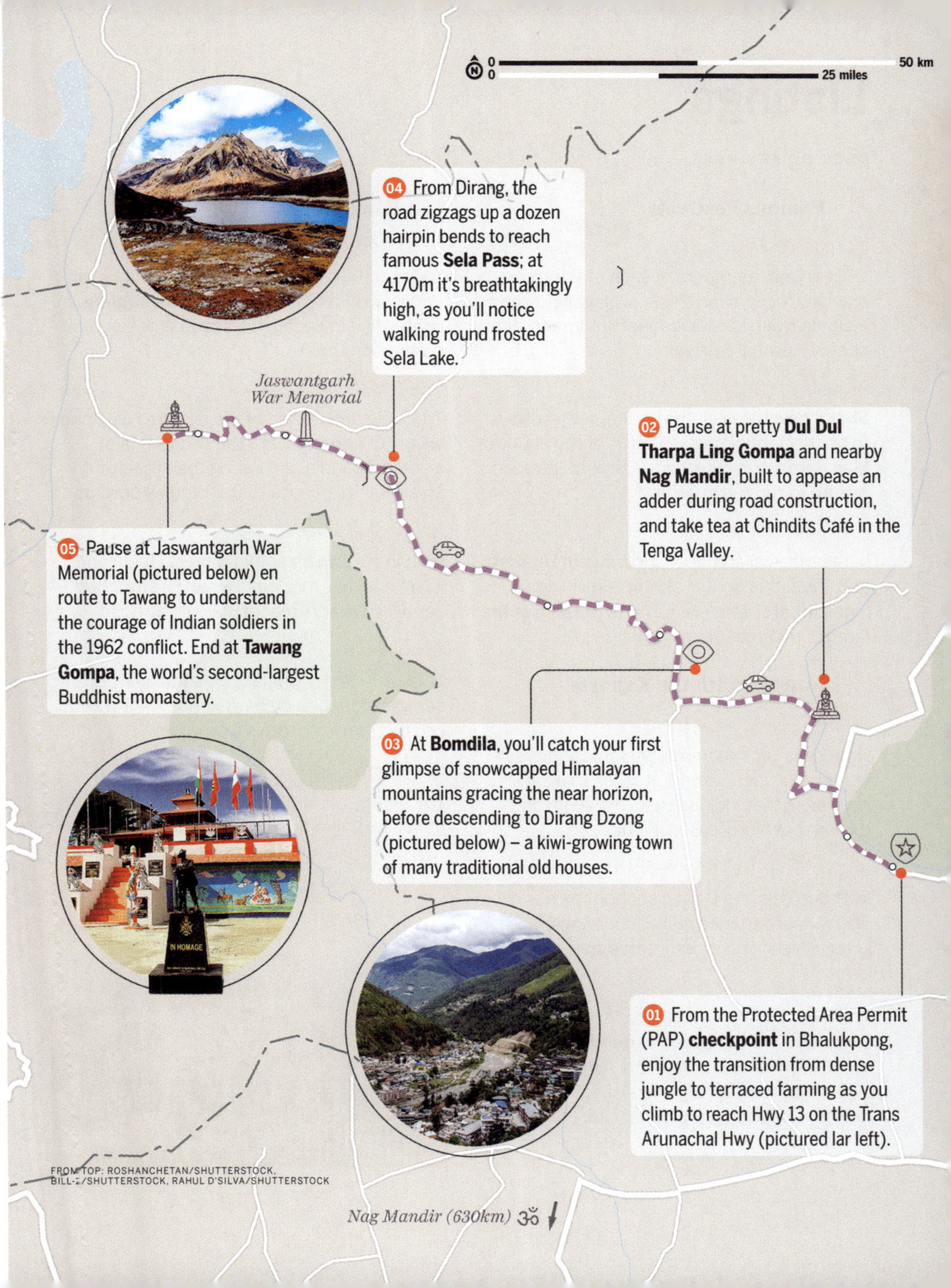

01 From the Protected Area Permit (PAP) **checkpoint** in Bhalukpong, enjoy the transition from dense jungle to terraced farming as you climb to reach Hwy 13 on the Trans Arunachal Hwy (pictured lar left).

02 Pause at pretty **Dul Dul Tharpa Ling Gompa** and nearby **Nag Mandir**, built to appease an adder during road construction, and take tea at Chindits Café in the Tenga Valley.

03 At **Bomdila**, you'll catch your first glimpse of snowcapped Himalayan mountains gracing the near horizon, before descending to Dirang Dzong (pictured below) – a kiwi-growing town of many traditional old houses.

04 From Dirang, the road zigzags up a dozen hairpin bends to reach famous **Sela Pass**; at 4170m it's breathtakingly high, as you'll notice walking round frosted Sela Lake.

05 Pause at Jaswantgarh War Memorial (pictured below) en route to Tawang to understand the courage of Indian soldiers in the 1962 conflict. End at **Tawang Gompa**, the world's second-largest Buddhist monastery.

FROM TOP: ROSHANCHETAN/SHUTTERSTOCK, BILL-Z/SHUTTERSTOCK, RAHUL D'SILVA/SHUTTERSTOCK

Listings

BEST OF THE REST

Famous Festivals

Hornbill Festival

Once a year, members of each of the 16 officially recognised tribes of Nagaland send a dance troupe to the capital Kohima for the annual Hornbill Festival.

Ambubachi Mela

Shakti devotees celebrate what they believe to be the annual menstruation of the goddess Maa Kamakhya causing the Brahmaputra in Assam to run red in June.

Ashokastami Festival

In the magical archaeological site of **Unakoti** in Tripura, this annual spring festival combines tribal custom with Hindu worship of the famous rock-cut images.

Touring with the Experts

Sikkim Peak Tours & Travels

Nothing is too much trouble for founder Madan Gurung – expert at tailor-making itineraries that include treks in Sikkim and throughout Northeastern India.

Khangri Tour Trek & Expeditions

Founder Tshering Dorjee Lachungpa has over 30 years of experience in pioneering Sikkimese treks and is committed to eco-tourism.

Xohojatri Travels

Going above and beyond to deliver the best service for his customers, the Assamese owner, Apurba Kalita (+9864625574), gives excellent advice on the Sister States.

Kingly Connections

Norbugang Park

A kingdom until 1975, Sikkim's first chogyal (king) was crowned in 1641 at **Norbugang**; a centuries-old cedar tree shades the open-air coronation throne.

Headman's Home

The 'king and queen' of the remote Nagaland village of **Longwa** have the distinction of sleeping in India and eating their meals in Myanmar in a house that straddles borders.

Neermahal Palace

Built in 1930 in a combination of Hindu and Islamic styles, this Tripura palace stretches across an island, reachable only by boat.

Talatal Ghar

This 18th-century palace was the heart of a complex founded by King Rudra Singha and can be seen in Assam's Sivasagar.

Solomon's Temple

The biggest of Mizoram's many churches, this huge building in Aizawl re-creates King

RAHUL D'SILVA/SHUTTERSTOCK

Solomon's Temple

Solomon's temple in Jerusalem and accommodates 2000 worshipers.

Homestays on High

Martam Village Homestay ₹

Rooms, with grand views of the famous Sikkimese rice terraces, are hotel quality but the experience is local and delicious.

Silnon Homestay ₹

A traditional village homestay with simple rooms beside Sikkim's Silnon Gompa – perfectly located for the monastery hike to Yuksom.

Lempia Ude Homestay ₹

Nothing beats sitting around the central fire in the kitchen of this Apatani homestay, except perhaps having breakfast in the winter sun on the terrace.

Seasons Homestay ₹

Forget the Hornbill Festival (within walking distance): the whole tribal experience of welcome, family customs and local foods is delivered at this Kohima favourite.

Risa Pines Homestay ₹₹

Don't miss the chance to join the family for dinner in this cosy homestay in Shillong, one of the best in Northeastern India.

First for Flavours

Elgin Nor-Khill ₹₹₹

Take tea from a silver teapot and where sugar is dropped in with tongs in this Gangtok hotel, originally built to accommodate royal guests.

Paradise ₹₹

This famous Guwahati restaurant serves traditional lunch thali featuring delicacies such as fish *tenga* (tangy curry) and gooseberry soup.

Ziro Degrees ₹₹

Reflecting Ziro's reputation as the rock capital of Northeastern India, this 1st-floor restaurant and bar is a favourite meeting spot.

SOMPOL/SHUTTERSTOCK

Enchey Gompa

More Monasteries

Enchey Gompa

One of the oldest and most revered Buddhist monasteries in Sikkim, this Gangtok monastery is believed to house a potent wish-fulfilling shrine.

Urgelling Gompa

Famed as the birthplace of the sixth Dalai Lama, a Monpa tribesman born in 1683, this small but beautiful monastery is in Tawang in Arunachal Pradesh.

Local Logistics

Raj Kumar Subba

To take the fear factor out of overlanding in Sikkim, call in a professional such as level-headed Raj (+6296955867), an expert driver who puts your safety first.

Mrinal Chandra Rag

Enlist this delightful driver from Assam (+9101171513), with experience of driving in all Sister States, to help you move around Northeastern India safely.

Banshailang 'Babit' Lynnong

Engage this excellent Khasi guide *(+9233211585)* to bring local insight to a visit to the mega-wet state of Meghalaya.

EASTERN INDIA

TEMPLES | HISTORY | WILDLIFE

RESEARCHED BY PAUL STAFFORD

MILOSK50/SHUTTERSTOCK

EASTERN INDIA
Trip Builder

Trace tigers in the mangroves, behold the birthplace of Buddhism and ride a historic toy train through emerald tea fields; Eastern India thrills with its jungle safaris, mystifies with its Himalayan mountain culture and indulges with its rich, meaty cuisine.

Ride a UNESCO-listed steam train from **Ghum to Darjeeling** (p174).
3hr from Siliguri

Taste Kolkata's **Bengali cuisine**, from street food to signature dishes (p176).
10min from central Kolkata

Join pilgrims at the **Mahabodhi Temple,** Buddhism's holiest site (p180).
45min from Gaya

Watch sculptors create *pandals* (marquees) for the Durga Puja at **Kumartuli** (p182).
15min from central Kolkata

Observe the intricate carvings of chariot-shaped **Konark Sun Temple** (p178).
2½hr from Bhubaneswar

Seek the elusive Bengal tiger at **Sundarbans Tiger Reserve** (p172).
+ *4hr from Kolkata*

CLOCKWISE FROM BOTTOM LEFT: PAUL STAFFORD ALEXREYNOLDS/SHUTTERSTOCK

Practicalities

ARRIVING

Netaji Subhash Chandra Bose International Airport is Eastern India's primary entryway, with flights to India's main cities.

Howrah Junction is India's largest metropolitan railway station; routes include Bhubaneswar, Patna and Siliguri.

FIND YOUR WAY

Map apps are fairly reliable, but West Bengal's hill-station towns are the exception. Pre-load maps whenever you have connection.

MONEY

Always negotiate prices before taking tuk-tuks. Save money by using public transport, or save time by hiring a car and driver.

WHERE TO STAY

Places	Pros/Cons
Kolkata	Megacity. Vast choice of accommodation. Good public transport. Expect crowds.
Bhubaneswar	Temple city and ethnographic museums. Some excellent upscale hotels.
Bodhgaya	Buddhism's main pilgrimage site. Plenty of passable budget hotels.
Darjeeling	Mountain views and heritage hotels. Fantastic tea. Peak-season overcrowding.

GETTING AROUND

Train & Metro Rail hubs are in Kolkata, Patna and New Jalpaiguri. Kolkata has a five-line Metro network.

Bus Routes connect every town and most villages; 4WDs take over in Darjeeling Hills.

TAXI

Taxi & Car Use rideshare apps in cities. Car and driver hire starts at ₹3500 per day.

TOP: AVIJIT BOURI/SHUTTERSTOCK
BOTTOM: STOCKIMAGEFACTORY.COM/SHUTTERSTOCK

EATING & DRINKING

Bengali and Odishan cuisines are freshwater-fish-centric. Mustard oil, fenugreek and nigella seeds predominate.

Try Bengal's sweets, such as creamy *mishti doi (pictured top left);* the Bengali street-food classic *kathi* rolls (stuffed paratha); or *aloo dum* (stuffed potatoes served with chewy *luchi* bread; pictured bottom left).

Best Eastern Indian cooking Kanika (p188)

Must-try kathi roll Kusum Roll's (p188)

OCT–NOV

Post-monsoon flourish: drier weather, cooler temperatures and the clearest mountain views.

DEC–JAN

Domestic tourism peaks; reserve well in advance. Mountain temperatures dip.

FEB–MAY

Warm days and perfect wildlife-spotting conditions. Odisha's humidity rises.

JUN–SEP

Monsoon season; the Rath Yatra festival takes place in Puri and Kolkata.

36 Swamp CATS

TIGERS | MANGROVE SWAMPS | BOAT TOURS

Humans have long struggled to broach the vast, inhospitable, root-tangled swampland covering the Ganges-Brahmaputra delta. Now protected as Sundarbans Tiger Reserve, the world's largest mangrove forest harbours the world's largest population of the beleaguered Bengal tiger. Boatloads of visitors furrow the waterways here hoping for a glimpse of these elusive cats.

PAUL STAFFORD

How to

Getting there Take a bus, ferry, autorickshaw and another ferry to reach the park fringes. Better yet, take a pre-arranged tour.

When to go October to February are peak months, although tiger sightings are anecdotally highest in March and April. Sundarbans Tiger Reserve closes on Tuesdays and in summer.

Overnight Boats Tours of at least one night are recommended. One-night, two-day trips start at around ₹6500 per person.

SOUMYAJIT NANDY/SHUTTERSTOCK

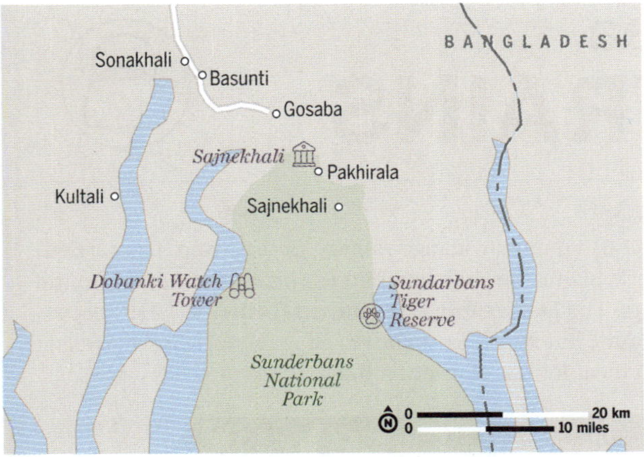

Into the swamp Roughly 101 Bengal tigers (as of the 2025 census) roam the **Sundarbans Tiger Reserve**. They spend most of their time ensconced in the swampy depths, stalking, hunting and sleeping far from the human gaze. But visit one of the reserve's watchtowers at **Sajnekhali** or **Dobanki Watch Tower** and their huge paw prints in the soft mud often tell of a recent presence. When extremely lucky, you might even spy one taking a drink from one of the reserve's many water channels. Learn more at Sajnekhali's **Mangrove Interpretation Centre**.

Reserve access is strictly limited. Most trips are spent aboard diesel-engined boats, which strike out at daybreak, plying the major channels. Spotted deer, wild boar, monitor lizards, crocodiles and macaques are commonly seen, while the bright electric blue of a kingfisher, a sweeping flock of whistling ducks or the waddle of a wading bird provide frequent moments of excitement.

To tour or not to tour? Sundarbans Tiger Reserve offers stark contrast to nearby Kolkata, which is among the world's most polluted cities. But reaching Satjelia Island, from which most Sundarbans boat tours depart, is complicated and often costs more if done solo than as part of a group. Group tours include all transportation, accommodation and meals, along with the boat tour to the Sundarbans Tiger Reserve and its watchtowers. Usually, tours include sunset cruises and night-time bioluminescence canoe trips into the mangrove forest.

Top left Mangroves boat tour, Sundarbans Tiger Reserve
Bottom left Bengal tiger

Bonbibi & the Tiger Widows

Shrines featuring a goddess riding a tiger depict **Bonbibi**, goddess of the Sundarbans. Both Hindus and Muslims supplicate to her, seeking protection from the tiger demon Dakkhin Rai. Official figures count roughly three people killed in tiger attacks here per year. Those figures only account for individuals who were legally permitted to be inside the national park at the time. Most fatalities by tiger occur while people are inside the protected reserve without permission. The thousands of local women who have lost husbands this way are called 'tiger widows'. Only those whose husbands were lawfully inside the national park when killed receive compensation.

37 Tea TRAINS

TOY TRAINS | MOUNTAINS | TEA

Darjeeling's UNESCO-listed narrow-gauge railway, or 'toy train', has carried passengers from the Gangetic plains, through emerald tea plantations and into the Himalayas for over 150 years. The **Darjeeling Himalayan Railway** (DHR) uses diesel engines for the full route, but steam locomotives chug on 'joyrides' between Darjeeling and Ghum, both ideal for tea-plantation tours.

PAUL STAFFORD

How to

Getting there New Jalpaiguri and Siliguri have key train stations connecting to towns and cities across India. From these two stations, you have direct access to the DHR.

When to go The crowds are greatest in December and January, but late October and November bring calm, warm weather and the clearest mountain views.

Joyrides Make sure you book a 'Steam Joyride' train with a 'Vista' carriage. These ensure a steam locomotive, and its carriages offer the best views.

BEIBAOKE/SHUTTERSTOCK

Part steam, full diesel Darjeeling dusts a Himalayan mountain ridge in the shadow of the 'Sleeping Buddha' **Mt Khangchendzonga** (the world's third-highest mountain; 8586m). Despite the altitude, its popularity as a hill station, particularly among people seeking to escape the Kolkata monsoons, led to the construction of an engineering marvel bringing trains from the low plains of India. The route climbs around 2100m (6900ft) in the process.

Today, the full DHR train route from New Jalpaiguri to Darjeeling is tackled by diesel engines, but trips with **steam locomotives** (irctc.co.in; ₹1500) such as the 804B, built in 1925, run at least three times daily between Darjeeling and Ghum. **Darjeeling Train Station**, where you can buy tickets if you haven't bought them in advance online, is charming in its traditional, ramshackle way.

Behind the caffeine curtain All along the route, the green-tea gardens are ripe with the fragrant leaves of orange pekoe. This delicate tea is best taken without milk and is much sought after worldwide. On the diesel trains south of Ghum in particular, you will see these tea gardens running right up to the edge of the tracks in places, interspersed with thick pine forest.

A great day trip involves taking the train and then hopping out to visit an estate. Among them, both **Happy Valley Tea Estate** (happyvalleyorganictea.com) in Darjeeling and **Makaibari Tea Estate** (makaibari.com) south of Kurseong have fantastic estates where factory tours, walks and tastings offer glimpses behind the scenes. Tours and tastings cost ₹100 at both.

Top left Tea tasting, Happy Valley Tea Estate
Bottom left Darjeeling Himalayan Railway

Talking Leaves

If you want to buy tea while in Darjeeling, I recommend buying loose tea from the standalone shops, not the packages of tea, where nobody can see what's going into it.

From my tasting experience, if you're looking to buy good tea and are looking at which garden it came from, the best gardens are Goomtee and sister garden Jungpana. Then the Goodricke Group that own Margaret's Hope and Castleton.

By former tea-taster **Moubani Roy Choudhury**

38 Bengali Cuisine IN KOLKATA

STREET FOOD | COOKING CLASSES | SWEETS

Bengali cuisine is some of India's most flavourful and interesting. With sharp-edged mustard oil at its core, dishes are composed of meats accentuated with coconut, fenugreek and cumin seeds, and plenty of vegetables. Street food ranges from light tiffin (snacks) to full combo meals; save room for dessert, because Kolkata is known as the 'sweet capital of India'.

How to

Getting there With its rapidly growing metro system, Kolkata is easily navigable, making trips to the upscale restaurants of Ballygunge or the time-tested holes-in-the-wall around Shyambazar a doddle.

When to go As soon as you're ready to eat again.

Grease lightening Street food in Kolkata is generally safe to eat. If in doubt, look for places frequented by locals and make sure fried items don't emerge looking darker than they should, indicating the use of old oil.

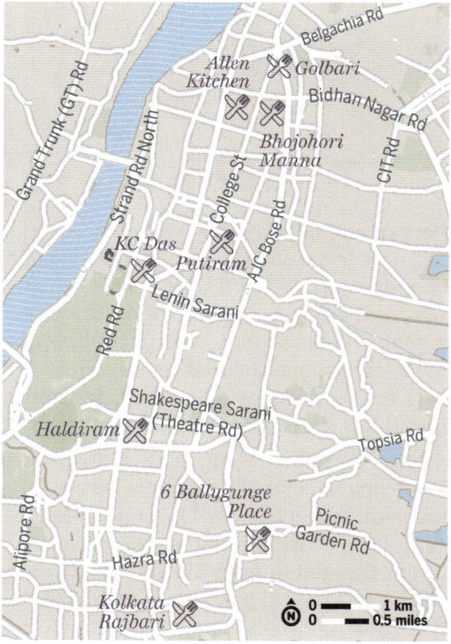

Five spices 'Bengalis look down on basmati rice' is a common refrain in Kolkata, where people take great pride in their cuisine. Their sticky, short-grain *gobindobhog* is West Bengal's most celebrated rice. Another pillar of Bengali cooking is *panch phoron*, a five-spice mix of fenugreek, nigella, fennel, cumin and mustard seeds.

You'll see Bengalis gathering together to taste these spices in a variety of dishes, including *macher jhol* (a fish, cauliflower and potato curry) and *shukto* (a vegetable stew made with bitter gourd and Indian flat beans). All of those dishes could conceivably be served together as a Bengali thali, starting with the vegetables and a bread, such as puffed *luchi*, then moving on to the rice and meat or fish curries. Great places to try these dishes include **6 Ballygunge Place** and **Kolkata Rajbari**.

VIKASH KUMAR RAI/SHUTTERSTOCK

From the streets Kolkata's street-food options range from entire meals, known as combos, to lighter snacks such as *phuchka* (aka *pani puri*, crisp *puri* filled with a mix of water, spices and veg). The middle ground is taken up by *kathi* rolls (a paratha fried with egg and filled with grilled onions, chilli and paneer or meat).

Sweet tooth Bengal is famed for its sweets, chief among them *mishti doi*, made with curd and sweet date-palm jaggery.

Purveyors of these tasty treats are held in high esteem, particularly **Haldiram** and the *rasgulla* (syrupy cottage-cheese balls) from **KC Das**, both found in Chowringhee.

Must-Try Street Food

Mutton curry (pictured) at **Golbari**: Mutton is red goat meat, which can absorb a lot of spices and flavours.

Prawn batter cutlet at **Allen Kitchen**: Started by a Scotsman, they use fish to make interesting culinary treats.

Golda chingri malaikari at **Bhojohori Manna**: A lobster prawn curry cooked in a delectable coconut sauce.

Mishti doi at **Putiram**: The only shop that serves it with a crystal white colour. There's no added sugar; they harness the natural sweetness of milk.

Avik Mitra, leader of food tours for A Chef's Tour, outlines his top recommendations for Bengali eats in Kolkata *@achefstour*

39 Sacred Sites OF ODISHA

TEMPLES | ART | CAVES

Odisha boasts some of India's holiest sites: Explore old Bhubaneswar's sandstone temples, discover the mighty stone chariot of Konark Sun Temple and witness the religious fervour at Jagannath Mandir in Puri, one of the four char dham Hindu pilgrimage temples.

PAUL STAFFORD

Trip Notes

Getting around Regular trains connect Bhubaneswar and Puri (two hours). Konark is connected by buses (the main stand is 1km east of the Sun Temple), which depart when full for Puri (one hour) and Bhubaneswar (2½ hours).

When to go November to February are the main months for visiting Odisha. Other months are exceptionally hot and humid.

Top tip Daylong coach tours to Konark and Puri from Bhubaneswar are operated by Odisha's tourism department (bookodisha.com; ₹660).

A God Who Dies

Jagannath has a wooden body, so every 12 to 19 years he dies. The *nabakalebara* is where his old wooden body is renewed. Although he is a god, he is like a family friend, so people go inside Jagannath temple to express their feelings to him.

Samar Pradhan *is tour manager at Heritage Tours Orissa @heritageorissa*

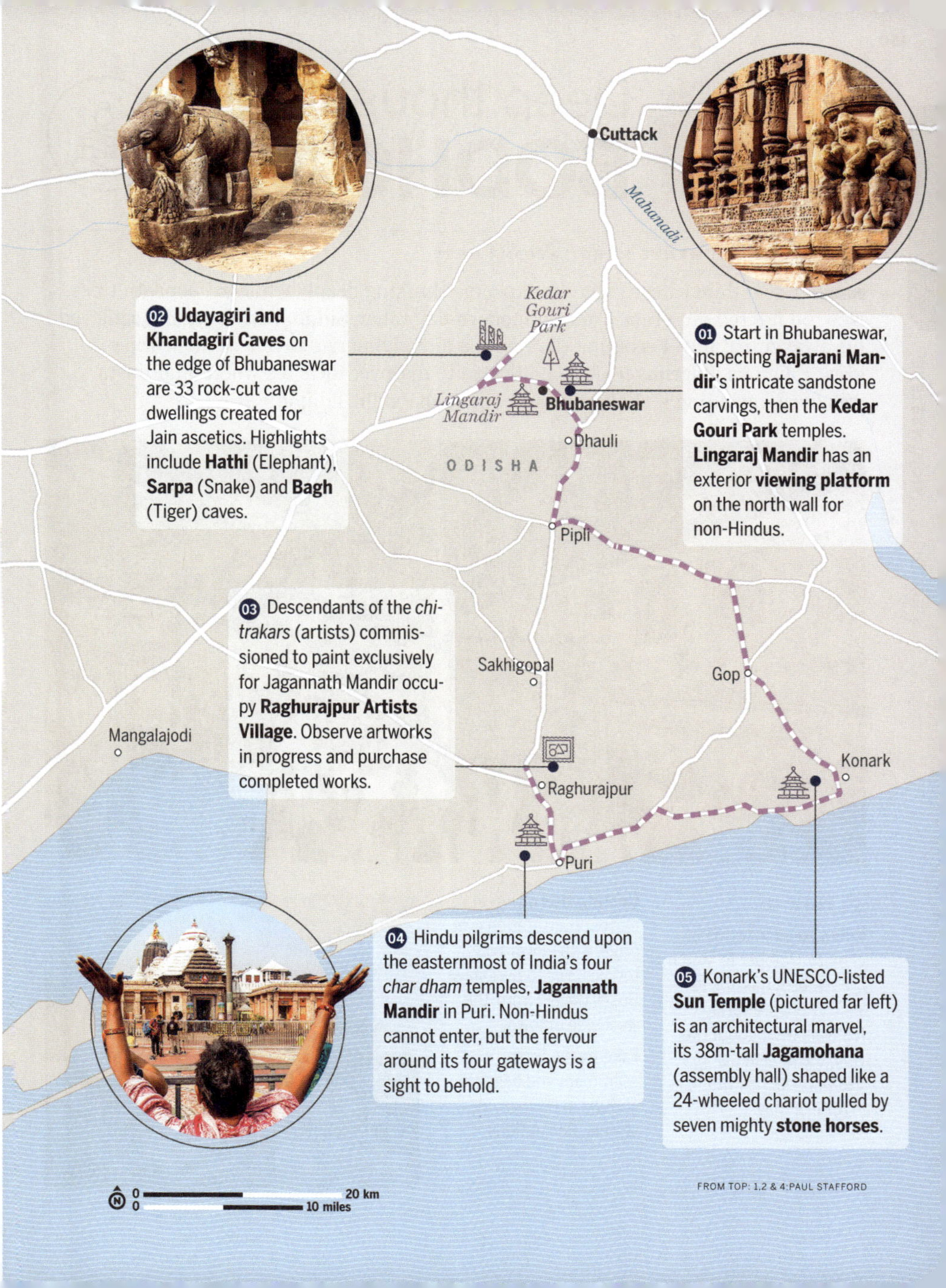

01 Start in Bhubaneswar, inspecting **Rajarani Mandir**'s intricate sandstone carvings, then the **Kedar Gouri Park** temples. **Lingaraj Mandir** has an exterior **viewing platform** on the north wall for non-Hindus.

02 **Udayagiri and Khandagiri Caves** on the edge of Bhubaneswar are 33 rock-cut cave dwellings created for Jain ascetics. Highlights include **Hathi** (Elephant), **Sarpa** (Snake) and **Bagh** (Tiger) caves.

03 Descendants of the *chitrakars* (artists) commissioned to paint exclusively for Jagannath Mandir occupy **Raghurajpur Artists Village**. Observe artworks in progress and purchase completed works.

04 Hindu pilgrims descend upon the easternmost of India's four *char dham* temples, **Jagannath Mandir** in Puri. Non-Hindus cannot enter, but the fervour around its four gateways is a sight to behold.

05 Konark's UNESCO-listed **Sun Temple** (pictured far left) is an architectural marvel, its 38m-tall **Jagamohana** (assembly hall) shaped like a 24-wheeled chariot pulled by seven mighty **stone horses**.

FROM TOP: 1,2 & 4:PAUL STAFFORD

40 Deep thoughts at BODHGAYA

BUDDHIST MONUMENTS | MEDITATION | HERE

Great things have come from people thinking deeply while sat beneath trees. Newton figured out gravity, and in modern-day Bihar, Siddhartha Gautama achieved his awakening, thus becoming the Buddha and giving rise to one of the world's great religions. Pilgrims flock to Bodhgaya to discover the sites where Buddhism was born, including its holiest shrine: the Mahabodhi Temple.

CASPER1774 STUDIO/SHUTTERSTOCK

How to

When to go In terms of climate, October to March are the best months to visit. There are various festivals throughout the year, the largest being **Vesak** (Buddha Purnima) in April or May.

Getting there The closest train station is in Gaya, with onward autorickshaws to Bodhgaya. Buses depart from the west side of town.

Fake gurus Touts, scammers and beggars abound in Bodhgaya's streets. Be cautious.

TINNAPORN SATHAPORNNANONT/SHUTTERSTOCK

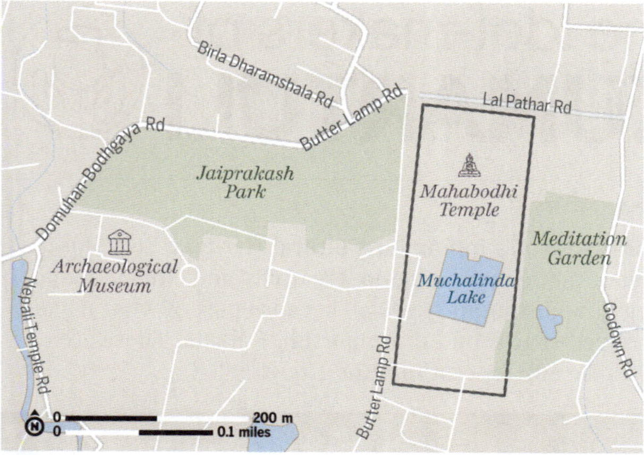

Top left Monks and pilgrims pray at the Bodhi Tree
Bottom left Mahabodhi Temple

The Great Tree In 528 BCE, a prince sat beneath a Bodhi Tree in deep meditation. It was here that he made a breakthrough, coming to a series of understandings that led to his enlightenment. Around that leafy nucleus, the temple town of Bodhgaya simmers with the fervour and industry of pilgrims and disciples. Although the original is long gone, the Mahabodhi (Great Bodhi) Temple Complex is structured around a 19th-century descendant of that Bodhi Tree. This is joined by the 6th-century **Mahabodhi Temple** (bodhgayatemple.com; free), with its beautiful 50m-tall stone tower, now a UNESCO-listed monument. It is sited on the exact spot the Buddha is said to have attained enlightenment.

Meditations and mantras Although the kind of serenity required for efficient meditation is not exactly ubiquitous amid the clamour and energy of pilgrims, Buddhist monks and nuns, yoga teachers and curious visitors (and all the industries they attract), it's worth diving into the streets surrounding the complex. But leave all electronics and bags in your hotel if planning to visit the temple. If you're keen to meditate within the complex, head for the Meditation Garden *(₹20)*. Throughout the site, you'll encounter groups reciting mantras and doing prostrations, particularly around the Mahabodhi Tree. Queues also form to see the temple's gilded icon. Southwest of the temple complex are a series of monasteries for various Buddhist sects, plus the Great Buddha Statue, an 18m-tall seated Buddha.

The Life of a Tree

Within Bodhgaya's small **Archaeological Museum** are remnants of a stone perimeter fence said to have been built by King Ashoka around the original **Bodhi Tree** under which the Buddha achieved enlightenment.

The tree had been carefully tended to by the Buddha's disciples until Tissarakkhā, Ashoka's wife, is said to have poisoned it, jealous of her husband's devotions. In a stroke of divine luck, a sapling from the original tree had been taken to Sri Lanka. A cutting was dutifully returned to Bodhgaya and planted on the site of the original. Its lineage is said to trace directly to the current tree.

41 The idol-makers of KUMARTULI

FESTIVALS | EFFIGIES | IMMERSIONS

Garnering a place on UNESCO's Intangible Cultural Heritage List, Durga Puja is a fervent expression of the region's religion, creativity and cuisine. But don't worry if you're not visiting during the festival, because part of what makes it special are the effigies created year-round in Kumartuli, Kolkata. There are many opportunities to see those effigies cast into the Hooghly River.

PAUL STAFFORD

How to

Getting there For Kumartuli, take Kolkata Metro Line 1 (blue) to **Shovabazar Sutanuti** station. **Potter's Lane** is a 10-minute walk northwest. For **Babughat**, buses run west from Esplanade.

When to go Durga Puja falls in September or October. Effigies are made year-round but are best seen in the weeks before Durga Puja. For immersions, visit Babughat during any religious or national celebration.

Top tip Calcutta Walks (calcuttawalks.com; ₹2,500) offers good tours of the Kumartuli workshops.

ROOP_DEY/SHUTTERSTOCK

Top left Sculptor, Kumartuli
Bottom left Durga Puja celebrations, Babughat

Straw gods Kumartuli is a neighbourhood of narrow, winding lanes in northern Kolkata. Here, scores of sculptors *(kumar)* create effigies (aka sculpture-idols) of deities in their **workshops**. Starting with frames made from tightly packed straw, the *kumar* cover them with clay, scooped from the banks of the **Hooghly River** (a distributary of the sacred Ganges). Gradually, the effigies come to life, particularly those of the 10-armed goddess Durga, often depicted riding a lion.

It is possible to observe the artistry in action, with **Potters Lane** (also known as Banamali Sarkar St) hosting the highest concentration of workshops. While some sculptors are taciturn, invested in their holy work, many are happy to welcome visitors in to look around.

Immersed idols Once finished, these remarkable, paint- and lacquer-covered idols are things of great beauty. Perfect, then, for throwing into the river. Once the Durga Puja celebrations begin, the effigies are placed inside *pandal* (temporary temple-like structures) until the final day of the festival, when they're carried to the Hooghly, accompanied by singing and dancing, and immersed. Most people aim for **Babughat**, which has a special concrete ramp leading down to the water's edge. Throughout the year, but particularly on weekend evenings during a national or Hindu celebration (of which there are many throughout the year), people come from all around carrying these effigies of varying sizes in order to hoist them into the sacred waters.

Durga Puja

The **Durga Puja** is Kolkata's most majestic festival and Eastern India's alternative to Dussehra, which ends on the same date. While both Hindu festivals celebrate the victory of important gods, Durga Puja centres on the defeat of the demon Mahishasura by the warrior goddess Durga. Swallowing up most of Kolkata in its celebratory embrace, the 10-day festival is a vibrant mesh of music, culture and food. Creative temporary structures known as *pandal*, erected throughout the city, are the main stages for the revelry. Every community has its own *pandal* and many families go back to the same *kumar* every year for their effigies.

ARTISAN
Crafts

01

03

02

04

05

01 Baluchari Silk
Hindu mythological scenes are replicated on colourful saris handwoven using resplendent silk on old Jacquard looms in Bishnupur, West Bengal.

02 Adivasi Tribal Jewellery
See the Bonda people's thick neck bands, coin necklaces of the Koya and waist chains of the Desia Kandha in Odisha.

03 Patachitra Paintings
Intricate renderings of Hindu folkloric tales on cloth scrolls, most famously from Odisha's heritage crafts village of Raghurajpur.

04 Nepali Gorkha Caps
These colourful hats, also called *Dhaka topi*, are a badge of Nepali identity common among the Darjeeling Hills Gorkha community.

05 Kantha
This Bengali embroidery craft is primarily used in the creation of saris or to repurpose old, worn saris into other textiles.

01, 03, 07, 08, 09, 10 PAUL STAFFORD, **02** AKELLA SRINIVAS RAMALINGASWAMI/SHUTTERSTOCK, **04** INIGOLAI-PHOTOGRAPHY/SHUTTERSTOCK, **05** UPRABHAT/SHUTTERSTOCK, **06** INDIAPICTURE/ALAMY

06

07

08

09

10

06 Sikki Grass Craft
Beautiful artworks and handicrafts made from dried grasses.

07 Terracotta Pottery
Figurines and pottery have been crafted in terracotta throughout Eastern India for generations. not to mention the terracotta temple carvings.

08 Chandua Appliqué Art
Handicraft combining embroidery, small mirrors and colourful fabrics into geometric, religious and floral motifs in Odisha's Pipli.

09 Dhokra Art
Tracing back to the Indus Valley, this bronze-casting art, often depicting animals, has endured in Eastern India.

10 Kala Bhavan Sculptures
Students past and present have left their mark on the grounds of Visva-Bharati university in Shantiniketan with murals and sculptures aplenty.

The long road to becoming a global power

A HISTORY OF EMPIRES ECHOES THROUGHOUT WEST BENGAL

West Bengal has been at the centre of frequent power struggles, with the fate of the subcontinent often at stake, and it has the ruins of many former empires to prove it. But it took colonisation by a power from a faraway land to inspire modern India's independence.

DAVID EVISON/SHUTTERSTOCK

Left Chamkan Mosque, Gaur
Centre Statue of Netaji Subhash Chandra Bose, Kolkata. **Right** Hazarduari Palace

Before the 13th century, West Bengal had largely known only Buddhist and Hindu rule, notably King Ashoka's Buddhist Mauryan empire in the 3rd century BCE. But the 13th century saw the arrival of Islamic rule, which slowly coalesced into the Bengal sultanate by 1352. The sultanate endured for more than two centuries, and the mosque, gateway and minaret ruins of its capital cities at Gaur and Pandua litter the countryside around the Bangladeshi border.

Those ruins exist largely because of the Mughals who, under Emperor Akbar in 1576, subjugated the Bengal sultanate into their own burgeoning empire. For many years, Bengal served as a vassal state, but the Bengalis had more to offer than their allegiance alone. The region grew to become a crucial player in the textile industry, bringing great wealth to Bengal and filling the Mughal coffers.

The Europeans

The international appetite for West Bengal's textiles, spices and saltpetre attracted suitors to the region. First, in the middle of the 16th century, came the Portuguese, who already had thriving settlements in Goa. They were swiftly followed by the French and Danes, who set up trading bases along the Hooghly River at Chandannagar and Serampore, then the Dutch and, finally, the East India Company of the British. They all paid duties to the nawabs; rulers of what became known as the Bengal State, who governed from Murshidabad, further north upriver. The Mughals, meanwhile, had become embroiled in costly wars, and the role of the Marwari Jain financiers who arranged Bengal's fealty payments to the Mughal emperors in Delhi grew in

SUBHAMAY ACHARYYA/SHUTTERSTOCK

SOUMITRA GIRI/SHUTTERSTOCK

importance. Murshidabad's stock was rising and the wealth was ploughed into ornate mansions beside the Hooghly. But these settlements all paled in comparison to what Calcutta (now Kolkata) would become.

The Freedom Fighters

The East India Company was run in such a way as to protect its interests by taking full advantage of the crumbling Mughal empire and the Indian subcontinent's fractured allegiances. Although Calcutta was only founded in 1690, the British went to war with the Bengalis and seized power in 1757. British rule would expand and come to dominate the subcontinent for almost two centuries.

British rule would expand and come to dominate the subcontinent for almost two centuries.

As British governance became more repressive and crackdowns on dissidence more brutal, Calcutta became the hub of an underground independence movement. Led primarily by intellectuals and children of wealthy merchants, the movement soon gained an appetite to fight back. Acts of civil disobedience saw many of these leaders imprisoned in Kolkata's infamous Alipore Gaol. Benoy Basu, Badal Gupta and Dinesh Gupta assassinated Colonel Simpson, who ran Kolkata's prisons, becoming martyrs for the cause. Their leaders, such as Mahatma Gandhi and Netaji Subhash Chandra Bose, are now national heroes, though their legacy remains contentious as India emerges as a global power.

West Bengal's History on Show

Fascinating historical attractions are littered throughout West Bengal in a chronological southward march towards the Bay of Bengal. Starting in the north, the ruins of **Gaur and Pandua** are spread out across an expanse of farmland. Highlights include Pandua's **Adina Masjid**, and Gaur's **Chika Masjid** and **Firoz Minar**.

Moving south towards Kolkata, **Hazarduari Palace** is a glaring pile built by the British for the then-compliant Nawab of Bengal. **Serampore College** and **Institut de Chandernagor** are European relics, while much of central Kolkata, with its churches, administrative buildings and **Victoria Memorial**, is open for visits. **Alipore Museum** is a fitting ode to the independence struggle.

Listings

BEST OF THE REST

Memorable Meals

Kanika ₹₹₹

For a taste of the wonderful, mustard-oil-cooked Odia cuisine in Bhubaneswar, this up-scale spot does a fantastic *chungudi chhecha* (river shrimp in garlic and chilli).

Kusum Roll's ₹

Buying a *kathi roll* at this popular hangout is practically a Kolkata rite of passage. Little more than a hole in the wall, there's usually a crowd here.

Noryang Tibetan Kitchen ₹

Traditional Tibetan food in Darjeeling where the noodles and *momo* are prepared by hand. Try the *mokthuk* (*momo* in a garlic and ginger broth) and *thukpa* (noodle-and-vegetable stew).

Dinner with Bomti ₹₹₹

Art dealer Bomti Iyengar invites guests into his beautiful Kolkata home for cocktails, an exquisite Bengali meal with all the trimmings and some erudite conversation. Reservations at bomtiyengar@yahoo.com.

Art Café ₹₹

Traditional dishes and snacks from the Darjeeling Hills such as *falay* (a Tibetan pie), plus great coffee. Runs a sustainable handicraft shop and offers village food experiences with local families.

Handcrafted Curios

Raghurajpur Artists Village

This artisan village near Puri in Odisha is inhabited by artists making *patachitra* (Orissan cloth) paintings and other crafts. You will be invited into the homes of these artists. Expect the sales pitch.

Anuvab

The Jacquard looms clank away in this Baluchari silk-sari shop's garden workshop in Bishnupur. Staff at Anuvab welcome visitors into the workshop to see the saris being made.

Cultural Jamborees

Durga Puja

The Hindu calendar's main event sees street parties centred on elaborate marquees known as *pandals*, where effigies of 10-armed warrior goddess Durga are placed before being thrown into the Hooghly River.

Rath Yatra

Aka the Car Festival, this Hindu celebration takes place regionwide. In Puri, three chariots lead a procession from Jagannath Temple, one carrying Jagannath himself, and one each for his brother Balabhadra and sister Subhadra.

Konark Dance Festival

This Odissi dance spectacle sees the once highly secretive art form performed before audiences in front of the huge Konark Sun

SHAIKHMERAJ/SHUTTERSTOCK

Konark Dance Festival

Temple. The main festival is in December, with a smaller iteration in February.

Mukteswar Dance Festival

Another chance to see the beautifully expressive Odissi dance takes place in Odisha's capital, Bhubaneswar, this time at **Mukteswar Mandir** in **Kedar Gouri Park**.

Must-See National Parks

Gorumara

Seek out the one-horned rhino in this large national park in the Dooars region, a few hours from Siliguri. If you have more time to travel, consider **Jaldapara National Park** as a rhino-rich alternative.

Bhitarkanika

Crocodiles number in the high hundreds, dragging their huge frames onto the muddy banks of the various waterways. Boat tours are the main way to get around.

Neora Valley

In Eastern India's best-preserved tract of Himalayan forest, you'll fnd exceptional views of **Khangchendzonga** excellent bird-watching and a chance of spotting red pandas.

Betla

Teak forest with a bamboo understorey, home to a variety of wildlife including elephants, deer and leopards.

Singalila

Best known for its multiday ridge trek that follows the montane border between India and Nepal, with Mt Everest often in view. Best place for seeing red pandas.

Sacred Sites

Shikharji

Join the Jain pilgrims in Jharkhand as they ascend **Parasnath Hill**. The site where more

PAUL STAFFORD

Bandel Basilica

tirthankars (enlightened ones) are believed to have reached *moksha* (nirvana) than anywhere else.

Nalanda

In its 7th-century heyday, this Buddhist university in modern-day Bihar was one of the world's greatest places of learning. Although destroyed by 12th-century invaders, valued remnants are displayed at Nalanda's **Archaeological Museum**.

Ashokan Rock Edicts

Following decisive military victory in 260 BCE near **Dhauli** in Odisha, King Ashoka embraced the non-violent customs of Buddhism. Eleven of his 14 subsequent decrees are still visible, etched into a boulder.

Bandel Basilica

Construction on this Portuguese church began in 1599, roughly 90 years before the British East India Company was established in Kolkata, making it the first known church in Eastern India.

Temple of the Vedic Planetarium

Looming over the Hooghly River in Mayapur, West Bengal, the Hare Krishnas started construction on what will be, when complete, Eastern India's largest temple.

WESTERN INDIA

FOOD | ARCHITECTURE | HERITAGE

RESEARCHED BY JOANNA LOBO

ARPAN/GETTY IMAGES

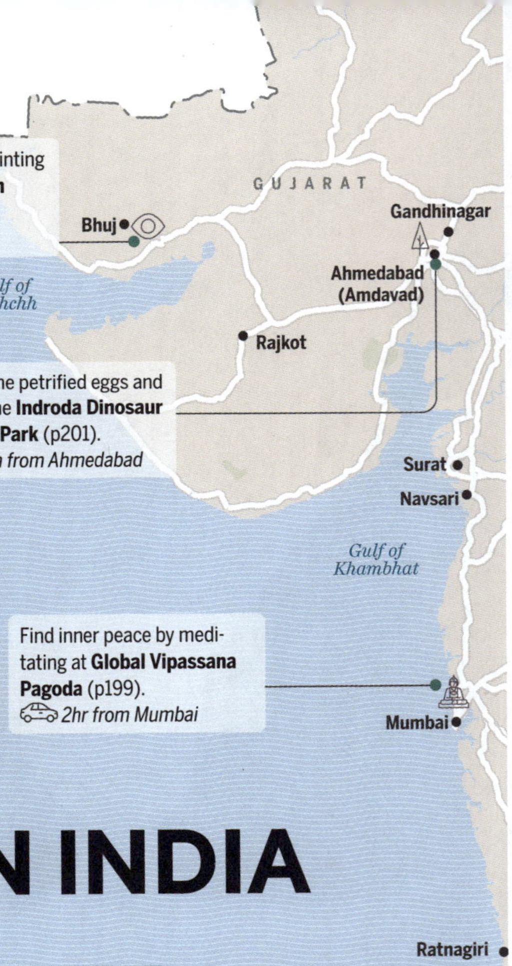

Learn how to do block printing at a workshop at **Sufiyan Ajrakh Studio** (p197).
20min from Bhuj

Marvel at the petrified eggs and fossils at the **Indroda Dinosaur and Fossil Park** (p201).
45min from Ahmedabad

Find inner peace by meditating at **Global Vipassana Pagoda** (p199).
2hr from Mumbai

WESTERN INDIA
Trip Builder

Western India is a culturally rich region along the country's west coast, encompassing Goa, Gujarat, Diu and Maharashtra. You'll need to come again and again to take in its architectural splendours, eat through the dizzying array of local food, visit its wildlife sanctuaries and national parks, and learn about its textile and art heritage.

CLOCKWISE FROM BOTTOM LEFT: SAIKO3P/GETTY IMAGES, DCHAUY/SHUTTERSTOCK, HEINRICH VAN TONDER/SHUTTERSTOCK, SAIKO3P/SHUTTERSTOCK

200 km
100 miles
Udaipur
Ratlam
Indore
Take a scenic winery tour at **Sula Vineyards** (p203).
30min from Nashik
Pench Tiger Reserve
Nagpur
Amravati
Akola
Admire the monolithic black-basalt **Kailasa Temple** at Ellora.
1hr from Aurangabad
Nashik
Aurangabad
Jalna
Akola
Maharashtra
Telangana
Ahmednagar
Nanded
Pune
Bidar
Nagpur
Satara
Hyderabad
Eat a traditional and hearty Goan meal at **Shubhra Shankhwalker's farm** (p207)
15min from Mapusa
Kolhapur
Bagalkot
Kolhapur
Goa
Karnataka
Drink some feni (Goan liquor) and learn about its importance at a **cashew farm** (p206)
20min from Margao
Andhra Pradesh
Arabian Sea
Sharavati Valley Wildlife Sanctuary

Practicalities

MRIDULABLOG/SHUTTERSTOCK

ARRIVING

Chhatrapati Shivaji Maharaj International Airport in Mumbai (Bombay) has flights conveniently connected to the rest of India.

Sardar Vallabhbhai Patel International Airport in Ahmedabad is a major airport connecting Gujarat to the rest of India and the world.

Manohar International Airport (GOX; pictured), or Mopa Airport, is the main airport in Goa for domestic and international flights. Use the GoaMiles taxi app.

HOW MUCH FOR A

Thali/rice plate
₹450

Street snack
₹60-100

Cocktail
₹500-1000

GETTING AROUND

Autorickshaws & Taxis In the main cities like Ahmedabad, Vadodara, Aurangabad, Pune and Nagpur, autorickshaws and metered taxis. Ridesharing apps (Ola, Uber) work too. Everywhere else, it's best to hire a taxi or a private car and driver. Goa uses the GoaMiles taxi app, and you can hail motorcyle taxis.

Metro & Trains Mumbai, Ahmedabad and Pune have functioning metro systems. In Mumbai, trains are the cheapest and quickest way to get around (except during the rains when the tracks flood causing delays).

Buses Fares are minimal (always carry change) but routes are slow and delays are frequent.

WHEN TO GO

NOV–FEB
Cold winter days, lots of festivals and peak season with Christmas and New Year

MARCH–MAY
The hottest months, ideal for beach days in Goa and Gujarat or for safaris in Maharashtra

JUNE–OCT
Monsoon season means humid, dark and cool days, a variety of monsoon festivals and much seasonal produce

TOP: MJPHOTOGRAPHY1/SHUTTERSTOCK
BOTTOM: JOANNA LOBO

EATING & DRINKING

Gujarat is primarily a vegetarian state, so an all-you-can-eat thali is the best option here. If you want something lighter, try Gujarati snacks like *fafda* (crispy gram-flour strips; pictured top right) and *dhokla* (steamed rice and gram-flour cakes).

Maharashtra's cuisine changes according to region. The coast is heavy on the seafood (best in a thali; pictured bottom right), while the interiors offer dishes heavier on the spice.

Goa's cuisine is a mix of coastal fare with some European elements. Definitely try a cocktail or two, ideally one with feni.

Best Goan food Goan Kitchen (p207)

Best Chef's Table Papa's (p210)

CONNECT & FIND YOUR WAY

Wi-fi works in hotels and some restaurants but it's best to buy a local SIM card with data. They're easily available at shops; ask your hotel if you need help finding one.

Navigation apps work fairly well, but not in more remote areas, so download offline maps. You can also ask for directions; local people tend to be helpful.

TRAIN PASS

If you are spending time in Mumbai and will travel by local trains, get a monthly pass (1st class/2nd class/air-conditioned ₹215/₹910/₹2050) on the Rail One app.

WHERE TO STAY

Western India straddles diverse areas, each with its own character and atmosphere. Whether you want to explore heritage sites or immerse in a local festival, you'll find a vibe that suits you.

Places	Pros/Cons
Ahmedabad	Bustling city, rich in museums and heritage monuments. Good for shopping and food.
Mumbai	Major centre of art, culture and films. Varied cuisine. Expect crowds.
Panaji	Cultural hub, home to many events. Great eating and drinking options. Easy access to the rest of the state.
Pune	Rich in history. Major destination during Chaturthi celebrations. Convenient spot for visiting nearby trekking spots and waterfalls.
Mapusa	Famous for its market. Local food. Easy access to hot spots in the North.

MONEY

Most places accept digital payments (UPI), but carry some change for local transport and markets. Markets often ask for a higher 'tourist rate'; you can usally bargain this down to a more reasonable price.

42 Textile Trail in KACHCH

CULTURE | SHOPPING | NATURAL

The villages surrounding Bhuj in Kachch district are a living museum of Gujarat's crafts and textiles. Each community is known for a specific art – embroidery (pictured below) is the most common, but there's also weaving, lacquer, *rogan* art (fabric painting), copper bell-making, *ajrakh* (block printing), and *bandhani* (tie-dye).

EMILY_M_WILSON/GETTY IMAGES

Trip Notes

Getting around It's safest to hire a driver and car *(per day approximately ₹4000)*.

When to go Go during the cool winter months of November, December and January.

Food There are hardly any eating joints on the way, so bring snacks and water.

Workshops Visits are possible anytime, but book beforehand if you want to get a demo at a workshop.

Tip Get a quick introduction to textile heritage and a chance to visit shops through NGOs Kala Raksha, Shrujan and Khamir.

Crafting Change

The three main NGOs working towards conserving and showcasing Kachch's rich textile heritage are **Kala Raksha**, **Shrujan** and **Khamir**. Kala Raksha has a small museum on-site. Shrujan runs the Living and Learning Design Centre, a craft museum with three galleries. Khamir has a campus for training craftspeople and a craft resource centre.

01 In the heart of **Bhuj**, **Sidr Craft** is home of the intricate work of *bandhani* (pictured above). This studio conducts workshops for visitors, and even runs internships for textile students.

05 Learn about *ajrakh* (pictured left) from artisans in **Ajrakhpur**, like **Sufiyan Ajrakh Studio**. This studio uses natural dyes and designs its own blocks; it also sells finished works on-site.

04 **Khamir** is a platform for traditional crafts from the region, which are displayed on the workshop campus. You can also watch the artisans at work.

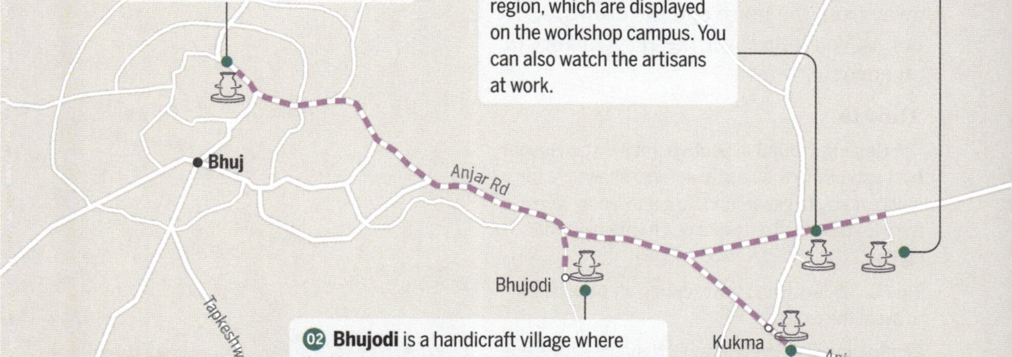

02 **Bhujodi** is a handicraft village where the Vankar community practises handloom weaving (pictured left). Master weaver **Vankar Vishram Valji** showcases weaving and dye-making demos.

03 **Tejsinh Dhana bhai** in **Kukma** village is the only known artisan practising *kharad* weaving (pictured left), making carpets from goat and camel hair. It's a family business and you can see the looms in action.

43 Unseen MUMBAI

ARCHITECTURE | HISTORY | RELIGION

Away from the usual tourist trail, Mumbai reveals some unusual sights, from hidden temples to caves. Often hidden in plain sight, these places are usually free but may require some effort to access. Strap on your walking shoes and explore India's financial capital, away from the noise and the crowd. As a bonus, you'll discover the city's history in an engaging way.

How to

Getting around In South Bombay, a taxi is your best option. In the suburbs, autorickshaws are the quickest way to get around. To get to Gorai, take a ferry from Borivali jetty or a bus from Bhayandar station.

Tips Go midweek and travel during off-peak hours to avoid the crowd.

Picnic time The Sanjay Gandhi National Park is one of the last green spots in the city and makes for a good day trip if you're hitting the caves.

Temple run **Kwan Kuang Temple** is Mumbai's only Chinese temple. It is located in a quiet lane in Mazagaon and occupies a room atop a small building; the caretakers live downstairs. Here you will find murals of Chinese gods, paintings, calligraphy and a brass bell. Go during Chinese New Year to catch the celebrations. The Anglican **Afghan Church** in Colaba (instagram.com/afghanchurchcolaba) is actually a war memorial of the First Anglo–Afghan War (1838–42), built in the Gothic Revival style.

Go underground Andheri is home to the **Mahakali Caves** (₹300), a series of 19 basalt caves that were used by Buddhist monks as far back as 2000 years ago. They're situated in a peaceful area with views overlooking the city; within the caves you'll find a *stupa*, some *chaityas* (prayer spaces) and *viharas* (monastic cells).

Over in the Sanjay Gandhi National Park in Borivali are

ABRAHAM NOWITZ/GETTY IMAGES

Mumbai's Best

Banganga, Walkeshwar: One of Mumbai's oldest sacred sites, at the heart of Walkeshwar lies **Banganga Tank**, surrounded by historic temples and shrines.

Pir Haji Ali Dargah: On an islet in the Arabian Sea, off the coast of Worli, is the marbled **tomb** of a 15th-century Sufi saint from Uzbekistan.

Mughal Masjid: The bylanes of Bhendi Bazaar have a 19th-century Persian Shia **mosque** with a blue-tile facade, geometric honeycomb patterns and Islamic art.

Holy Name Cathedral: One of Mumbai's **oldest Catholic churches**, noted for its frescoes and stained glass.

Pooja Ashokkumar, *public historian and researcher.* *@thoughtsofmadrasi*

the **Kanheri Caves**. You can reach them on rental bicycle (₹300) or with a shuttle (₹15) – but be prepared for long walks and many stairs after you enter. Hike to the top of the hill for great views.

Sanctuary of stillness The **Global Vipassana Pagoda** (globalpagoda.org) in Gorai is the largest meditation hall in the world, with capacity to seat 8000 people. The largest dome here is a pillarless structure containing the bone relics of Gautama Buddha and a spire of gold. The temple offers free *vipassana* meditation courses throughout the year.

Above Sculptures, Kanheri Caves

44 Discover the MUSEUMS

MUSEUMS | FUN SPACES | CULTURE

Museums aren't just quiet, stoic places anymore: Maharashtra and Gujarat are home to places that go beyond showcasing dusty artefacts and offer a fascinating lens to tap into the state's cultural legacies. It's not just art and history, but textiles, dolls, utensils, even fossils, from both public and private collections. Go with an open mind and prepare to be surprised.

How to

Tip Many museums are privately owned and, as such, opening hours and rules may be different. Read through their websites or social-media profiles before visiting.

Food Museums will not allow food inside, but you can carry water.

When to go Ideally, come after 10am in the morning and before lunch. Many museums will shut during lunchtime until 1pm or 2pm.

Hobby collectibles One person's hobby is another's museum. Many museums in the western region are based on hobbies, and feature personal collections. Over in Rajkot, over 1600 dolls from over 102 countries make up the **Rotary Dolls Museum**. In Ahmedabad, you can find a collection of brass and copper utensils of every kind at the **Veechar Utensils Museum**, and there are textiles, musical instruments and, for no reason at all, an elephant skeleton at **Shreyas Folk Museum**.

Wheels of time If you have a keen eye for transport, Maharashtra is your destination. In Pune is the private **Vikram Pendse Cycle Museum**, open only on weekends, with vintage bicycles and cars. **Joshi's Museum of Miniature Railways** has model trains, including a miniature train setup that's perfect for children. Mumbai also has

Unusual Museums in Gujarat

Dr Chandarana Dental Museum Perhaps one of its kind in the entire world, this **museum** in Vadodara opened a few years back to much applause and interest.

Oriental Institute The museum in Vadodara is one of the world's richest **repositories** of rare, ancient manuscripts (over 30,000) and printed books.

Hansiba Museum This Radhanpur space is the first **museum** in Gujarat owned and managed exclusively by women artisans of SEWA (Self Employed Women's Association).

Patan Patola Museum This purpose-built **museum** is an excellent place to see Patola silk-weaving in action.

Chirag Munjani, *tour guide and founder, Rural Pleasure Journeys*

SAM PANTHAKY/AFP/GETTY IMAGES

the **BEST Museum**, located in a bus depot and dedicated to the city's iconic red buses.

Dinosaur stories Raiyoli village in Balasinor, Gujarat, is one of India's most significant sites for fossil discoveries, which include eggs from 13 different dinosaur species, and a new species discovered in 2003, *Rajasaurus marmadensis*. You can learn more about these at the **Balasinor Fossil Park**. Nearby, Gandhinagar's **Indroda Dinosaur and Fossil Park** has petrified eggs and fossils uncovered from the Kachch Basin and other regions of Gujarat.

Above Fossilised brontosaurus eggs, Indroda Dinosaur and Fossil Park

45 Say 'Cheers!' in NASHIK

DRINK | CULTURE | FESTIVALS

Maharashtra's Nashik District is India's premier wine-growing region. Often called India's Wine Capital, it has numerous wineries and big players offering tours, tastings, restaurants and vineyard stays for those seeking a well-rounded wine holiday. The wines have distinct profiles, are affordable and offer depth in variety.

KIRAN-SHARMA/SHUTTERSTOCK

How To

Getting around Apps are unreliable and autorickshaws will refuse to take you outside the city. The best option is to arrange a private car and driver through your hotel.

When to go January to March are harvest months, abuzz with activity and stomping sessions. There's SulaFest in February, and the Nashik Grape Festival in March.

Tip If you fly into Nashik, show your boarding pass at Sula for a free wine tour and tasting.

ANMOL GOYAL/SHUTTERSTOCK

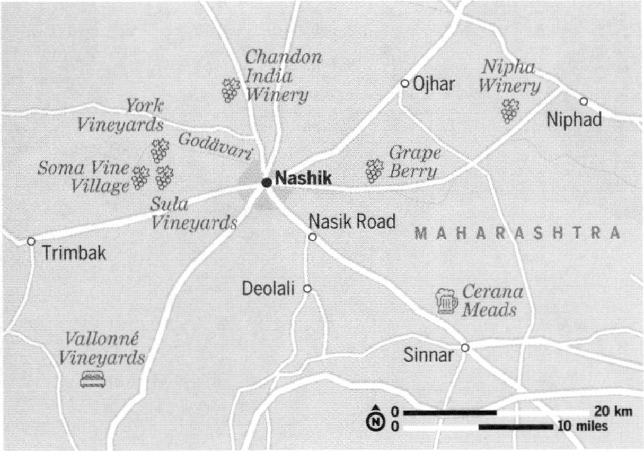

Uncork & Unwind

The simplest way to explore Nashik's wineries is to divide them according to location, as the wineries are grouped together in clusters. Keep aside three days for this itinerary.

Start at the most popular – the stretch on the Gangapur Savargaon Rd. This cluster contains , which is the most comprehensive in its offerings and a great place to snap photos. Visit during **Sulafest**, an annual music festival held in February. Nearby is **York Winery**, which offers a quieter tasting with great views of the Gangapur Dam. **Soma Vine Village** is the only winery making fruit wines like litchi, pomegranate and mango.

The second cluster is in Igatpuri. **Vallonné Vineyards** has the best views in the region, overlooking the Mukne lake and the Sahyadri Hills. It also runs extremely informative tours, and like other vineyards here has its own restaurant.

Close by, about a 15-minute drive away, is **Grover Zampa Vineyards**, Nashik. India's second-largest wine producer also has a space in Nandi Hills, Karnataka. The vineyard here is under renovation but open to visits (if booked a few days in advance).

Away from the city centre on the east are two more small wineries: **Grape Berry**, which produces a unique honey-based wine, and the family-run **Nipha Winery**, which is open during harvest season for wine tastings and wood-fired pizzas.

Top and bottom left Wine tasting, Sula Vineyards

Beyond the Vine

Nashik isn't only about the grape. In the hills of Anjaneri is **Cerana Meads**, which has a taproom showcasing the honey and fermentation process used in its meads, as well as tastings of its different varieties – blue pea lavender, Pinot Noir, Chenin Blanc, pomegranate vanilla, jamun and yule spice. There's also a healthy brewing scene in the region, kickstarted with Topchi, which set up base in an old artillery centre to brew its own craft beer; you can also attend tours of the microbrewery. The taproom at **Topchi Brewing Outpost** has 12 beers on taps, as well as cider and mead.

46 Goa on A PLATE

GASTRONOMY | SPIRITS | CULTURE

In Goa, they don't say hello, but *jevpak kitem asa* – 'what's there to eat?' Goans love their food, and whyever not? It's a vibrant, spicy, tangy, seafood-rich blend of coastal flavours, local ingenuity, seasonal produce and the heavy imprint of colonisation. Fish, curry and rice are staples, as are the local spirits of feni and *urrak*.

JOANNA LOBO

Top left Goan thali
Bottom left Mapusa market

NAME/CREDIT

How to

Getting around The easiest way to travel in Goa is by renting a motorbike. Ridesharing apps like GoaMiles and Uber are convenient if you need a taxi.

When to go Goa's monsoons showcase the state's lush natural beauty, and are a time for a variety of festivals. Winter is peak season for tourists, and ideal if you want to attend events and parties.

Cheap eats Food trucks are common here, dishing out some staple snacks like cutlet *pao* (beef or chicken cutlet in bread), *ros* omelette (chicken curry served with an omelette), fish cutlets and more.

Soul Food

'What fish are you eating today' is a great conversation-starter in Goa, where culinary life revolves around the day's catch. A seafood thali is the ultimate Goan experience, available at tiny joints advertising specials on a board, at shacks on the beach and at fancy restaurants as the token Goan preparation. A thali usually contains a seafood curry (prawn is common), *kismur* (dried-shrimp salad), a *tisreo sukka* (dry spiced clams) salad, local vegetables and fried fish. The more local spots will offer homemade pickles made of fish, aubergine or mango in the thali. Always ask what's the catch of the day before deciding on the fish in your thali. Some great spots to grab a thali include **Kokum Curry**, **Spice Goa**, and **Bombil**. Pro tip: the small bars and restaurants typically have the freshest fish.

OLEG SHULDIAKOV/GETTY IMAGES

To the Market

Markets are a great introduction to the diversity of Goan produce. The **Mapusa** Friday market draws sellers from across the region; **Panaji** is great for *purumenth* (monsoon provisions); and **Pernem** and **Banastarim** buzz during the Ganesh Chaturthi festival for their *Matoli* (canopies of fruits and flowers strung above the idol of Ganesha).

Fun with Feni

Cocktails made with feni (Goan cashew-nut liquor) and *urrak* (the first distillate of cashew nut) are now commonplace in Goa's buzzing cocktail scene and in neighbourhood bars like

Quinta Cantina

To learn more about feni and *urrak*, meet Hansel Vaz, the owner of **Cazulo Premium Feni**. At his cashew farm in Cuelim, Vaz invites guests to try different feni expressions and cocktails while he imparts his deep knowledge of the spirit. This **Floating Feni** experience also includes food pairings and a glimpse behind the scenes at the cashew farm.

Goa's old watering holes or tavernas are good places to get the freshest *urrak* or feni. Many tavernas can be experienced through tours conducted by **Soul Travelling** (soultravelling.in) and **Local Beat** (thelocalbeatgoa.com). Some one-time tavernas have undergone makeovers and are now hip bars (p211).

Exciting Drinking Destination

Goa is one of India's most compelling drinking destinations. Bars operate with a level of freedom that allows for real experimentation across craft spirits, ingredients and formats. The result is a cocktail culture that feels bolder and more assured than elsewhere.

Flavour, unique ingredients and technique show up not just in headline venues but also in small bars. From **Bar Outrigger** in Panjim to **Mister Merchant** in Moira, there's a cocktail experience for everyone. With a crowd that's a mix of domestic travellers and international visitors, the scene is constantly in motion.

Kimberly Pereira, *chief operating officer at spirits company Maya Pistola Agavepura @kim.brew.licious*

Not Another Restaurant

In Goa, some of the best food can be found outside restaurants. In the quiet village of Camurlim, **Shubhra Shankhwalker** (instagram.com/shubhra_shankhwalker) offers a long feast of dishes originating from the Goan Saraswat (a Hindu caste). She sources and cooks everything herself; go on an empty stomach because there will be at least 18 dishes (her maximum is 29).

Attend a concert at the **Centre for Indo-Portuguese Arts** in Panaji, and you'll not only get to listen to Portuguese-rooted musical forms of *fado* and *mando*, but also to eat some Portuguese delicacies like *rissois* (savoury pastries), *fofos* (savoury cakes) and *pasteis* (custard tarts).

Goan Kitchen serves up a feast of treats in the courtyard of a home in Loutolim. Co-founder Crescy Baptista will show you her her kitchens and teach you how to stuff Goan sausages or *choris* and bake *bebinca* (a layered sweet) without an oven.

Below Portuguese-style pasteis de nata

FROM LEFT: JOANNA LOBO, NATALI ZAKHAROVA/SHUTTERSTOCK

GOAN
Goodies

01

02

03

04

01 Azulejos
These hand-painted glazed ceramic tiles are a unique architectural feature of Goan homes, they can be bought as murals or nameplates.

02 Cashew nuts
One of Goa's famous exports, cashew nuts are found in every market in shelled, roasted, salted, and even masala avatars.

03 Coconut /coir craft
The husk of the coconut, and shell, polished and smoothed out, are turned into cute curios and even spoons and cups.

04 Choris
Goa's very own pork sausage is a spicy treat that can last a while. Pungent in aroma, with lingering vinegar notes, it is a delicious cooked treat.

05 Feni
Goa's state spirit makes for a good gift, especially the miniatures. Try the coconut feni and infusions. Choose well-known brands.

06 Ghumot
The traditional percussive instrument is

05

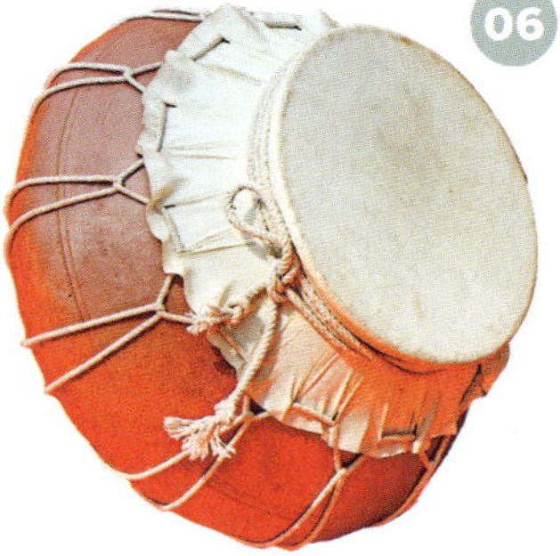

06

07

08

09

made of earthenware and used to be covered in lizard skin; today, the membrane is synthetic.

07 Homegrown alcohol

An increasing number of craft spirits are being produced in Goa, especially gin. Good, cheap and there's a variety on offer.

08 Mario Miranda art

Goa's legendary artist and cartoonist was known for his quirky, colourful depiction of the local life and characters. His art now features on clothes, magnets, postcards, games, bottles and more.

09 Seashell jewellery

Common to flea markets and beachside shops, seashells make their way into easy to wear jewellery like earrings, rings, anklets and necklaces.

01, 05 & 08 JOANNA LOBO. **02** FLOORTJE/GETTY IMAGES. **03** RINI SAID/SHUTTERSTOCK. **04** ERROL_ALPHONSO/SHUTTERSTOCK. **06** MATJOE/SHUTTERSTOCK. **07** MARIYANA M/SHUTTERSTOCK. **09** NAKSH K/SHUTTERSTOCK

Listings

BEST OF THE REST

Chef's Tables

Papa's ₹₹₹

Reservations are hard to get for chef Hussain Shahzad's 12-seater restaurant in Mumbai, but the food makes up for it: Indian at heart, but high on technique and theatrical in its presentation.

Praça Prazeres ₹₹₹

Goan chef Ralph Prazeres dishes up technically brilliant and comforting European food. The chicken liver pâté demands repeats. The bar upstairs does live music and excellent picantes.

Aragma ₹₹₹

The restaurant takes the phrase 'ingredient-forward' to heart. Chef Amit Ghorpade's themed tasting menus change often and will challenge your idea of Indian ingredients.

Accentuate Food Studio ₹₹₹

This kitchen serves as a reservations-only lab for chef Mohib Farooqui's culinary experiments. The eight-seater space showcases changing global and local menus.

Skilful Storytellers

Local Beat

Tour group organising picnics on private properties, usually by a water body, across Goa (instagram.com/thelocalbeat_goa). The location is never publicised, and there's a lot of Goan food on offer, plus refreshing feni cocktails.

Konkan Travel Club

This club (konkantravelclub.com) conducts immersive trips in the Konkan belt (in the south of Maharashtra). Trips vary according to season, they focus on history, and always include stops at local businesses.

Sohail Wazir

Photographer and textile enthusiast Sohail (instagram.com/sohail_wazir_) has vast knowledge of Kachch's textiles and personal relationships with many of the local artisans. He organises and customises individual and group tours.

Parks & Recreation

Mollem National Park

Monsoons are a good time to visit this wildlife site in Goa. Rich in biodiversity, you can spot a variety of amphibian and insect life, including bioluminescent fungi.

Gir National Park and Wildlife Sanctuary

The only place to find Asiatic lions in the wild. A sighting at this Gujarat park is said to be almost guaranteed; you may even get to see the playful cubs.

Tadoba-Andhari Tiger Reserve

Go here for the best chance to spot the Royal

RAVI THEJA/500PX

Asiatic lion, Gir National Park and Wildlife Sanctuary

Bengal tiger in Maharashtra. Safaris are a visual delight, as the park has a rich butterfly and bird population.

Velavadar Blackbuck National Park

The beautiful park near Bhavnagar is a stretch of grassland and wetlands between rivers, home to blackbucks, the critically endangered and migratory lesser floricans and migratory harriers.

Cool Cafes

Gazra Cafe ₹₹

An LGBTIQ-friendly space by the lake in Vadodara doing special Maharashtrian and Gujarati snacks and food. Definitely try the seasonal *undhiyu* (mixed vegetables cooked in earthen pots underground) and the refreshing drinks.

Larder & Folk ₹₹₹

Chef Priyanka Sardessai's cafe in Goa is beloved for its hot-honey doughnuts and addictive cookies. It is a work- and pet-friendly space.

Marz-o-Rin ₹₹

Old-school cafe on the happening MG Rd in Pune offering a selection of drinks and tasty, affordable snacks like chutney sandwiches, chicken sandwiches and macaroons.

Candies ₹₹

A villa converted into a cafe in Mumbai, this space is an old Bombay haunt. Go here for a casual, arty vibe with filling snacks and sandwiches, and to attend a host of events.

Zen Cafe ₹₹

Cute outdoor cafe in Ahmedabad with wholesome, healthy food, teas and coffee. A bonus is the location next to an underground museum, Amdavad ni Gufa, decorated with artist MF Husain's paintings.

DCHAUY/SHUTTERSTOCK

Blackbucks, Velavadar Blackbuck National Park

Trendy Tavernas

Cajy Bar ₹₹

Neighbourhood bar with straight drinks (no cocktails), and home-cooked Goan food that includes beef and pork. The decor includes upcycled items, and the vibe is warm and friendly.

Peter Tavern ₹₹

Family-run space attached to a house offering a selection of Chinese-Indian and Goan food, straight pours and cocktails. The space hosts regular events like quiz nights, karaoke and parties.

Pablo's ₹₹

Popular spot in North Goa known for its cocktails, beers on tap, small bites and regular bar takeovers. The bar hosts Holi, Diwali and other festive parties. It's a pet-friendly space.

Joseph Bar ₹₹

The original taverna-turned-bar remains a hit with tourists, especially for its location in the pretty Latin quarter of Fontainhas. It still retains much of its old-world furniture and decor. Great feni cocktails and Goan snacks made by neighbourhood aunties.

SOUTHERN INDIA

TEMPLES | ART & CULTURE | BEACHES

RESEARCHED BY CHARUKESI RAMADURAI

DOCTORS PHOTOGRAPHY/SHUTTERSTOCK

SOUTHERN INDIA
Trip Builder

Cast aside everything you think you know about India – from the Bollywood movies you may have watched, to the takeaway curries you may have eaten – and be ready to be surprised by the mishmash of languages, cuisines and cultures that are uniquely southern.

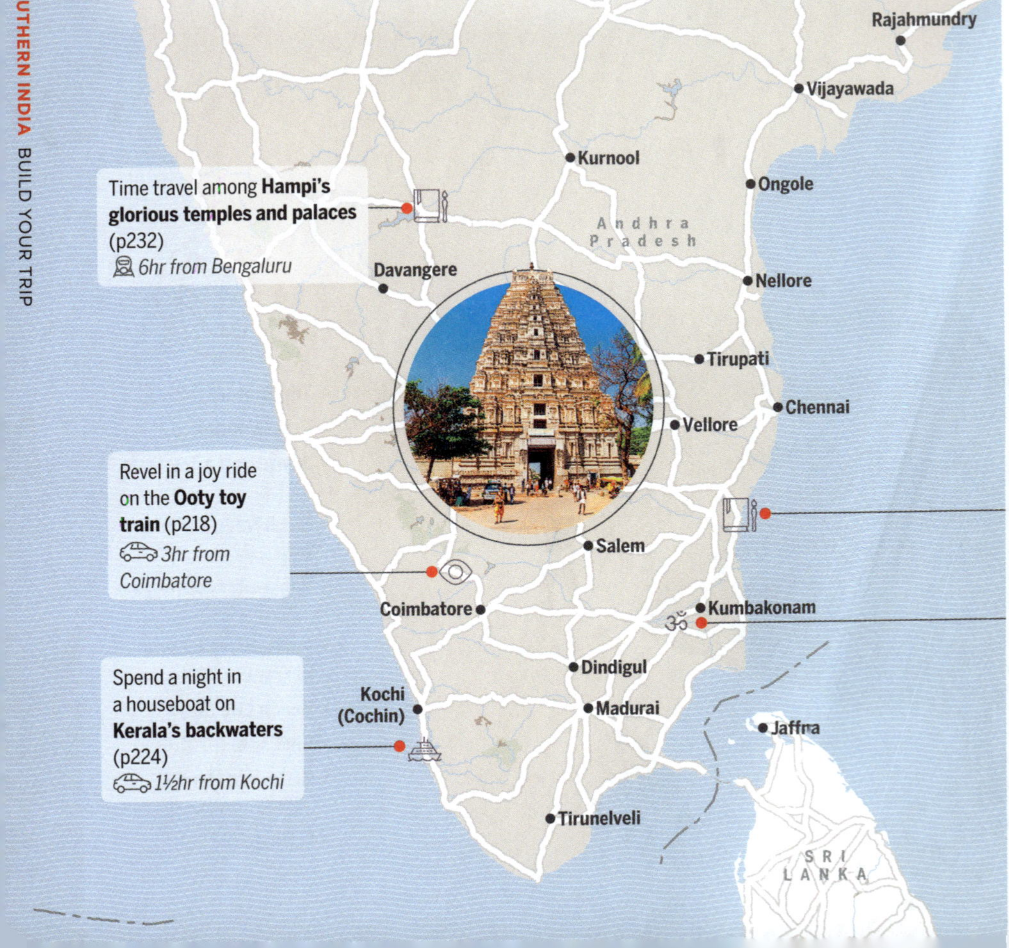

CLOCKWISE FROM BOTTOM LEFT: SAIKO3P/SHUTTERSTOCK, EXPLOREWITHINFO/SHUTTERSTOCK, MALCOLM P CHAPMAN/GETTY IMAGES, KIRAN-SHARMA/SHUTTERSTOCK

Practicalities

SNEHIT PHOTO/SHUTTERSTOCK

ARRIVING

There are several international airports across the southern states, with the larger ones at **Chennai**, **Bengaluru** (Bangalore; pictured), **Kochi** (Cochin) and **Hyderabad** connecting to the Middle East and onwards to Europe and the USA. There is an excellent train network to cities like Thanjavur, Madurai, Coimbatore, Chennai, Bengaluru and Kochi, from where you can take a bus or cab onwards to Puducherry, Alleppey or Hampi. For the Andamans, a flight from Chennai to **Port Blair** (recently renamed Sri Vijaya Puram) is your best option.

HOW MUCH FOR A

Filter coffee
₹20

Masala dosa
₹60

Tuk-tuk ride
₹100+

WHEN TO GO

SEP–OCT
Shoulder period, beginning of festival season.

NOV–FEB
Cooler temperatures, with many cultural and religious festivals all over the region.

MAR–MAY
Sweltering summer months, with uncomfortably high heat and humidity.

JUN–SEP
Monsoon season, but the days can be pleasant with intermittent showers.

GETTING AROUND

Taxi Taxis hired from reputable travel agencies are the best way to cover longer distances and even to travel between cities in South India. For travel within cities, app-based services like Uber and Ola are available everywhere.

Autorickshaw Tuk-tuks or autorickshaws (usually shortened to 'auto') are your best friend for navigating through traffic congestion, so feel free to hail these three-wheeled rockets. Make sure to negotiate your price before starting the ride.

Walk Given traffic and road conditions, walking is really not a great option in the larger cities. But smaller towns like Madurai, Thanjavur, Puducherry and Hampi are best explored on foot, so expect to wear out your shoe leather.

EATING & DRINKING

Expect to eat a lot of rice and rice-based dishes like dosa (paper-thin lentil-flour crepe), *idli* (spongy, round, fermented rice cake), *idiyappam* (string hoppers) and *puttu* (rice powder and coconut, steamed in a metal or bamboo holder; pictured top right) served with a variety of aromatic chutneys and stews. And then there is the unmissable biryani (fragrant spiced steamed rice with meat or vegetables; pictured bottom right) with subtle regional variations, and all the fresh seafood in Kerala.

Best ghee podi dosa Murugan Idli Shop

Must-try masala grilled fish Brunton Boatyard

WHERE TO STAY

Although there are international chain hotels in the big cities, book a room in one of the restored heritage hotels for a feel of this region's unique culture.

Places	Pros/Cons
Chennai	Wide range of options, makes for a good base to explore the whole region
Kochi	Fort Kochi has cute cafes, art galleries and quick access to the backwaters
Hampi	Stay within town close to the main attractions for ease of navigation
Ooty (Udhagamandalam)	Find a converted British-era bungalow for a laid-back stay
Thanjavur (Tanjore)	Excellent base for the Tamil Nadu heritage trail, with high-end boutique hotels
Puducherry (Pondicherry)	Plenty of guesthouses and boutique hotels in the old Tamil and French quarters

CONNECT & FIND YOUR WAY

Wi-fi is available for free at most hotels, restaurants and cafes, although it is a good idea to buy a prepaid SIM card, so you have internet on the go for booking taxis and finding directions. Google Maps works fairly well in south India, although asking a local for directions still remains a fun (if occasionally unreliable) thing to do.

GET A GUIDE

Authorised tourist guides don't just have the best stories and anecdotes, but can also help you navigate through the overwhelming cultural maze of south India, so hire one wherever possible.

MONEY

Credit cards are accepted at the bigger shops, hotels and restaurants, but it's always a good idea to keep cash at hand, especially in smaller towns. ATMs are readily available if you need to make a withdrawal.

47 Joyride on a TOY TRAIN

SLOW TRAVEL | NATURE | VIEWS

Several times a day, a narrow-gauge train runs up and down the green slopes of the Nilgiri mountains in and around Ooty (short for Udhagamandalam) past lush tea plantations, charming old train stations and through long, dark tunnels. Fondly called the 'toy train', the Nilgiri Mountain Railway has been transporting tourists and locals alike for over 125 years.

DANEY DANEY/SHUTTERSTOCK

How to

Getting around Fly into Coimbatore (roughly 90km away) and take a cab up the winding roads for the three-hour drive to Ooty.

When to go Visit any time of year, but note it can get crowded during school holidays in the summer months between April and June.

Top tip If you want the fun, but can't spare time for the entire five-hour journey, opt for the hour-long ride to Coonoor, and return by cab or bus.

BALAJISRINIVASAN/SHUTTERSTOCK

DENIS.VOSTRIKOV/SHUTTERSTOCK

Slow Travel

Taking nearly five hours to cover a mere 46km between Ooty and Mettupalayam, this 'toy train' is a throwback to the glorious days of slow travel, when the journey was the whole point and not the destination. This is one of those rare travel experiences that allows you an up-close-and-personal glimpse of local life in India's small hill towns.

Board early and grab a window seat so you can have your nose pressed to the glass as the train crosses 250 bridges and 16 tunnels along the route, manoeuvring over 200 steep curves. The scenery is the stuff of picture postcards, the hillsides covered with **tea gardens** from where the tenderest of tea leaves make their way to local factories to be processed into fine export-quality teas.

Get off to stretch your legs at the stops along the way, if only to admire the old architecture of the railway stations, which often come with brightly painted sheds, red tiles and white eaves. Many of the town names – **Wellington**, **Runnymede**, **Lovedale** – have been retained from the era they were named in by British colonial rulers.

And while the train does not have a catering car, don't miss the chance to sample hot and sweet milky chai and fried goodies like *vada* (spiced lentil fritters) from itinerant vendors.

Far left top and left Nilgiri Mountain Railway ('toy train')
Far left bottom Railway station, Lovedale

Oh Fudge!

People don't only visit this popular high-altitude 'hill station' to escape the scorching summer heat of the plains, but also to shop for excellent home-made chocolates and rich fudge in delectable flavours like chocolate, coffee, caramel and peanut butter. As you walk along the main market area, peep into the chocolate shops for a sample, and perhaps pick up a few blocks to take back home (or munch on the train, if you will). **King Star Chocolates** is one of the most famous local brands, while **Moddy's** is another golden oldie that also sells other assorted artisanal products from the region like nuts, spices, honey, tea and coffee.

48 Tamil Nadu TEMPLE TRAIL

ARCHITECTURE | CULTURE |

The stars of Tamil Nadu's temple circuit are the triumvirate in Thanjavur (Tanjore), built by the Chola kings. Now over a thousand years old, the three form a UNESCO world heritage site collectively known as the Great Living Chola Temples.

CHECCO2/SHUTTERSTOCK

How to

Getting around

The nearest airport is in Trichy (Tiruchirapalli), from which the 60km drive to Thanjavur takes about an hour. Set up base at **Svatma** hotel in Thanjavur and hire a cab to visit the other towns.

When to go

Visit the temples early in the morning or late in the evening for an authentic local vibe.

Good to know

Wear modest clothing that covers the knees and shoulders, and comfortable slip-on shoes.

SATISH PARASHAR/SHUTTERSTOCK

Temple-Hopping in Thanjavur

Although there are hundreds of temples of all sizes scattered across the state, the Thanjavur trio stand out for their ornate towers, intricate carvings and other remarkable architectural elements. Not surprising, given they were built by the Chola dynasty, who from their base at Thanjavur politically and culturally dominated this fertile region for several centuries. Look beyond the frenzy of devotion into these quiet corridors and courtyards, and you will discover vignettes of silence, grace and beauty.

The Great Living Chola Temples

Start with Thanjavur's **Brihadishwara Temple**, simply referred to as the *periya koyil*, or 'big temple', by locals, for its unmatched glory and grandeur. As soon as you enter, your

EDDIE GERALD/LONELY PLANET

Make it Happen

For a deeper understanding of the significance of these temple towns both in the past and at present, sign up for the Chola Trail with **Courtyard Tours** *(courtyard tours.in)*. **Madurai Magic** *(maduraimagic.com)* also offers various tours, focusing on culture, crafts, textiles and food.

Top left Brihadishwara Temple
Left Fresco, Brihadishwara Temple
Above Airavatesvara Temple (p222)

eyes are drawn to the imposing tower with a dome on top that's hewn from a single granite block weighing over 80 tons. If nothing else, spare a few minutes to ponder over how they hoisted this monolith up 216ft (66m) all those centuries ago.

And then spend some time admiring the frescoes on the walls and ceilings, with brilliant renderings of both divine and prosaic themes.

Just an hour away is the equally splendid but often overlooked temple at **Gangaikondacholapuram**, with its spacious courtyard, and surrounded by paddy fields. And located between these two giants is the smaller **Airavatesvara Temple** at Darasuram, a quiet beauty with lush stone carvings. Look for the statues of the *yali*, a mythical creature with the body of a lion and the face of an elephant, symbolising the might of the Chola dynasty.

When Temple Fatigue Hits

Most prominent temples in Tamil Nadu are surrounded by bustling bazaars, where locals shop, eat and catch up. Take a break from your temple-hopping by wandering through the market lanes. You never know what you will find – perhaps a workshop where master and apprentice are making the ancient stringed instrument known as the *veena*, or a home where a couple is busy at a loom, spinning absolute splendour out of local silk and cotton. Or simply sit down at a roadside tea shop for a soothing cuppa. In most places in south India, that means strong and sweet coffee, or *kapi* as it is known here.

Left Brihadishwara Temple (p221)
Below Mansion, Tamil Nadu

Magnificent Mansions in Chettinadu

For a change of scene, head on to Chettinadu, two hours' drive away. This is a cluster of over 75 villages and towns filled with grand mansions, each with over 100 rooms stretching across several corridors, connected through square open-air courtyards. These mansions, built over a century ago, are so massive that their front entrance is on one street and the back door in the parallel one. Peep in for a look at the original architecture and artwork from those times, including colourful wall frescoes, intricate woodwork, teak pillars from what was then Burma, chandeliers from Belgium and stained glass from Venice.

The big draws in Chettinadu are the towns of Kanadukathan and Karaikudi – so book a room at **Visalam** or the **Bangala**, heritage hotels repurposed from these grand residences. Each offers a glimpse into the almost-forgotten way of life of the old residents here, who enjoyed ample leisure time and elaborate meals (speaking of which, make a reservation for lunch at either hotel for a taste of piquant Chettinadu cuisine). Another couple of hours' drive gets you to Madurai, for the last stop on the temple trail, at the **Meenakshi Amman Temple**, with its magnificent statues and murals of gods and goddesses, devotees and demons.

49 Backwater JOURNEYS

BOATING | BACKWATERS | LAGOONS

The most fascinating feature of Kerala is the backwaters, a labyrinthine network of brackish canals and lagoons flowing inland from the Arabian Sea, through villages and along paddy fields. While rowboats are the most common mode of transport for locals, you can enjoy a more upscale experience on traditional *kettuvallam*, houseboats that have been spruced up with a kitchen and bedrooms.

How to

Getting here The two most popular backwater hubs of Allepey (now officially Alappuzha) and Kumarakom are both less than two hours' drive from Kochi. Public buses and taxis are best for travel between cities, while nothing can get around the inner roads of towns and villages like an autorickshaw can.

When to go If you can brave the fierce monsoon rains, the annual **Nehru Trophy Boat Race** in mid August is an unparalleled sporting spectacle.

An overnight cruise on the backwaters is one of the most popular travel experiences in Kerala, and indeed all of India. As you settle down on the *kettuvallam*, you get to watch local life on and along the water: children going to school, housewives washing clothes, men going to the market, fisherfolk out for a catch and much more.

Of the two main destinations, Alleppey has the classic narrow channels and scope to observe village life, and Kumarakom has the more expansive views of Vembanad lake. While there are plenty of local operators, **Spice Coast Cruises** offers a deluxe experience lasting from two to five days, with a chance to interact with local communities along the way.

For a more detailed and immersive trip spanning several

GRAHAM KING/SHUTTERSTOCK

locations on Kerala's fertile Malabar Coast, **Pandaw** (pandaw.com) has an eight-day, seven-night cruise taking in temples, churches, food, art, culture and crafts. To explore the backwaters away from the tourist hordes, try a quieter alternative like Ashtamudi Lake in Kollam (Quillon), five hours south of Kochi, with **Southern Backwaters**.

If the idea of staying on a boat for two days is not appealing, then book a stay at one of the resorts located on the banks of the backwaters. **Taj Kumarakom Resort & Spa** is perfect to sit back and relax, with restaurants serving fresh Kerala cuisine and the option of shorter boating excursions through the backwaters.

Go kayaking

For an up-close-and-personal experience, slip into a kayak to quietly glide on the surface and take in a whole new perspective of the backwaters ecology and the local way of life. For a luxe waterfront stay, along with kayaking or stand-up paddling adventures (or lessons) on Kumarakom's lagoons and Vembanad Lake, book a villa at CGH Earth's **Coconut Lagoon**, which has tied up with **Jellyfish Watersports**, a local company. **Kalypso Adventures** also offers one- and three-day kayaking expeditions in Kochi and Allepey, stopping at interesting historical and cultural sites along the way.

Above *Kettuvallam* houseboats

50 Puducherry's taste OF FRANCE

HISTORY | CULTURE | FOOD

More than seven decades after Puducherry (formerly Pondicherry) ceased being a French colony, the town still retains its French legacy, blended in with its original Tamil heritage. This is reflected in myriad ways, like the competing aromas of freshly baked croissants and piping hot *idlis* (steamed rice cakes) on streets with names like Rue De la Marine and Rue Calve Subraya Chetty.

How to

Getting around You can fly into Chennai and take a cab or bus onwards (three hours), or take a train to Puducherry from Chennai (16115 Auroville Express) or Bengaluru (11005 Puducherry Express on Monday, Tuesday and Saturday). Within town, walking or autorickshaw rides are the best ways to navigate the narrow, crowded lanes.

When to go Puducherry is good to visit through the year, although arguably best over the somewhat cooler period in December and January.

Begin your exploration of the French Quarter (earlier known as the 'White Town') at **Sri Aurobindo Ashram**, the secular spiritual hub founded by Indian philosopher and freedom fighter Aurobindo Ghose, along with his French disciple, painter and spiritual leader Mirra Alfassa. Pay silent homage at their *samadhi*, or final resting place, and find a shaded corner for a moment of meditation.

The streets in this neighborhood are laid out in a neat grid and are home to several interesting French colonial-era buildings, usually painted in a cheery yellow. Buildings like the **Chambre de Commerce** on Rue Suffren and the **Notre Dame des Anges** church on Dumas St are both open to visitors and offer a fascinating glimpse into Puducherry's French past. Some of the repurposed heritage boutique hotels like **Palais de Mahe** on Rue de Bussy or **Gratitude**

A Global Community

Just outside Puducherry is the town of Auroville, which was founded in 1968 with Mirra Alfassa's vision of a secular, international community where people could live together peacefully as global citizens. As of now, Auroville has 3300 temporary residents, and over 2500 daily visitors, including artists and farmers, potters and sculptors, writers and poets. Begin at the Visitor's Centre to get an idea of what you can see and do within Auroville – from shopping for handcrafted paper products to sampling organic south Indian food – but make sure to book a slot to visit **Matrimandir**, the striking globe at the heart of Auroville, meant as a place for deep and introspective meditation.

GABRIELA BHASKAR FOR LONELY PLANET

Heritage on Rue Romain Rolland also have the best Indo-French architecture, so just walk in and ask politely at the reception for a quick tour of the interiors.

An even better way to understand the complex history of this town is by tasting Creole-French cuisine, often mixed in with local Tamil flavours. Restaurant **Chez Francais** at the Hotel De L'Orient and Terrace Dining at **Maison Perumal** offer fine Franco-Tamil food; but a home-style Creole meal at **Chez Pushpa** is even better (only through advance phone reservations).

Above Notre Dame des Anges

51 Beach LIFE

BEACHES | MARINE LIFE | WATER SPORTS

The remote Andaman archipelago, a collection of hundreds of islands (of which only a handful are inhabited), is the stuff of picture postcards: powder-white sandy beaches, swinging palms, glorious sunsets and lush forests. And then there is a whole underwater world with pristine corals and all manner of marine life, from dugongs and dolphins to reef sharks and manta rays.

How to

Getting around Once you fly into **Veer Savarkar International Airport** at Port Blair (direct from Chennai, Bengaluru or Kolkata), boats and ferries are your only way to get from one island to the other.

When to go While the Andaman is an all-year destination, it is smart to avoid the monsoon months from June to September, when the heavy rains and choppy waters may disrupt ferry services and water activities.

Havelock Island This island (renamed Swaraj Dweep a few years ago) is the most famous of Andaman's islands, and rightly so. Get to the star attraction, **Radhanagar Beach**, at sunset, and you will see why this one regularly finds a place in lists of the world's best beaches.

The island has some of the best diving sites, and trusted operators like **Barefoot Scuba**, **Lacadives** and **Dive India** offer lessons and packages for both beginner and advanced divers. Non divers, never fret, for there is plenty of other stuff for you, like snorkelling at **Elephant Beach** and kayaking through lush mangroves. This island also has some of Andaman's prettiest resorts, like the **Jalakara** and **Barefoot at Havelock**.

Other islands An hour away is the quieter Neil Island (Shaheed Dweep), also with excellent diving and snorkelling, while **Butler Bay** in

JAMES R.D. SCOTT/GETTY IMAGES

Way Up North

It's admittedly a trudge getting to North Andaman (unless you can splurge on a chopper ride), but if you brave the long and tedious road trip or irregular ferry from Port Blair, you will be rewarded with stunning, secluded white-sand beaches with great snorkelling and trekking options. You will also want to get to **Kalipur Beach**, just outside the main settlement of Diglipur, to see the turtle nesting site, where in the dry season between November and March, four different turtle species gather to lay eggs. Sign up for a late-night beach walk led by forest officials to witness this magical sight.

the even more remote Little Andaman, nearly eight hours by ferry from Port Blair, has been quietly making waves (literally) as a world-class surfing destination.

On your way in or out, make a trip to **Mahatma Gandhi Marine National Park** for some snorkelling at Red Skin or Jolly Buoy Island (in the best responsible tourism practice, the two are opened alternately to allow corals time to regenerate). And when you absolutely can't stand being in the water any longer, you can hop onto a glass-bottomed boat for a joyride.

Above Scuba diving, off Havelock Island

52 Surf's UP

SPORTS | BEACHES | LOCAL LIFE

With a coastline stretching for thousands of miles and with dozens of unspoiled beaches, South India has become a premier surfing destination in the last decade. Whether you are a beginner looking for basic lessons, or an experienced surfer seeking new thrills, the beaches of Tamil Nadu, Puducherry, Kerala and Karnataka have something just right for you.

SWATHI SANKAR/SHUTTERSTOCK

How to

When to go When the monsoon hits the west coast between June and September, shutting down surfing, the east coast offers perfect conditions. So there is some place for you to go surf at any time of the year – but watch for cyclone warnings in Tamil Nadu and Puducherry in December and January.

Competitions Time your visit to one of the exciting surfing competitions like the Covelong Surf, Music and Yoga Festival (August/September) or the Varkala International Surfing Festival (April).

DMITRY RUKHLENKO/SHUTTERSTOCK

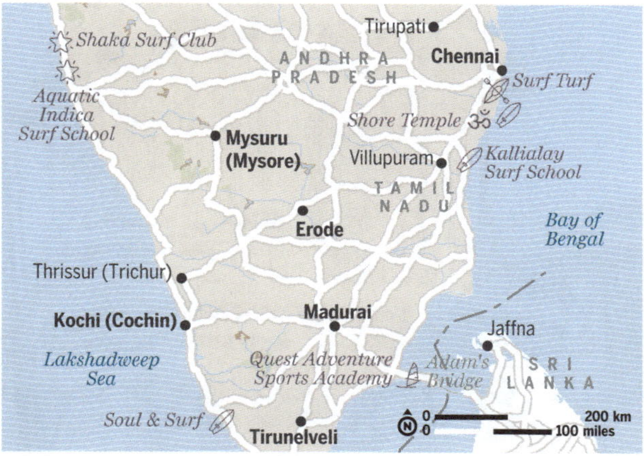

Along with its 8th century **Shore Temple**, Mamallapuram (Mahabalipuram) is known to have the best waves in the region, if not the entire country. Sign up for surfing, stand-up paddleboarding or kayaking with **Surf Turf**, which has another outpost at Covelong (also called Kovalam, not to be confused with the beach of the same name in Kerala), just 15 minutes away. Another two hours to the south is Puducherry, where **Kallialay Surf School** offers both lessons and equipment.

If you are an absolute newbie (or would like a spot of post-surf yoga), the **Soul & Surf** in Varkala in southern Kerala is a good bet. But the superstar of the south-Indian surfing scene is the coast of Karnataka near the temple town of Udupi. This is where it all started, with American Jack Hebner setting up **Mantra Surf Club** in 2004. Now there is also the **Aquatic Indica Surf School** in Mulki, which comes highly recommended for beginners. The sleepy village of Kodi Bengre is also emerging as a surfing hotspot, thanks to the **Shaka Surf Club**, run by India's first professional female surfer, Ishita Malaviya.

And for a totally secluded surfing experience among shallow coral-reef breaks, head to the Lakshadweep archipelago on India's west coast (a 90-minute flight from Kochi), particularly Kiltan, Kadmat and Minicoy for consistent high waves.

Top left Surfing, Karnataka
Bottom left Shore Temple, Mamallapuram

Wind Surfing

South India's surf story goes well beyond the obvious. While I take first-time surfers to Mulki for its sandy bottoms, forgiving waves and solid instructors, my personal favourite is Rameshwaram. This comes as a surprise to most people, because it is known primarily as a temple town. But it's home to **Quest Adventure Sports Academy**, and it's a place where steady winds and shallow waters create excellent conditions for windsurfing. And Tuticorin stands out for kitesurfing, with flat waters and consistent winds; **Aqua Outback** (aquaoutback.com) provides top-notch instruction. Together, these places are quietly reshaping how people see South India's coast.

Kripa Poonacha, *founder of Fit Oyster, an adventure travel company for women travellers (fitoyster.com)*

59 History in HAMPI

MONUMENTS | PALACES | ROCKS

In the former capital of the prosperous Vijayanagara Empire, discover a land with nearly 1600 monuments, royal ruins, palaces and temples scattered along the banks of a river and right in the midst of barren granite hills.

SOUVIK BHATTACHARYA/GETTY IMAGES

How to

Getting around The smallish Jindal Vijayanagar Airport, just 40km away has daily flights from Bengaluru and Hyderabad, but the better option is the overnight train (16592 Hampi Express) from Bengaluru to Hospet.

Festive fervor For two days every February, the entire region comes alive to a festival of traditional music, dance, art and cultural events during the Hampi **Vijaya Utsav**.

WAJ/SHUTTERSTOCK

The Religious Circuit

Start at the early-15th-century **Virupaksha Temple**, which soars to the skies in the heart of Hampi. Still functioning as a live place of worship for locals, this temple dedicated to Lord Shiva takes on a particularly mesmeric vibe during early-morning and late-evening prayer times. The temple elephant is usually around in the courtyard, her trunk ready to proffer blessings in exchange for a few bananas (and some cash, please).

The other unmissable religious monument is the **Vittala Temple** downriver, where the dancing hall known as *maha mandapa* is held upright by 56 granite pillars that emit musical notes when struck with the hand or a stick. The temple is a pleasant walk along the Tungabhadra river from the main town, or a short ride away by coracle (circular bamboo boat).

NEELSKY/SHUTTERSTOCK

A Local Touch

Spend some time at the **Kishkinda Trust** in Anegundi to learn more about the organisation's work with local communities in education, sanitation and conservation. You can shop for souvenirs from the crafts project, with banana fibre woven into enticing baskets, hats, handbags and home-decor items by village women.

Top and bottom left Vittala Temple
Above Virupaksha Temple

The Royal Circuit

For a slice of history, head into the **Royal Enclosure** of Hampi, away from the temple trail, to see how the Vijayanagara kings (and queens) lived. The **zenana** area, once a secluded area for royal women and their companions, provides a particularly charming peep into the past, with its soft pink **Lotus Mahal** at the core, an enclosed pavilion with arched domes, and the **Queen's Bath** – a glorious sunken bathing area, for the queen and her attending ladies to spend languid afternoons.

Another unmissable spot is the main step-well, **Pushkarani**, worth visiting both for its pleasing geometry and engineering design that allowed rainwater to be collected and stored in this mostly arid region. Nearby is the sprawling **Mahanavami Dibba**, a raised platform that the king ascended during royal ceremonies and processions.

A Time for Sloth

Spare an evening to visit the sloth-bear sanctuary at **Daroji** (21km away; 30 minutes by rickshaw), the first of its kind in India, for a glimpse of these endangered shaggy black bears. The sanctuary is open only between 4pm and 6pm, when the bears come out to explore the surrounding rocks. Be sure to take a binoculars or telephoto lenses, since visitors are allowed to watch only from a distant viewing platform. If you are lucky (and have keen eyes), you may also spot a few of the porcupines, jackals, hyenas, wild boars and leopards that live in this rugged region.

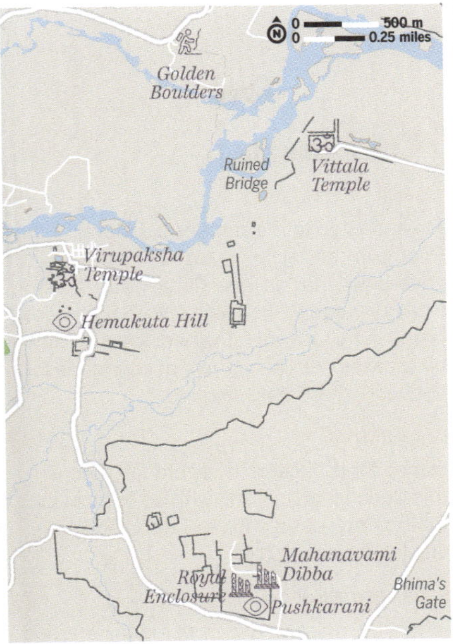

FROM LEFT: GANGADHAR A G/SHUTTERSTOCK, HENNING MARQUARDT/SHUTTERSTOCK

Stories in Stone

Don't forget to make a stop at the **Hazara Rama Temple**, once the king's private place of worship within the royal enclosure. This temple has some of the most intricate and impressive statues and bas-reliefs on the walls and pillars, most of them depicting scenes from the Ramayana epic.

For Adventure Addicts

The massive granite boulders of Hampi are just calling out to be conquered, if the dozens of rock climbers who arrive every day are to be believed. While climbing is not allowed in the historic core of Hampi, head outside to neighbouring towns like Anegundi to get a feel of this incredible landscape. **Golden Boulders** is a reputable company offering climbing and bouldering sessions for all skill levels.

Even if you are not into hardcore bouldering, there are easy hikes in and around town: walk up **Hemakuta Hill** right next to Virupaksha temple at sunset for an aerial view of the brown (and in rainy season, green) countryside, or up **Matanga Hill** at sunrise, when you are likely to have the place to yourself. Hampi's market also has several shops that rent out bicycles and motorbikes for a leisurely exploration at your own pace.

Left Sloth bear and cubs, Daroji bear sanctuary
Above right Relief carvings, Hazara Rama Temple

Listings

BEST OF THE REST

Walk on the Wild Side

Nagarhole Tiger Reserve

For a sighting of the magnificent Bengal Tiger, this protected reserve on the banks of the Kabini River is a great option. There are two daily jeep safaris as well as a boat safari that takes you close to the large herds of bathing and frolicking elephants on the banks.

Eravikulam National Park

The ecosystem of the larger Nilgiri Biosphere Reserve, where the park is located, is one of the richest and most complex anywhere in India. Go to look for the endangered Nilgiri Tahr, a goat-like ungulate that is found only in this region. Once every twelve months, the rare kurinji flower blooms here, carpeting the hills in purple.

Thattekad Bird Sanctuary

This small park spread over just 25 sq km is home to more than 300 avian species, making it a bird-watcher's delight. Apart from the usual suspects like darters, flycatchers, woodpeckers and hornbills, Thattekad also has rarer species including the Ceylon Frogmouth and the Oriental Dwarf Kingfisher.

Honnikeri Reserve Forest

Not a common name in the wildlife circuit, the Honnikeri Reserve Forest near the main town of Bidar is a compact stretch of protected land where endangered blackbucks, with their long and twirling antlers, are found. And then there are wild boars, porcupines, black-naped hares, peacocks and parakeets all around.

Best Thali Meals

Mavalli Tiffin Rooms ₹₹

Most folks go to the century-old Mavalli Tiffin Rooms in central Bengaluru for its crispy, ghee-laden *masala dosa* (large South Indian savoury crepe stuffed with spiced potatoes) or the fluffy *rava idli* (steamed, savoury semolina cakes), but head there at lunchtime for the hearty Karnataka thali.

Annalakshmi ₹₹₹

Famed for its 'fine-dine' vegetarian menus, this Chennai restaurant, with an outpost in Coimbatore, has a choice of thali, including one for those on a diet!

Rayalseema Ruchulu ₹₹

Ignore the massive a la carte menu here, and order yourself a special non-veg thali, choosing from chicken, mutton or seafood (or even just egg, if you want to keep it simple).

GYANA_GRAPHY/SHUTTERSTOCK

Oriental Dwarf Kingfisher

Museum-Hopping

Salar Jung Museum

These 39 galleries containing a magnificent collection of art, sculpture, metalwork and manuscripts from all over the world, were amassed and curated by Mir Yousuf Ali Khan, who served as an influential minister in the local nizam's court. Don't miss the marble sculpture of the *Veiled Rebecca* and the wooden sculpture of *Mephistopheles and Margaretta* in the European Art Gallery.

Government Museum

Although the exhibits are not well curated or labelled, this Chennai museum is still worth a visit for its fabulous collection of bronze idols from the Chola era, housed in a separate annex building.

Napier Museum

Housed in a late-19th-century mansion painted in bold and bright colours, this tiny museum has an impressive collection of ivory and wooden artefacts showcasing the glory of the erstwhile Travancore kingdom.

Nimhans Brain Museum

For a change from all the art and culture, drop by this quirky museum to understand the workings of the human brain by peering into preserved brains with and without neurological disorders.

Wellness with Ayurveda

Arya Vaidya Sala

For an immersive (and – fair warning – demanding) Ayurveda (Indian herbal medicine) experience, sign up for a detoxifying Panchakarma treatment at this nearly-125-year-old hospital.

NESRU MARKMEDIA/SHUTTERSTOCK

Napier Museum

Somatheeram Ayurveda Village

Set on the beachfront in southern Kerala, providing authentic Ayurveda in an upscale resort setting, and particularly known for stress-management therapies.

Kalari Rasayana

Think rejuvenation in the midst of a coconut grove and floating islands, as well as treatments aimed at immunity boosting, weight management and specific physical complaints.

Kairali – the Ayurvedic Healing Village

Provides Ayurveda treatments along with yoga and meditation, specifically suited for chronic aches and pains, including migraines, spinal rehabilitation and neurological problems.

Niraamaya Retreats

Focus on mind-body balance at this resort on the shores of Vembanad Lake, with traditional Ayurveda therapies and five-star luxury.

Amal Tamara

The Kashayapura Experience here allows you a rare peek at the herbs, instruments and processes that go into making Ayurveda medicines.

Practicalities

Right Pune Junction railway station (p194)

Indian Railways
12:43

EASY STEPS FROM THE AIRPORT TO THE CITY CENTRE

Most international travellers arrive by air into Delhi (DEL) or Mumbai (BOM; pictured below), followed by Bengaluru (BLR), Chennai (MAA) and Hyderabad (HYD). India's main airports are modern with dining, ATMs and SIM counters in arrivals. IndiGo and SpiceJet are the main budget airlines, though you often find deals on Air India and Vistara. Immigration queues can be long – especially during early-morning arrivals – so allow time.

AT THE AIRPORT

SIM CARDS
Official SIM card counters are located in international arrivals, usually operated by Airtel or Jio. Expect to pay from ₹600 to ₹1200 with passport paperwork and possible activation delays; larger cities and towns will have multiple stores with faster setup and better deals. Digital SIMs work well in India.

CURRENCY EXCHANGE
Currency exchange counters are available in the arrivals hall, but you won't get the best rates. ATMs are a better option. For larger amounts, wait to exchange cash at bank branches or authorised money changers in city centres, where rates are typically better and more transparent.

TUKARAM.KARVE/SHUTTERSTOCK

WIFI
Free and fast at major airports, though it's typically timed access and requires a local SIM card for verification.

ATMs
ATMs are found in all airports. State Bank of India (SBI) and ICICI are the most reliable for foreign cards.

ELECTRICITY
Charging points are available in terminals and lounges. Plugs are Type C, D and M; power is 230V/50Hz.

ENTRY/EXIT FORMALITIES

Visas Most travellers require a tourist visa before arrival, with e-visas available to many nationalities. Your passport must be valid for at least six months with two blank pages.

Restricted items Drones are heavily regulated and may be confiscated without prior approval. Professional filming equipment and large sums of cash must be declared.

GETTING TO THE CITY CENTRE

METRO AND EXPRESS TRAINS
Delhi and Mumbai have direct airport metro or rail links into the city. These are fast, inexpensive and avoid traffic, with journey times of 20 to 40 minutes and fares usually under ₹100, making them the quickest option during peak hours.

AIRPORT BUSES
Most major airports run city buses on fixed routes and schedules. They are a great budget option, but can be slow, crowded and affected by traffic. Useful if you're travelling light and not in a hurry.

PRIVATE TRANSFER
Many hotels offer airport pickups for a fixed fee. This is often the best option after a late flight. Prices vary widely, so confirm the cost and meeting point in advance.

HOW MUCH FOR A...

Taxi
₹600
1.5hr

Bus
₹70
1.5hr

Metro
₹54
25min

TAXIS
Prepaid taxi booths operate at most airports, with fixed fares by zone. Pay at the booth, not in the car, to avoid disputes on arrival.

RIDESHARE APPS
Uber and Ola are widely used in Indian airports and have designated zones for pick up. Prices can spike at busy times or late at night.

TICKETS, PAYMENT & TRAVEL TIME
Traffic can dramatically affect journey times, particularly at rush hour and during festivals. Intercity rail tickets often sell out, so book ahead. Rideshare apps need mobile data and sometimes local payment methods – cash works well. Screenshots of bookings save stress if connectivity drops.

OTHER POINTS OF ENTRY
India is accessible by ferry, overland routes and international trains. These routes, however, are far less common and require careful planning for international travellers.

E-visas are valid only for entry through designated airports and seaports. Travellers planning to enter India overland will generally need a regular visa issued in advance by an Indian embassy or consulate, even if they hold an e-visa for air arrival. Overland crossings are possible from Nepal, Bhutan and Bangladesh at designated border points, but facilities and procedures vary widely.

The Maitree Express train links Bangladesh and India, from Kolkata to Dhaka. But these routes require prearranged visas and tickets booked well in advance. Rail links from Pakistan remain suspended, and overland routes from Myanmar are currently restricted.

Sea entry is rare for international visitors. Passenger ferries between India and Sri Lanka operate, though services are seasonal and weather dependent.

TRANSPORT TIPS TO HELP YOU GET AROUND

India's size makes your transport choices very important. Trains do the heavy lifting for long distances, while flights help when time matters more than scenery. In cities, autorickshaws and rideshare apps like Uber and Ola are easiest. Outside urban centres, a hired car with a driver is often the simplest way to get around without losing days to logistics.

TRAIN

Trains are the backbone of travel in India. They're affordable, social and reach almost everywhere, but popular routes sell out quickly. Book as early as you can, choose air-conditioned classes for comfort and use overnight services to save on both time and accommodation.

BUS

Buses go where trains don't, including remote towns and hill regions. Private sleeper buses are far more comfortable than state-run services, especially overnight. Most travellers book through aggregators like RedBus (redbus.in) or AbhiBus (abhibus.com), which accept international cards.

HOW MUCH FOR A ...

Car & driver
₹3-5,000/day

Scooter rental
₹300-600/day

Express train from ₹500 on major routes

Left-luggage facilities in India vary by city. Most large railway stations have a cloakroom, usually open 24/7 – check timings on arrival. Major airports also offer storage: Bengaluru airport charges around ₹1000 per day, while Delhi's 24-hour cloakroom starts at about ₹600 for large bags. Many hotels and guesthouses will store luggage free of charge before check-in or after check-out.

Planes Domestic flying is widespread, with frequent connections by local carriers like IndiGo, Air India, Vistara, Akasa Air and SpiceJet. You can find great deals if you book early enough; delays and schedule changes are not uncommon.

City Transport Autorickshaws and rideshare apps are the easiest way to get around most cities. Fares are low, but traffic can be slow and unpredictable. Metros work well where they exist, especially in Delhi, Mumbai and Bengaluru.

DRIVING ESSENTIALS

Drive on the left and always choose full insurance.

100 Speed: 100–120km/h on highways and 40–60km/h in cities.

The legal driving age is 18. India has a zero-tolerance drink-driving law.

Expect frequent horn use and animals on the road.

Road signs are typically in the state language, Hindi and English. Offline maps and a local SIM are essential.

BIKES Scooters are often the best way to navigate beach towns and smaller centres, with rentals common in Goa, Hampi, Mysuru (Mysore) and parts of Rajasthan beyond the city centre. Expect minimal paperwork, with scooters typically renting for ₹300-600 per day; larger motorbikes cost more. Helmets are legally required, though not always provided. Only ride if you're experienced and comfortable navigating the busy local traffic.

AUTORICKSHAWS Motorised rickshaws are the quickest way to cover short distances in towns and cities. Some use meters, many don't – agree on the fare before you set off. They're cheap, flexible and good for traffic.

DRIVING Most travellers don't drive in India. Traffic is dense, conditions vary and local driving habits take time to adjust to. Mountain roads are narrow, with landslides common during the monsoon season. Foreign drivers need an International Driving Permit.

KNOW YOUR CARBON FOOTPRINT Your transport choices have a big impact. A flight from Bengaluru to Goa emits roughly 182kg of carbon dioxide per passenger, compared with 51kg by bus and around 10kg by train. Trains are the most efficient option for long distances. To compare journeys, use a carbon calculator like carbonfootprint.com or myclimate.org.

ROAD DISTANCE CHART (KMS)

	Guwahati	Kolkata	Chennai	Kochi	Bengaluru	Goa	Mumbai	Jaipur	Agra	Delhi
Delhi	1955	1495	2290	2700	2160	1965	1425	330	235	0
Agra	1735	1275	1965	2500	1935	1775	1300	240	0	235
Jaipur	1980	1520	2070	2480	1940	1715	1165	0	240	330
Mumbai	2645	1905	1315	1320	990	565	0	1165	1300	1425
Goa	2950	2100	885	770	565	0	565	1715	1775	1965
Bengaluru	2830	1900	350	535	0	565	990	1940	1935	2160
Kochi	3260	2305	690	0	535	770	1320	2480	2500	2700
Chennai	2700	1665	0	690	350	885	1315	2070	1965	2290
Kolkata	1015	0	1665	2305	1900	2100	1905	1520	1275	1495
Guwahati	0	1015	2700	3260	2830	2950	2645	1980	1735	1955

DANGERS, ANNOYANCES & SAFETY

India is generally safe for travellers, but scale, climate and infrastructure can shape how you move through the country. From understanding local customs to navigating public spaces, knowing what to expect helps keep you safe and confident while exploring.

AIR POLLUTION

Smog can be a real problem in big cities, especially Delhi and Mumbai where air quality often dips between November and February. If you have asthma or respiratory sensitivities, keep an eye on daily AQI readings and plan outdoor sightseeing for clearer days. Many travellers benefit from wearing an N95 mask.

WEATHER

Monsoon season (June to September) cools things down but can affect travel significantly. In the Western Ghats and the Himalayas, heavy rain can shut trekking routes and trigger landslides. Roads flood and trains get delayed. Build flexibility into itineraries and check local conditions before embarking on trips or treks.

TRAVEL PERMITS & ACCESS

India's most remote corners don't always reward spontaneity. Some states in Northeast India require Inner Line Permits (ILP) and long distances can take far longer than expected. During the monsoon, landslides may cut off roads entirely. Phone signal and data aren't guaranteed making apps less reliable.

Road India's roads can be intense. Traffic mixes cars, buses, bikes, people and animals, often with little warning. Trains and daytime travel are generally safer for longer distances – don't forget to wear your seatbelts and helmets.

RADIOKAFKA/SHUTTERSTOCK

VYSTEKIMAGES/SHUTTERSTOCK

Tap Water Tap water isn't considered drinkable. Stick to sealed bottles or filtered refills, and be cautious with ice. In rural areas, many travellers also use bottled or purified water for brushing teeth.

MOSQUITOES

These menaces are part of daily life, especially after rain. Bites aren't just annoying – they can lead to dengue or malaria. Repellent matters, evenings are peak time and breezy or air-conditioned rooms make a noticeable difference.

DRUGS

India is not relaxed about drugs, whatever you might hear on the road. Laws are strict, enforcement varies and tourists aren't exempt. Avoid drugs altogether, especially anything framed as spiritual, local or quietly acceptable.

QUICK TIPS TO HELP YOU MANAGE YOUR MONEY

CASH & CREDIT CARDS
India is functionally cashless in cities – until it suddenly isn't. Credit cards work at hotels, restaurants and big stores, but markets, street vendors and local transport often use cash. Mobile payments via UPI dominate daily transactions, though most international visitors can't use it. Carry small notes for autorickshaws and tips; breaking large bills is harder than expected.

BANKS & ATMs
ATMs are everywhere, yet can be unreliable. Machines regularly run out of cash, reject cards or impose low daily limits.

TIPPING
Tipping isn't required, but it's common to round up or leave small change. In hotels and on tours, tips are increasingly expected.

CURRENCY
Indian rupee (₹)

HOW MUCH FOR A...

Takeaway coffee
₹20-50

Latte in a cafe
₹250-400

Dinner for 2
₹1200-2500

CURRENCY
The Indian rupee (₹) is a closed currency and can't be exchanged abroad. Change money or withdraw cash at an ATM upon arrival.

HAGGLING
Bargaining is normal in markets and for autorickshaws, but not in fixed-price malls, supermarkets or restaurants. Keep it light, know when to stop and don't confuse negotiation with confrontation.

ON A BUDGET
India is easy on a budget if you travel like a local. Eat street food, use trains and avoid peak holiday periods. Off-season travel often means better prices, fewer crowds and greener landscapes.

TAXES
Goods and Services Tax (GST) is usually included in displayed prices, particularly at hotels and restaurants. Most restaurants charge 5% GST on food, while those in higher-end hotels may add 18%, depending on the room rate. Unlike many countries, tourists generally can't claim tax refunds on purchases. Larger hotels may add additional service charges or local taxes, which should be itemised on the bill. Check invoices before paying and question anything that looks unexpected.

INDIA'S ECONOMY
India's economic growth is driven by services, tech, manufacturing and a rapidly expanding middle class with rising wages and spending power. In cities, this shows up in app-based work, digital payments and new consumer habits – think contemporary cafes and large shopping malls – while informal, cash-based labour still underpins everyday life, often side by side.

UNIQUE & LOCAL WAYS TO STAY

Accommodation in India spans everything from spare, family-run guesthouses to luxuriously restored palaces, havelis and wildlife lodges. What makes it distinctive isn't just price range, but variety: where you stay often shapes how you experience a place. Expect strong regional differences, uneven standards and some of the best value-for-money stays anywhere – if you choose carefully.

HOW MUCH FOR A

Guesthouse
₹1,500-3,500

Heritage hotel
₹6,000-15,000

Wildlife lodge
₹10,000-25,000

ULTIMATE TRAVEL PHOTOS/SHUTTERSTOCK

HERITAGE HOTELS

Staying in one of India's heritage hotels usually means sleeping in a former palace, *haveli* (traditional residence) or colonial-era bungalow – with all the quirks that implies. Comfort levels vary; some feel museum-like, others quietly luxurious, but the appeal lies in the scale, architecture and sense of place. Many weren't designed with lifts or level access, so expect stairs, uneven floors and long walks between rooms and common spaces. But even mid-range heritage properties deliver experiences that would be unaffordable elsewhere.

GUESTHOUSES

Small guesthouses still define travel across much of India. Many are family-run, informal and lightly staffed, from simple rooms in temple towns to leafy retreats in the hills. Comfort can be uneven, but hosts often step in by organising transport, sharing home-cooked meals or pointing you towards places you'd never find on your own.

WILDLIFE LODGES

Wildlife lodges are built around access rather than convenience – with guided drives and experienced naturalists available for the duration of your stay. They range from bare bones to ultra luxurious, and because they're often remote, most operate as self-contained stays with meals and activities included. Once you arrive, expect early mornings and set safari times.

REVATI AND CHARLES VICTOR/SHUTTERSTOCK

ITIPRITHUL/SHUTTERSTOCK

HOMESTAYS

Homestays in India are rarely just spare rooms. More often, they're working households that fold guests into daily routines. Culture, food and daily rhythms shift not just from state to state in India, but often from one city to the next. Staying in someone's home brings travel down to that scale. Rather than a standardised room, you're stepping into how things actually work. Conversations fill in context no guidebook can – about festivals (such as Holi, pictured), prices, politics or why something is done a certain way here but not two towns over. Homestays are especially prevalent in the hills, plantation regions, the northeast and in smaller towns, where hotels can feel disconnected from local life. Standards vary widely. Some feel closer to boutique inns or bed and breakfasts, while others remain resolutely domestic. Bathrooms might be basic. Power cuts happen.

What you gain is context. Food reflects the region, not a menu. Hosts explain how things work – permits, buses, festivals – because it's their life, not a service offering. In remote areas, homestays often solve practical problems too, arranging transport or introductions that would otherwise stall a trip.

They aren't for everyone. But for travellers curious about how India is lived – not just visited – homestays offer a level of access that's hard to replicate elsewhere.

BOOKING

When booking accommodation in India, consider the plethora of options available, from no-frills guesthouses and homestays to heritage hotels, beach resorts and wildlife lodges. Your expectations should shift accordingly. Recent reviews matter more than star ratings. A good-looking room can still have unreliable water, patchy power or serious noise issues.

Book ahead in peak season and around festivals, particularly in popular destinations and near national parks. In smaller towns, it's common to ask to see a room before committing, though quality can vary wildly.

During the monsoon, always confirm access. Hill roads wash out, ferries stop running and 'nearby' can mean something different on the ground. When in doubt, call or message directly.

Booking.com The widest spread of accommodation options across India, from basic guesthouses to luxury hotels.

Agoda Often competitive on mid-range hotels and last-minute availability.

Airbnb Best for longer stays, apartments and select homestays. Quality varies widely; recent reviews matter.

HILL STATIONS

India's hill-station towns are dominated by bungalows, small retreats and legacy hotels. Climate and views do the work. In the summer, tourism spikes fast, with availability tightening and prices rising, sometimes overnight.

RESPONSIBLE TRAVEL

Tips to leave a lighter footprint, support local and have a positive impact on local communities.

ON THE ROAD

Choose small, locally-run stays. Small guesthouses, homestays and heritage properties usually have lighter footprints, and your money stays closer to the community. Hotel groups such as CGH Earth (cghearth.com) have a long track record in low-impact design, local employment, regional food systems and sustainable initiatives.

Travel by train. India's rail network connects most regions at a far lower carbon cost than flying; overnight services also save on time and accommodation.

Travel sustainably. State buses and shared taxis reduce fuel use, particularly in hill regions. Walk whenever possible.

Be aware of fuel consumption. If hiring a car, choose a hybrid or electric model when you can.

Reduce waste on the move. Refill filtered water at hotels and stations, carry a cloth shopping bag and avoid single-use plastics sold at tourist sites.

VICTOR TYAKHT/SHUTTERSTOCK

GIVE BACK

Support conservation-led experiences. In coastal Goa, organisations such as Terra Conscious (instagram.com/terraconscious) run expert-led marine walks and wildlife-spotting trips that follow strict ethical guidelines rather than chase close encounters.

Support social enterprises. Across India, craft-led organisations create livelihoods by keeping regional skills alive. In Karnataka, Sandur Kushala Kala Kendra works with rural artisans to produce handwoven textiles using natural dyes.

Eat with impact. Social enterprises like The Good Ocean (thegood ocean.in) support coastal livelihoods by promoting sustainable seaweed harvesting and local food systems.

Donate wisely. For wildlife protection beyond your itinerary, Indian NGOs such as Nature Conservation Foundation (ncf-india.org) publish clear research and impact reports.

DOS & DONTS

Dress modestly. Cover shoulders and knees at temples, mosques and in rural areas; lightweight layers make this easy.

Ask before photographing. People or rituals; this is especially important at religious sites.

Use your right hand. For eating or exchanging money and items.

Avoid public displays of affection. They're uncommon outside major cities.

LEAVE A SMALL FOOTPRINT

Think small when choosing where to stay. Guesthouses, homestays and older heritage properties tend to use less water and energy than purpose-built resorts.

Be water aware. In many parts of India, water shortages are seasonal and acute, so short showers and reusing towels make a real difference.

Limit energy use. Switch off lights and air-conditioning when leaving your room; power cuts are common outside major cities.

Tread lightly. Stick to marked paths in forests, deserts and hill regions, and keep a respectful distance from wildlife.

VINAYAK JAGTAP/SHUTTERSTOCK

SUPPORT LOCAL

Buy with intention. Region-specific crafts – handwoven textiles, metalwork, pottery and natural-dyed fabrics – are best purchased where they're made, directly from artisans or cooperatives.

Eat what's grown nearby. Seasonal thalis, street snacks and market produce reflect local food systems.

Spend small, often. A coffee at a neighbourhood cafe or a paperback from an independent bookstore often matters more than a single big souvenir.

CLIMATE CHANGE & TRAVEL

Lonely Planet urges all travellers to engage with their travel carbon footprint, which will mainly come from air travel. While there often isn't an alternative, travellers can look to minimise the number of flights they take, opt for newer aircrafts and use cleaner ground transport, such as trains.

One proposed solution—purchasing carbon offsets—unfortunately does not cancel out the impact of individual flights. While most destinations will depend on air travel for the foreseeable future, for now, pursuing ground-based travel where possible is the best course of action.

The UN Carbon Offset Calculator shows how flying impacts a household's emissions:

The ICAO's carbon emissions calculator allows visitors to analyse the CO2 generated by point-to-point journeys:

RESOURCES

canopybythecoast.in

heritagefirstgoa.com

instagram.com/coorg conservationcollective

keystone-foundation.org

anetindia.org

ESSENTIAL NUTS-AND-BOLTS

DRINKING WATER

Tap water is not safe to drink. Use sealed bottled water or filtered refills, and avoid ice unless you're confident about the source.

PUBLIC TOILETS

Squat toilets remain common in stations and rural areas. Don't expect toilet paper or soap to be provided – carry tissues and hand sanitiser.

SHOES OFF

Shoes are removed at temples, mosques and most homes; socks help on hot stone floors.

FAST FACTS

Time Zone
GMT+5.5

Country Code
+91

Electricity
230V/50Hz

GOOD TO KNOW

India's e-visa allows entry only through designated airports and seaports.

Pharmacies are plentiful and well stocked. Many medications are available without a prescription.

Passport and visa details are needed to buy a local SIM.

Power outages are common outside major cities; hotels often use generators.

Indian rupees cannot be taken in or out of the country, so exchange money on arrival and departure.

ACCESSIBLE TRAVEL

Uneven pavements, steps and crowds remain common, especially in older neighbourhoods, though newer airports, metro systems and large hotels are improving access.

Wheelchair-friendly rooms are most likely to be found at international-chain and upscale hotels; always confirm details in advance. Metro systems in cities such as Delhi, Mumbai and Bengaluru have elevators and staff assistance, but buses, trains and taxis are rarely adapted.

Ramps or alternative entrances are available at many monuments and temples.

Braille signage and tactile paving are limited. Audio guides are uncommon outside major museums.

Sign language is not widely understood, and visual announcements are rare.

Visit accessibletoursindia.com for bespoke tours across India. For tailored trips, Enable Holidays (enableholidays.com) and Sage Traveling (sagetraveling.com) specialise in accessible itineraries across India.

SMOKING

Smoking is banned in many public places, though enforcement varies; designated smoking areas are common in hotels.

GPS

Google Maps works well in cities, but on rural routes can be unreliable. Asking locals often gets better results.

CASH

Though UPI dominates, cash is still essential for transport, markets and in smaller towns. Carry small notes.

FAMILY TRAVEL

Book family-friendly stays at larger hotels and resorts with interconnecting rooms and pools.

Kids often receive discounts or free entry at monuments and museums, though age cut-offs vary by site.

Child seats are rarely available in taxis or hired cars.

Strollers are often impractical due to uneven pavements and steps; baby carriers work better.

Food is flexible – plain rice, rotis, dosa and curd are widely available and suit young travellers.

FESTIVALS CAN TRANSFORM LIFE

During events such as Diwali, Holi or Durga Puja, expect packed trains, road closures and sold out hotels and other accommodations. Book transport well in advance and make sure to allow for extra travel time – disruption is part of the experience.

SOLO FEMALE TRAVEL

Travelling alone as a woman in India means being visible. Curiosity is common. Dressing modestly helps you blend in, especially outside big cities. Trust your instincts, ignore catcalls and don't hesitate to seek out other women or families if you need help.

SUVENDU DAS INDIA/SHUTTERSTOCK

LGBTIQ+ TRAVELLERS

Same-sex relationships were decriminalised in 2018, but there are no nationwide anti-discrimination protections or marriage rights.

Public displays of affection are uncommon regardless of gender or orientation.

Everyday attitudes and acceptance varies by region. Large cities such as Mumbai, Delhi and Bengaluru have visible queer communities, events and nightlife.

Stay informed through local LGBTIQ+ collectives and social media, which are useful for current events and safe space. Follow *instagram.com/out_and_about___*, India's first queer-inclusive travel collective.

Index

000 Map pages

P

000 Map pages

R

S

T